"A vibrant, engaging real life story t. to savor bite after bite, each morsel eve: I cheered the authors on while giving m me in the process. This is a heartwarming, delicious must read for anyone asking the question, Is that all there is? This courageous family crafted their own answers and by example inspires and guides you to your own authentic recipe."

—*Diane Sukiennik, FoodandWineAccess.com*

"Take one croissant in the morning. And let this charming, well-written book simplify your life for the better!"

—*Nancy Mills, Founder of The Spirited Women.com*

"The authors are great storytellers. This is a book for anyone who has considered a change in their life but didn't quite have the guts to begin. This may just be the push you need!"

—*Beverly Kaye, CEO Career Systems International*

"*Courage and Croissants, Inspiring Joyful Living* is a triumph! Through their journey of love, humor, honesty and courage, this in-spiring family teaches us that, by following our hearts and dreams, we can break through the bondage of empty societal conventions to live a more authentic, fulfilled life. I highly recommend this book to anyone who is looking for the inspiration, and practical tools, to live a more joyful life."

—*Laura Roppe, Award-winning singer/songwriter*

"If you dream of it, do it! Suzanne and Jean take you on an inspir-ing journey of the heart and mind by sharing their story of living life fully, with the conviction of following through on their dreams and putting the perception of risk in its place. You'll be encouraged to take the plunge!"

—*Kristin Andress, author of Imagine Being in a Life You Love.*

"I'm a big believer in the power of vision to lead us where we never knew we could go. *Courage and Croissants* invites us to re-examine our lives, our priorities, and how we are living--and discover the unexpected vision. Never before have we so urgently needed inspiration and ideas on how to value the simple pleasures in our lives wherever we live. From California to the south of France we journey with Suzanne, Jean, and their daughter, Zoé-Pascale—and we are simultaneously given the courage to step out of our comfort zones and create the life we want to live."

—*Rev. Karen Russo, award-winning author, The Money Keys: Unlocking Peace, Freedom and Real Financial Power.*

"Part memoir and part how-to manual, Saxe-Roux, a husband and wife TEAM have written an affecting story about how they found the courage to step outside the insanity of their hard-working lives in the states to pursue their dream of living in Southern France with their young daughter. Filled with sensuous descriptions of life abroad as well as concrete advice about how to embark on a similar journey, this is an invaluable guidebook for those who dare to dream of stepping off the U.S. merry-go-round of high pressure and achievement to discover the true joy of being a family."

—*Elisa Bernick, author of The Family Sabbatical Handbook*

"This book reminds me that dreams can be your reality if you let them come true. Suzanne and Jean are inspirational role models for all of us who want to live life to its fullest and need the courage from those who have broken the traditional mold. This book helps us realize what it takes to truly live your dream - it's not easy, but it's worth it."

—*Nick Clayton, Harvard Publishing*

"I could feel the laughter, triumph, and difficulty as I read *Courage and Croissants* late into the night. Anyone can find inspiration in this book to follow their dreams abroad or in their own home by appreciating what is really important in this life."

—*Mindy O'Toole, Mercer Consulting*

"Read this book! Whether you seek inspiration to claim the life you have always dreamed of or just want to savor a well written novel, you will devour *Courage and Croissants*. This real life story evoked powerful new insights for me in and enchanting and surprising way! Delicious."

—*Ann Herrmann-Nehdi, CEO Herrmann International*

"An inspiring story written in a charming voice about unplugging from the grind and diving heart first into one's passion."

—*Karen Leland, best selling co-author of Watercooler Wisdom: How Smart People Prosper in The Face of Conflict, Pressure and Change*

"This book evocatively chronicles the Roux family's move from the hectic pace of Silicon Valley to Southern France, where they created a new life focused on living in the moment, appreciating the bounties of the French countryside and embracing the local culture. By sharing their personal experiences in discovering more joyful living, and providing easy to follow tips and suggestions for making lifestyle changes both large and small, this family show us how delightfully rich and full life can be."

— *Melissa Dyrdahl, Social Entrepreneur*

Courage And Croissants

Inspiring Joyful Living
A Story and Life Guidebook

Suzanne Saxe-Roux, Ed.D.,
and Jean P. Roux, Ph.D.

St. Rémy Press | Tiburon

This book is available at special quantity discounts for bulk purchases, sales promotions, premiums, fund-raising events or educational use. Special books or book excerpts can also be customized to fit specific needs. Info@StRemyPress.com

Courage and Croissants, Inspiring Joyful Living
A Story and Life Guidebook

St. Rémy Press
Tiburon, California
Email: info@StRemyPress.com
415. 272.0169

ISBN 978-0-9826909-0-1

We dedicate this book to our
magnificent daughter,
ZOÉ-PASCALE

I want to go to the south of France, sit in a café under poplar trees and watch the world go by. Buy a colorful straw basket and fill it with salmon and olives and sun-warmed tomatoes and a baguette and bring it back to a stone bungalow and eat it out on the patio under the warm sun and curl up with a novel in a hammock.

I want to sculpt... make a giant imperfect ceramic mug out of which to drink my coffee and tea from now until it cracks and I have to glue it together and then for many more years after that.

I want to paint purple swirls and blue birds with red beaks out on the mailbox. I want the passing world to see that inside lives someone whose creativity has been unleashed and there is nothing that can be contained in a box or anywhere else.

I want to traipse all over the world... starting in my back yard and ending up at the Angkor Wat temple and from there climb up a mountain in Tibet, commune with the ravens, sit in meditation and get up and spin in circles.

I want to drive... down the coast then across the country. Windows down, wind in hair, music up, my voice singing along in a scream. Not knowing where I'm going but trusting that my next stop will be more magnificent than the last.

I want to love... spread love, make love, be love. Have love be the thing that radiates forth from me and drives my every action. Unabashed adoration of the world and everyone in it.

I don't want to sit here any more. Time to get up and move. Time to rebloom and make miracles in my world. Time to swim across the bay of confusion and climb up on the shore of carefree get-a-move-on land of the living.

Contents

How to Use This Book

WELCOME TO THE JOURNEY of courage, self-discovery, and finding joie de vivre!

Get comfortable, put-up your feet, pour a glass of wine, and come along with our family on the ride from San Francisco to the south of France (and beyond) and then back again.

We take you in search of taking back your life and the simple joys of living that so many of us have lost sight of.

The first portion of this book is the story of our journey and summarizes many of the lessons we learned.

- *Part I* chronicles our lives leading up to the decision to make a change. (You might feel twinges of recognition as you read!)

- *Part II* details the first days and weeks of our transition into our new life and, more importantly, out of our comfort zone.

- *Part III* contains various vignettes from our time in France: the new customs and valuable life lessons we have folded into our every day lives. They are broken out into various themes on which much of our learning was centered: creativity, sensuality, healthy living, and travel.

- *Part IV* deals with yet another transition: deciding how to bring our experience of learning and growth into the next phase of life.

The second portion of this book contains 15 "Life Guidebook Tips" exploring topics such as courage, taking risks, creativity, simpler living, healthy living, or embarking on an adventure of your own, whether it be big, small, staying right at home, traveling, or living abroad. This portion concludes with an essay on the American Dream; how it was created, what it has meant and how it is changing. We have purposely added this perspective at the end of the book as background for those of you who are interested in the larger context of this story.

While the two pieces of the book are meant to be used together, you are welcome to skip back and forth—particularly if there is a piece of the story that speaks to you, and you'd like more specific tips for moving forward in your own life.

Throughout, it is important to keep in mind that this story and the tips we provide are based on our experience: the resources that were available to us, our personalities, and all that was and is unique to our lives in a particular time in history. For every idea we provide in the guidebook, there are a thousand others available to you. Most importantly, however, is the idea that you can attract anything you want into your life if you believe in it enough and do the footwork that is well-documented by dozens of self-improvement authors.

Even though our story recounts a large change that may dwarf anything you ever want to do, we hope this book inspires you to make small changes as well that move you towards living a healthy, joyful life in whatever way is just right for you.

Bon courage!

SUZANNE and JEAN-PIERRE

Prologue: Hot Croissants

Live in the present
launch yourself
on every wave,
find eternity
in each moment

HENRY DAVID THOREAU,
American Author and Poet (1817-1862)

As THE CLOCK TOWER strikes 7 a.m., we awaken to sun shining through the long rectangular window of our upstairs bedroom. Shadows of small, swift, black swallows dart about as though they are playing hide-and-seek, and the smell of the fresh, cool lavender drifts in with the breeze.

Our three-story stone house is situated smack in the center of a quaint village in the south of France, which prides itself on being *tout commerce* (having all necessary services). There is one of every shop one needs for daily living, all compacted along narrow cobblestone streets. Jig-jagging old stone houses and shops, built two and three stories high, lean against each other in solidarity against the winter mistral winds.

Our home sits around the bend from the village's *pâtisserie*, *boucherie*, and *fleuriste*. It is across from the *Mairie* (Mayor's office), with its three flags flowing in the breeze: the European Union flag, with its cobalt blue background and circle of twelve golden stars; the red-, white- and blue-striped French flag; and the local red Occitan flag with the golden Cross of Languedoc, a badge of independence for people of the region. The street leads to the 11th-century Catholic cathedral poised tall at the crest of the hillside just above the Grand Rue, whose tolling clock tower can be seen from miles away. Nestled down the hill are the village school, the small grocery store, and the *Bar du Marché*—a place for a café, a glass of Côte du Rhône or a workingperson's hot lunch.

Slipping on shorts, T-shirts, and flip-flops, we run down the narrow stone road to the *pâtisserie* for our first hot, buttery croissants right out of the oven. Nibbling away, we saunter silently and slowly back up the cobblestone street, gazing at the antiquated stone houses that interlock like a puzzle. We can't stop grinning at each other. Our next-door neighbors poke their heads out the window and yell, "*Bonjour*," asking why we were arriving so late in the season.

"We are staying for a year!" we tell them, with broad smiles on our faces.

"*Bravo!*" our neighbors reply, expressing their pleasure.

Our neighbors aren't chic, sophisticated Parisians, but rather a mix of artisans, masons, electricians, doctors, teachers, storekeepers, chefs, and farmers. It is an active village of about two thousand people, with one American couple and a few English families who had moved south for retirement, the sun, or the same change in life we had come here seeking.

For the next year or more, this would be our home.

It was more than we could ask for.

〜〜〜〜

Two years earlier...

There must be a different way, I thought, as I sipped my Evian water and nibbled on a leftover energy bar as my Mercedes SUV idled quietly. I was surrounded by sleek BMWs, Lexuses, and Porsches, all stuck on Highway 101 in Silicon Valley—a thoroughfare lined with industrial parks, glass-and-steel buildings, billboards that no one read, and big-rig trucks. The radio announced an orange alert for the Golden Gate Bridge—in the aftermath of September 11, there were constant alerts, scares, and warnings—and I sat, immobilized, in the evening rush hour traffic. I tried to stay calm and relaxed, but my frustration was slowly mounting. I felt irritable and desperate. Even though I had left my client meeting two hours ago, I was still far from home, and I could forget about making it to the gym.

My cell phone light was beeping. "You have twenty-three messages," the automated voice said. All twenty-three had arrived since noon. The first message was from a client.

"I have to change our appointment. Can you fly in to meet with us tomorrow morning?"

I cringed thinking about waking up at 4 a.m. to catch a 7 a.m. flight to Los Angeles. Privately I wondered whether the client was worth that extra effort.

After listening to the twenty-third message, I called my husband Jean-Pierre (Jean for short—pronounced more like Sean or John in the French way) to discuss what to have for dinner: a frozen, pre-packaged meal or take-out from the Chinese restaurant? Scribbling sideways on the back of the envelope propped up against the steering wheel, I wrote, "Buy fresh vegetables."

"I just got out of an emergency meeting," he said. "We have to lay off another group of people tomorrow and I have to stay late to get the layoff packages ready. Go ahead and eat without me."

"Okay—but I have to fly out early tomorrow, so if you aren't home by ten, I may be asleep. And don't wake me," I told him, "because I'm exhausted."

"Leave me a note so I know where you are," Jean said. "Give a kiss to Zoé-Pascale and let's make a date for Friday night. I love you."

On the radio, accidents and traffic jams into San Francisco were announced. My mind went into action, plotting the fastest route home via side streets. Next, call the nanny to let her know we'd be late. My breathing finally began to slow down when I rolled into the driveway at 9 p.m., barely missing the garbage can. I grabbed my briefcase, laptop, and leather purse and scrambled down the path to the house. I dumped my load in the entranceway, our nanny whispered a quick "hello and goodnight," and I ran down the hall to the baby's room. Bundling Zoé-Pascale in the pink silk blanket draped over her crib, I cradled her close to me, carrying her down the narrow hallway, through the dining room alcove and into the kitchen, praying silently she wouldn't wake up. With my right hand I reached into the freezer and grabbed the nearest frozen dinner, poked holes in the plastic wrap, and pushed the reheat button on the microwave. I scanned the mail on the counter, added the unopened bills to the increasing pile, kicked off my black leather Ferragamos, and tiptoed into the bedroom with Zoé-Pascale wrapped around my neck. I flipped through my crowded closet, shook out the black gabardine pantsuit just back from the cleaners, and hung it in the bathroom. In less than six hours I would be starting it all over again.

When had everything gotten so out of control?

Traffic jams; commuting nightmares; insane work demands; take-out food; lack of sleep; Starbucks addiction; airport hassles; payments to the nanny, cleaning woman, meal delivery service, dry-cleaners, bookkeeper, and masseuse; and little time with our precious baby girl: this is what our life had become. Outwardly, we were successful and inspiring; inwardly, we were completely drained. Daydreams involved sitting down at 6 p.m. for a family meal, or mundane tasks such as going shopping at Nordstrom's—actually getting to try on a pair of shoes versus ordering them off the Internet late at night after a long day of work. There simply wasn't enough time for our family, each other, or ourselves. We answered only to the demands of work.

Jean and I had both been told that if we went to university and applied ourselves, we could have it all: great jobs, balance of work and home life, a spacious house, sporty cars, opportunities for travel, weekends filled with cultural and outdoor activities, plenty of money, and even children if we wanted. We were determined planners and goal-setters, and everything in our past led us to believe that we could have whatever we put our minds to. It was what we late Boomers had been raised to expect. The thought of life not turning out exactly as we expected was the furthest thing from our minds. And yet here we were.

When we first moved to San Francisco in the early 80s, we thrived on the drama and stimulation of city life. At our cores, we were both avid learners, and we gravitated toward the endless personal and professional growth workshops offered in the area. Though Jean was born and raised in South Africa and Namibia, and was often puzzled by how Americans do things, the opportunity for continuing his education and living in an international city comforted him enough that he was beginning to feel that San Francisco was his home. I was grateful that his adaptable and curious personality helped him to find his own way and made him willing to build a life with me in the San Francisco Bay area.

Separated from my family by 500 miles, and from Jean's by oceans and continents, we formed our own family of friends with whom we spent a great deal of time. We hiked, skied, walked on the beach, visited the wine country, and soaked in thermal hot springs. We ate in great ethnic restaurants, traveled widely, and attended movies, art fairs, and musicals. It was a time of opportunity, economic growth, and globalization, and we were young, successful, urban professionals.

Over time, we moved up the corporate ladder, acquired advanced degrees, and established ourselves in our fields through persistence and hard work. Our careers were demanding, but energizing and satisfying. Jean had evolved into a senior Human Resource manager and was enjoying the security of the job and the prestige of being a leader. I, on the other hand, had left a big training and management consulting firm to found a similarly niched company with a woman colleague before this had become popular. Working under the regime of the white male culture had left me disillusioned, and I was thrilled to be an entrepreneurial, independent businesswoman living by my own rules.

Now, as we entered our mid-forties with a late-in-life toddler, we found ourselves talking about our quality of life and shifting priorities. The problem was not our purpose in life, but *how* we were living—working constantly and spending outrageous amounts of money outsourcing our domestic chores so that we could work more.

We began asking deeper questions. How do we want to live our life? What is most important now? The "American Dream" for which we had fought now seemed hollow inside. Sure, we seemed to have it all, but at what price?

Living at this insane pace for fifteen to twenty more years began to seem unfathomable. The post-dot-com business slump was forcing me to work twice as hard for half the income. Jean was tired of reengineering, outsourcing, and laying off employees and dismantling companies. Our country tilted so far to the right that we hardly recognized it. Reason was replaced with self-righteous arrogance and fervor, and the trajectory of a growing economy seemed precarious. More and more, life seemed too short to continue on a path that was not making us happy.

We realized that our choices were no longer ours—we were working just to support the lifestyle we had created with little time to enjoy it. The American Dream was costing us dearly; it was time for a major reevaluation of what was truly important.

The inevitable question that followed, then, was "If not this, then what?"

Part I

Old Ways

Oh, my ways are strange ways and new ways and old ways,
And deep ways and steep ways and high ways and low,
I'm at home and at ease on a track that I know not,
And restless and lost on a road that I know.

HENRY LAWSON,
Australian Writer and Poet (1867-1922)

If life is not working, recognize it and make a change.

We shrink from change; yet is there anything
that can come into being without it?

MARCUS AURELIUS,
the last of the five 'good' Roman emperors. (121-180 A.D.)

Change is threatening, frightening, and challenging. For many years, life smoothly sails on, with the wind blowing us easily along. Our careers gain momentum, we are passionate about our work, our family is healthy and happy, the world is peaceful and safe, and the future looks bright.

Then something inevitably derails our life plans: a lost job, an illness, a divorce, total exhaustion, the demands of raising a family, the death of a loved one. One or even two of these events might be handled with the help of loving, supportive family and friends, but when several confounding, agonizing circumstances creep into our lives, stress accelerates, and questions emerge we never thought we'd ask ourselves: How do we truly want to live our lives? What is holding us back from doing what we want to? How much will we regret it if we don't follow our dreams? These thoughts become ever more nagging and insistent. In times of crisis and transition, such topics weigh heavily on our minds, requiring time for reflection, and usually demanding that we make a change.

During these life transitions, we often try to make time—stuffed into a weekend workshop, a therapy or coaching session, or some other diversion from our daily routine—to plan for our next phase. While these approaches do help (and we know—we've done them all), giving ourselves permission to really step outside our normal routines, change our pace, and focus on ourselves is not only the most rejuvenating and rewarding, but also can be the catalyst for personal and professional growth, and the kick we need to fully live our dreams.

The irony is that taking a break from your regular grind can actually be less expensive than dealing with the financial fallout from a divorce, an illness, depression, or the money spent on pampering yourself in order to cope better with daily stresses.

While shifting your life to focus on yourself and your family may come with feelings of guilt, seeming like a luxury rather than a priority, consider this: would you rather spend the coming years continuing to react, respond, and struggle to hold life together? Or would you prefer to create, dream, and savor the gift of life?

Chapter 1

The Pursuit of Happiness

Believe nothing just because a so-called wise person said it.
Believe nothing just because a belief is generally held. Believe
nothing just because it is said in ancient books. Believe nothing
just because it is said to be of divine origin. Believe nothing just
because someone else believes it. Believe only what you yourself
test and judge to be true. [paraphrased]

BUDDHA
(circa 563 BCE to 483 BCE)

WE ARE A COUPLE, happy and somewhat unconventional, striving to taste and experience all the abundance life has to offer. Jean and I met in our early twenties while we were backpacking through Europe and Israel. I had come from California, traveling alone with my burnt-orange burlap backpack and matching down sleeping bag tied on top. Jean had a dark denim duffel bag stuffed with Levi's 501s, flannel shirts, t-shirts and an elegant brown Pierre Cardin suit. He said he brought the suit and tie along from Africa in case he needed to dress up for a social event—a product of his upbringing and readiness to fit into any type of situation.

Standing in the dining room of a Kibbutz surrounded by orange groves in the north of Israel, I spotted Jean, with his huge head of brown, curly hair and a smile a hundred miles wide. He turned slowly and my heart pounded in my chest. Who was this adorable, strong man with the musical accent from halfway around the world?

Over the following year, a whirlwind romance ensued on the shores of the Red Sea, with a few stops and one long sojourn in London. Jean then followed me back to Palo Alto with my assurances that, if he didn't like living there, I'd buy him a ticket back to London. Living like college students, we settled into a studio garage apartment with books piled to the ceiling and mushrooms growing through the carpeting each time it rained. However, we were young and in love, so a little fungi was not about to deter us.

The big city of San Francisco soon beckoned to us, and we moved to a small one-bedroom apartment in the Marina District, right on the bay. San Francisco was a city built for young urban professionals with an international flair. We took the Union Street bus to our jobs downtown and left work promptly at 5 p.m., our new leather briefcases empty except for our day planners, newspapers, and the latest novel we were reading. The idea of bringing work home had not yet occurred to us (or to our bosses), and cell phones and the Internet had not yet invaded our lives.

At noontime, the urban parks were filled with employees eating their lunches, and the restaurants were packed with friends enjoying meals together. Having a work meeting during lunch was unheard of, and knocking off at 4:30 p.m. on Friday was commonplace.

One day, Jean came home thrilled. "What's going on?" I asked.

"I get to travel," he answered, laughing a bit. Working in international banking at the time, Jean had grand ideas of flying to Geneva and Paris. However, the following day he would be traveling to the great metropolis of San Jose, fifty miles down the peninsula.

The next morning, dressed in his blue pinstripe suit and wide-eyed with anticipation, Jean set off with his boss for the "big trip." Skipping the bus, I laced up my running shoes and walked to the Financial District in my fitted dark-grey wool suit, yellow blouse, and yellow-and-grey paisley bow tie. Passing the famous San Francisco Victorian homes painted in various shades of bright color, I would think back to growing up as a sheltered "Valley girl" in Southern California and thank my lucky stars for being able to live in one of the most beautiful cities in the world.

Life was easygoing, full of simple pleasures, and bursting with possibilities. We had no doubts that we were headed for great things.

Though we'd grown up on two distinct continents, we had both been raised to believe that there were few limitations in life, and that it was meant to be lived fully and with passion. Traveling on $10 a day throughout the world was commonplace, not to mention a rite of passage. Women were gaining recognition in the workplace, and marriage was viewed as an equal and evolving partnership. Women kept their own names or hyphenated them, built solid careers, and maintained their own bank accounts. Our relationship—and others like it—was a result of the women's movement and freedom of choice. We were focused on meeting goals, acquiring degrees, growing as people, building careers, and enjoying time with friends. We were both extroverts who craved deep conversations, connection with others, and stimulating debates.

With time to devote to our careers, we both climbed the corporate ladder. Nothing exceptional, just following a similar route to those of millions of others of our generation: the professional good life. Our drug was self-improvement—from management training to 12-step programs to addressing childhood trauma in rebirthing workshops to vision quests. We did it all and loved it. Jean grew tired of dry numbers and fell in love with psychology, fascinated to learn more about both himself and others. I came to recognize that my strengths were in motivating, facilitating, and coaching others to grow personally and professionally. We were pushed further to grow, develop, and find our places in the world.

In our spare time, we fixed up an old cottage we had bought across the bay in nature-loving Marin County. The property was surrounded by Mt.Tamalpais, the blue bay water, majestic redwood trees, and the stormy Pacific Ocean just over the cliffs. On days off, we laced up our hiking boots and hit the trails, sped up to Lake Tahoe (before the days of four-hour-long traffic jams), read piles of books, and indulged in inexpensive local and diverse cuisines. Travel was no longer a luxury, but an affordable necessity. With other couples we ventured to Taos, New Mexico, flew down the wild rapids of the Grand Canyon, and bathed in the warm waters of Mexico. On longer vacations we traveled further, to visit Jean's family and revisit his childhood spots out in the African bush. Each summer we traveled to France and parts of Europe, falling in love with the sunflower fields and hillside stone villages that dotted the countryside.

The world—quite literally—was ours. We didn't need it to change, and we never dreamed of how life transitions and the ways of the world would push us to reexamine our life, our priorities, and what was important.

Chapter 2

Waking Up

We don't understand life any better at forty than at twenty,
but we know it and admit it.

Jules Renard,
French Author (1864-1910)

B Y THE SUMMER OF my forty-second birthday and Jean's fortieth, we had been married for fifteen years. We had traded up to another Marin house—one with a water view in the harbor town of Tiburon. On a whim, we also had purchased an old village house in need of a great deal of *bricolage* (do-it-yourself handiwork) in the south of France, close to where Jean's paternal family had originated. Vacationing in the old villages of Provence, Jean had reconnected with his heritage and spent hours looking at the pictures of little houses in the windows of the real estate shops. "I'd love to have a little stone house here," he would comment. One day we found ourselves asking, "Why not?" It was a magical area: close to the sea, rivers, and mountains; culturally fascinating; and boasting terrific food. The property was very affordable, the exchange rate was good, and our frequent flyer miles were piling up and would last us many years.

Escaping each summer for four to five uninterrupted weeks of Provençal sun, we felt free, like caterpillars emerging from their cocoons and spreading their wings. We managed the time off by working hard and forgoing additional income for vacation, which was worth the sacrifice. France had become our deserted island—a place that replenished our energy for the other eleven months of the year. It was becoming our creative *pied à terre* where we were able to hear ourselves talk, listen to each other, and find lost parts of ourselves.

That year, the conversation turned to the topic of babies. Up to that point, we had pretty much forgotten about having children. It just wasn't on our radar as our careers seemed to take an exorbitant amount of time, and to us, life was about working hard and playing hard.

Then, on a weekend jaunt to Las Vegas, my fun-loving and successful friend Kirsten surprised us with the news that she was pregnant at age forty-one. Meanwhile, Shelley, my feminist best friend from graduate school, who convinced me at twenty-one that it was imperative to keep my own last name, unexpectedly adopted a baby girl, Alix Li, from China and asked us to be the godparents. At forty-two, I realized it was now or never for me, and began reconsidering our decision not to have a family. Could it be possible to have a career, a child, and a balanced life? What would having a child do to us financially? Could I be a loving, patient mother? Could Jean be a good father? Could we still live the life we had known? Could we still travel with a kid? Using the well-honed left, analytical sides of our brains, we began to assess the pros and cons.

Jean was the first to admit that he liked being the most important person in my life. He was afraid that a child would take over his world and that he would lose himself, me, and our unbridled liberty. Then he would add a few global statements, such as "The world is overpopulated anyway. Why add to the misery?"

I knew that what he said made sense, and would try to focus more on work and enjoying life as a couple. I'd listen to friends complain about how they rarely either finished a conversation or had sex with their husbands, and I would wonder whether our life was just perfect as it was. Then I would see a little girl playing on the swings, or eating an ice cream cone with chocolate all over her face. My hormones would surge and my heart would burst, seeping like a cracked egg. During one such unexpected bout of maternal longing, Jean said, "This emotion isn't going to go away, is it?" I responded by bursting into tears. Finally, we decided we would let nature take its course with no attachment to the outcome.

Then, that summer, my boobs blossomed into melons and I was pregnant. Scared, nervous, and elated, we flew back from France and made a doctor's appointment for one month hence. Jean had to leave for a business trip on the day of the appointment, and I naively went alone. I laid on the table and stared at the emotionless face of the doctor as he felt my tummy, glanced at the sonogram, back at the stethoscope on my stomach, and back at the monitor once again. "I'll be back in a minute," he said, and I knew something was horribly wrong. As the door creaked open, I bolted up off the exam table and blurted out, "What's happening?" In slow motion, I saw him shift his glance and begin to reach his arm out to put his hand on my shoulder. "What?" I yelled, shaking him off. "What?"

"I am so sorry," he replied. "The fetus died. Can I call your husband?"

Sobbing, I left a voicemail for Jean and called Kirsten to come meet me at home. We'd barely had time to absorb the idea of being pregnant, and now the gift had been grabbed out of our hands. How could I even sleep with a dead baby in my stomach? All I wanted to do was get it out of me.

Kirsten walked in my door an hour later armed with a basket of avocados, honey, and cucumbers. She announced. "You can cry for 20 minutes; then it is time for pampering. I'm here to give you my homemade avocado and honey facial." What could I do but smile? She was there to take care of me when Jean was traveling.

Four months later, as we fit intensive therapy sessions in between Jean's work trips to Malaysia, Singapore, and Hong Kong (places he'd only dreamed of traveling ten years earlier), Jean's mother was diagnosed with a rare uterine cancer, and within the year her longtime companion died of kidney cancer. Through her resilience and the grace of God, she went into remission. Though this was no less heart-wrenching, tragedy and death were familiar to Jean since the sudden shocking death of his father years earlier, but it was altogether new to me. All of a sudden, life took on a new sense of urgency. We had crossed the forty-year threshold, and come to the shocking realization that our lives were almost half over.

Chapter 3

Twists and Turns

Making the decision to have a child—it's momentous. It is to decide forever to have your heart go walking outside your body.

ELIZABETH STONE,
author, literature teacher, and mother of 16 children

IN THE WAKE OF one perspective shift after another, we decided to try one last time to have a baby. Since I was now forty-four, it was recommended that we try a new and awkward infertility treatment called egg donation. We sat in the living room of the egg broker, leafing through a dozen photo albums of women who were willing to donate their eggs for a fee.

"This is too weird. Do we choose someone who looks like me, or someone I *wish* I looked like?" I asked Jean.

"Let's definitely go for long legs," he laughed. But after a few minutes of flipping through and starting to feel like he was reading a pared-down version of a Victoria's Secret catalog, he said, "Let's get out of here."

We left the pile of albums on the coffee table and ran out the door.

Later we shared our story at the fertility center with the intake counselor, a woman with whom we both felt a strong connection. She had my same coloring and chocolate-brown eyes. Her intelligence, wit, and warm personality resonated with us in comparison to the flat photographs and embellished resumes we'd seen in the catalog. It was an awkward subject to broach, but we asked whether she had ever considered egg donation.

After a few discussions, she agreed. She had donated eggs before, she said, and could use the money as she was leaving her job soon to go back to college. Cautiously optimistic, we began the process of getting pregnant once again.

I was examined and given fertility drugs, an expensive daily injection that Jean administered alternately into my right and left thighs. After weeks of hormone surges, anticipation, and occasional attacks of second thoughts, the day came to hear the results of the final blood tests, which had been done to ensure we were prepared to move forward with the transfer of the fertilized eggs into my womb. We sat anxiously across from the sophisticated fertility doctor. She was in her early forties with a pretty face and firm body beneath the white lab coat.

"I'm sorry, "she said. "I will have to stop the fertility treatment. Your husband has tested positive for HIV 2."

"What are you talking about?" Jean demanded.

"Well, this is not the kind of HIV we see in the United States. It is a rare version called HIV 2, and it is found in Africa. Since you are from Africa, I must assume you contracted it while living there."

Jean was rattled, but continued in a soft voice, "I have not lived in Africa for 20 years. It doesn't make sense. Yes, we have been in

Africa but I've had repeated blood tests—they have always come up negative."

"Well, the test was done by an excellent lab that does not make errors," she said, snapping shut our manila file. "I have no option but to call the treatment off."

Standing side by side in the descending elevator we stared at each other in disbelief. Jean, shaking his head from side to side, kept repeating, "I don't believe this." Meanwhile, I flipped into my unemotional, take-charge mode, repeating, "We will deal with it. It will be okay. You will get retested immediately."

Over the next few days, Jean sunk into despair and began reading *The Final Exit* by Derek Humphrey—a book about preparing to die through assisted suicide. As we waited for new test results, he talked endlessly to two of our doctor friends and my warm-hearted business partner, Virginia, who had been battling recurring ovarian cancer. They locked themselves in the den talking with bent heads, laughing and wiping away wet tears until after midnight. Jean's spirit was shut down; he was preparing for the worst. He was on the edge of despondency and I felt I needed to hold on to the only acceptable outcome: life.

Finally, the results for the repeated tests taken months apart confirmed a negative status. The lab doctor speculated that some other organism in Jean's blood might have triggered a false positive. I had known in the bottom of my heart that things would turn out fine, but Jean had accepted the inevitable by now, and was shocked at the realization he was not going to die. Over the next few weeks, he had to get used to the idea of embracing and planning for life again. Suddenly, it just didn't seem so important anymore to have a baby, as long as we had each other. We were soul mates, best friends, lovers, and partners, and what mattered most were our commitment to each other, our health, and our shared journey through this life.

Chapter 4

The Yin and Yang of Life

I wanted a perfect ending. Now I've learned, the hard way, that some poems don't rhyme, and some stories don't have a clear beginning, middle, and end. Life is about not knowing, having to change, taking the moment and making the best of it, without knowing what's going to happen next. Delicious Ambiguity.

GILDA RADNER,

American Actress and comedienne, (1946-1989)

THE NEXT WEEK, VIRGINIA—my beloved friend and business partner—called early one morning and asked me, in a weak voice, to take her to her cancer clinic. She wasn't feeling well and her life partner wasn't home to drive her. I shoved my paperwork into my briefcase, hoping that our trip to the hospital would be quick, and simultaneously berating myself for thinking that. But having lived with her cancer for almost eight years, I had numbed myself, and the doctor's visits had become routine. I needed to believe that this time was no different.

As she shuffled from her bedroom to the bathroom and then

to the front door, I saw how very tired she looked, with huge bags under her eyes and a pained expression on her face. Having seen her go through so many ups and downs, I told myself that this was just one more down, and that she would make it through.

We had been working together for ten years to build our vision of a great company that would utilize and celebrate our women's intuition and honest, open, enthusiastic style of communicating. Although we were as different as two people could be, Virginia and I complemented each other in personality, temperament, and skills. We shared a deep love for what we were doing and were determined to make a difference. She was my soul mate in business, my partner, my friend, and the one person I probably talked to more than Jean. We worked out of our home offices, overseeing a virtual team that was based across the country. We seemed to be pioneers in everything we did. Both our life partners were supportive and understanding of the fact that our business was our "baby," and that we, as its "parents," had to nurture it so that it would grow and flourish.

After helping Virginia into a hospital bed, where she waited for the doctor, I plopped myself on the floor and spread my work out before me: a reading pile, a review pile, and a respond pile.

"I love that about you. Never wasting a moment, always on the go," Virginia said, smiling wanly. "You know I'm pretty sick, Suzanne."

"I know," I said, looking up at her from the sterile tile floor. "But you'll get better. You always have."

"I'm not so sure this time. I think I'm coming near the end. I don't want to leave you alone with the business. We had so many dreams. We have so many things still to do, and we have had such a good run."

I sat there on the cold gray linoleum, tears rolling down my cheeks. Virginia had never spoken to me about this; she knew I was in denial about the prospect of her death. I pushed up onto my knees to reach her, crawled onto the bed, and we hugged and clung to each other as long as we could, both of us crying, my heart aching with unbearable pain. I was learning the lesson that was being presented to me repeatedly: that some things were just beyond my control.

Virginia stayed in the hospital for another week. We talked daily, and I visited as often as I could while running the business and traveling to client meetings. In the midst of it all, I called Kirsten to tell her about our decision to move on with life and forget about having a child.

"If you have made a decision to be childfree, we need to help you let go of the idea completely," she told me. "I'm taking you on a hike this weekend."

The following Saturday morning, the sky was luminous, unclouded, and shiny blue. Kirsten and I hiked up a deserted trail off Lake Lagunitas on the side of Mt. Tamalpais.

"Today is about how you are going to fill your life without children," Kirsten told me. "So you can focus on new meaning and be content with your decision, as hard as it may be. Besides," she said with a big smile, "you can borrow my daughter any time."

We talked and walked, crying at the loss and laughing at the possible gain. I painted a picture of everything I wanted in my life going forward. I left the mountain with a lighter heart and a new sense of hope and joy as I thought about all the things Jean and I were going to do with our life now that the decision to be childfree was finally made and I had fully accepted it.

Two months later, I asked Kirsten to meet me at the shopping center for a quick lunch.

"Kirsten, our ritual had a flaw in it."

"What do you mean?"

"I'm pregnant!"

It was true. At forty-four, I was pregnant, without fertility treatment, and stunned by the turn of events. On one end of my life, Jean was saved but Virginia was dying, and on the other, I could be having a baby—or I could not. Because of my age, there were so many risk factors, so many things that could go wrong. With Kirsten as the only holder of the secret, we waited for the jury to announce its verdict.

During week twelve of my pregnancy, we walked into the specialist's office for a Chorionic Villus Sampling (CVS)—an early genetic test. The counselor called two days later. "We have found an abnormality on one of the chromosomes that we have never seen before," she said in a serious tone. "We checked the data again and sent it to three renowned labs around the world to have it evaluated, but no one has much information to offer. We need to test both of you to see if it could be a genetic anomaly."

After the tests showed nothing, we met with the counselor in her office. "I'm not sure what else to tell you, except we suggest you do an amniocentesis at sixteen weeks, four weeks from today, during which we will test the fluid in the amniotic sac," she explained. "It could be a fluke and everything could be fine with the fetus, but we will need to wait for the test results to know for sure."

Four tense weeks crawled by. Worn down by all that had happened, we hibernated, communicating very little with the outside world. I turned forty-five that April, though it felt like time had stopped for us as we awaited the next test, the next verdict.

Finally, the doctor called. "The amnio is normal. Whatever abnormality there is, is most likely confined to the placenta. We will just have to watch you carefully, and we will double-check you at five months to assess the development of the brain, lungs, and heart of the fetus. At that time, we will know for sure the viability and health of the fetus."

We started to breathe again, but still felt we were just treading water until the next big wave approached. When the next set of results came, and the survival of the fetus was more sure, we would tell the world; until then I wore looser shirts and hoped those around me would just think I gained a few pounds.

One day, Virginia called. "Suzanne, the doctor says that I have leukemia as a result of the chemotherapy. I thought I would die of ovarian cancer, but now it looks like I'll die of leukemia. I have to go into the hospital for one month straight."

After the news settled in and a tearful conversation ensued, she asked, "Can you handle everything at our business okay?"

"Sure," I replied, crying softly. "The team will chip in and I'll figure it out. I can call in regularly while I'm on vacation."

Two days before our plane left for our annual trip to France, I was scheduled for the critical five-month sonogram. "I think everything is okay," I told Jean. "It has to be."

"Let's remain optimistic," he said, squeezing my hand. "How's Virginia doing this week?"

"She knows she's dying." I said. "I don't want to talk about it. Okay?"

The ice-cold sonogram camera moved over my swelling belly as we watched the neonatal specialist's face for some reaction.

"Brain looks normal, lungs look good, and heart is in place, growth on target. The baby is small, but developing well. Congratulations, you are going to have a little miracle. Go to France, and don't worry. Enjoy yourselves and buy your daughter some gorgeous French outfit."

Calling Virginia, I told her Jean and I wanted to come to see her before we left. Lying on the couch, her head bald but with a smile on her face, she greeted us warmly.

"Virginia, we have something to tell you." I said. "We're going to have a baby." With a swoosh of her arms, I received a weak bear hug and congratulations to last a lifetime. The three of us embraced and cried softly with a strange sense of deep gratitude; as one life was taken and fading, another had been granted and would enter this world.

"A new baby in our family? I love babies. I love kids. I love you!"

Virginia yelled as loud as she could in her Arkansas drawl. "Yes, a new baby for all of us." Tearfully, we hugged again, knowing that we were standing right in the middle of the circle of life.

We flew to France and wrote postcards home to all our family and friends. The message said simply, "Guess what, we're having a baby!" It was one postcard they would never forget.

Chapter 5

Circle of Life

It's the circle of life, and it moves us all, through despair and hope, through faith and love, 'till we find our place, on the path unwinding.

SIR ELTON JOHN,
British Singer and Composer (1947-)

WEARING MY PROFESSIONAL BLACK gabardine wool pregnancy pantsuit, I led a group of participants through an exercise in a consulting skills workshop. It was a beautiful, sunny September day, and physically, I was feeling terrific, but my heart raced every time I heard a phone ring or saw the door opening into the classroom. I dreaded the call that would tell me Virginia was gone forever. The night before, Jean and I had gone to the hospital to say goodbye to her for the last time. We felt in our hearts that it would be a matter of hours, not days, before she would pass on. After pressing through the cluster of relatives who had flown in for her last breath, I was finally alone with Virginia for fifteen minutes of privacy.

"Remember, I'm always sitting on your shoulder. You can talk to me any time of the day or night," Virginia whispered through severe pain. "We've had a great journey together! I love you, I loved our time together, and I love Jean. Take care of all of you, including our new baby girl. Gosh, I wish I could be here to see her and help raise her."

Crying softly and caressing her thin, silky hands, I whispered into her ear, "I just can't believe you will no longer be here. I don't know what I'm going to do without you. I love you so much."

Tears rolling down both of our faces, I squeezed her bony fingers as she faintly smiled. "You're strong and smart and you'll be just fine. Besides, I'll be sitting on your shoulder watching." Just like Virginia—she was the one comforting me. Wasn't it supposed to be the other way around?

Jean and I walked out the swinging hospital room door, waving goodbye, crying, throwing kisses, and whispering "I love you" to her for the last time. There would never be another Virginia. I remembered back to when I first met her at an interview, fifteen years earlier. She had on a powerhouse red wool jacket and matching skirt, and sat at the picture window of her eighth-floor office overlooking Market Street in downtown San Francisco. She looked me in the eye and said. "I play the part, but what it's all about is having a great time with the people you work with. I can tell you'd be fun to work with." She was truly one of a kind.

At noon, the phone rang twice. Apprehensively, I pushed the answer button, knowing that the page was about to turn on a major chapter in our life. Virginia was gone forever. Silently, I sent out a prayer of eternal gratitude for having had her as my female soul mate and knowing that she was out of her misery. But another part of me was angry as hell that she died. What was I supposed to do now, with a new baby on the way, a business to run alone, and an empty hole in my heart?

Two weeks later, still consumed with the profound loss of Virginia, I found myself in the doctor's office. I had the feeling that something wasn't right in my grieving body.

"The baby's doing okay, but we are concerned she is not getting enough nutrients and is below normal in size," said the doctor. "Wrap up your business—we may have to help her into this world sooner than later."

With the time until our daughter's due date suddenly reduced from two months to mere days, I forged ahead to complete client projects, delegate tasks to the staff, and wrap up the purchase of Virginia's half of the business from her life partner. Jean painted the baby's room, we borrowed a crib from a friend, and we went on a quick shopping spree to purchase an assortment of diapers, baby clothes, blankets, and a car seat. In the meantime, we endured frequent doctor's appointments, experienced two heart-stopping false alarms, stayed a night in the hospital to monitor the baby's vital signs, and had a steady case of nerves. Plus I was being bombarded with drugs to help develop our daughter's lungs.

For his part, Jean was trying to hold it all together, worrying about how my grief over Virginia might be affecting the baby, working long, irregular hours so that he could escort me to my appointments, and keeping our fretting families informed of the baby's progress.

On October 16, 1999, an Indian summer Saturday morning, I decided I just didn't want to go the hospital for more tests and would skip my doctor's appointment. I wanted to spend time with my high school girlfriends, who had flown up to San Francisco for the weekend, their visit serving as a pseudo-baby shower for me.

Putting his hand on my stomach, Jean said quietly, "She's not moving. We're going in. Right now." Unbeknownst to me, the doctor had told him to watch for signs of movement and distress.

Trying to keep calm in the midst of my escalating hysteria, we sped to the hospital and ran to the maternity ward, demanding to see a doctor immediately.

"Sorry, there are no beds available right now," we were told in no uncertain terms. "Please sit in the waiting room until something opens up."

"You've got to be kidding!" I screamed at the nurse. "Get me a bed! I don't care if it's in the psychiatric unit!"

"The psychiatric unit?" Jean whispered in my ear. "You're losing it."

Jean waved down a nurse we knew, who, seeing my state, immediately took charge of the situation and found us a bed in a private room.

By 1:30 p.m., Zoé-Pascale was born by emergency caesarean, seven and a half weeks premature. She was a beautiful girl, weighing in at three pounds, six ounces. Other than being very tiny and unable to nurse, she was healthy, breathing on her own and had all ten fingers and toes. With the help of the wonderful intensive care nurses and a lot of love from our family and friends, our little miracle gradually gained weight and was home in a few weeks' time. Meanwhile, we had to rise to the occasion and learn how to care for a tiny premie.

We knew in our hearts that Virginia and Zoé-Pascale had met in passing somewhere in the ether, and that our beautiful daughter had a special angel watching over her.

Chapter 6

Something's Got to Give

*The dream was always running ahead of me. To catch up, to
live for a moment in unison with it, that was the miracle.*

Anaïs Nin,
Cuban-French author and feminist (1903-1977)

A FEW WEEKS AFTER the baby was born, I re-engaged with the
company a few hours a day via phone and e-mail. After two
months, I was back at work four days a week. Business was booming
with the dot-com growth. I hired more staff and wrote a business plan
to grow the company. Virginia's absence weighed heavily on me, as I
not only took over her duties, essentially working two full-time jobs,
but I was now solely financially responsible for the entire company,
for the staff, and for filling her shoes. I now had two babies who were
growing very fast and competing for my attention. I was missing Virginia at work and torn from being with my new baby at home.

Jean reached halfway around the world to South Africa, finding us a nanny who loved and adored our new baby, had raised four children of her own, and was willing to help keep the house neat, do the laundry, cook dinner, and be part of our family.

Jean was also working endless hours, fighting political battles by day, elbow-deep in outsourcing and endless reorganizations, and helping with Zoé-Pascale all through the night. He had fallen deeply in love with our daughter and became her protector, playmate, and guide. One day, he was so exhausted from being up all night with our baby that he nodded off during an important meeting. His boss, a one-company career man with a stay-at-home wife and grown children, told him in all seriousness that taking care of a newborn was women's work. Dumbfounded, Jean didn't quite know what to think. He couldn't comprehend leaving all of the nighttime childcare duties to his working wife.

Then came September 11, 2001. Our innocence and sense of safety were torn asunder, and the dot-com bust came crashing down on my business. I laid off over half my staff and went heavily into debt as I attempted to reorganize. To keep the company afloat and meet payroll, I was once again traveling regularly around the country to work with clients and bring in revenue.

One day I called Jean from the airport, crying. "I hate this," I said. "I can't do this any more. I miss Virginia, I miss Zoé-Pascale, and I miss you. I don't want to be sitting in O'Hare waiting for the next flight. I want to be home with you."

"We'll figure it out," Jean replied. "Just come home as soon as you can."

The world had changed since we began our careers, with Jean in his three-piece suits and I in my paisley bow tie. We went from leaving work at the office to taking it home—or, in my case, actually having my office *in* my home. The advent of e-mail facilitated the expectation to be on call 24 hours a day, in all time zones. With the addition of cell phones, laptops, electronic calendars, Blackberries, and required business travel, work had taken over our entire lives. Yes, we could do more and we had increased our efficiency and effectiveness, but at what price?

Pushing our heads under the pillows to smother out the 5:45 a.m. alarm bell, we swore, "just another 10 minutes." At the next snooze alarm, we'd scramble out of bed for a quick shower while one of us fed Zoé-Pascale. Watching Jean sit by the window singing her a French lullaby, *Une Souris Verte*, my heart would melt and tears would slowly well up in my eyes. However, by the time we finished our morning routines, we clamped down our hearts and emotions, handed over Zoé-Pascale to our capable nanny, and rushed out the door to work.

When I wasn't at a client site, I could pop up from the home office to see my daughter for a few minutes during the day. I would watch the nanny bundle her into her blue-and-white polka-dotted stroller and start off for a walk to the park. Hormones or not, I'd tear up again and, trying not to sink into a funk, stomp back down the stairs screaming silently to myself, "You've got it all! Be happy!"

On the weeks one of us traveled, the other took on double duty as a single parent. To accommodate Zoé-Pascale's schedule, the stay-at-home parent needed to be home promptly at 6 p.m., for there was dinner to be made, dishes to be washed, a bath to be given, a story to be read, lullabies to be sung, and another two hours or more of work to be completed before the next day. The one traveling was exhausted from long airport security lines, late-night client meetings, delayed flights, and working intense full days to get home as quickly as possible. Jean and I would always end up in a silly argument right before one of us left for the airport, adding more unnecessary agony, but making the separation psychologically easier. We had a California mortgage to pay, retirement and college to save for, life insurance policies, fulltime childcare, and other lifestyle expenses. What choice did we have but to keep going?

The many days I traveled to client sites, which were often two hours away by car or further by plane, I wouldn't arrive home before 7:30 p.m. However, Friday was supposed to be *my* day: a special day for my daughter and me. The morning began hopefully: a quick call to the office, which usually lingered until mid-morning while I half listened, half watched Zoé-Pascale rock in her mini-chair. *This child is sitting in a tomb,* I'd think. *Get off the phone.* "Got to go," I'd say. "Got to go."

By noon we'd get to the zoo and my phone would ring again. I'd ignore it and it would ring repeatedly. *No, I'm not answering it.* Pushing Zoé-Pascale in her stroller, I would murmur to her, "I'm sorry babe; I'm here with you today. Let's go talk to the giraffes." Lost amid my irresolute thoughts, I suddenly burst into laughter realizing I was jealous of the graceful, ten-foot-tall spotted giraffe standing in the sun and nibbling at the leaves hanging from the trees, her new baby nestled against her. The wire fencing enclosing her world notwithstanding, from my vantage point, it looked like a pretty good life.

Saturdays were for errands, a run to Home Depot, grocery shopping, a quick bite to eat, following up on e-mails and, if we were lucky, one of us would get to go to the gym while Zoé-Pascale slept. We tried as best we could to reserve Sundays for uninterrupted time outside in nature, with no cell phones, no e-mails, no workshops, no work, no chores. We were swirling in a hurricane of pressure and busyness with no end in sight.

Chapter 7

The Signs

One of the definitions of sanity is the ability to tell real from unreal.
Soon we'll need a new definition.

ALVIN TOFFLER,
American Writer and Futurist, (1928-)

O NE MORNING IN LATE September, Jean called from work. "I have some news," he announced. "It seems that I have reorganized myself out of a job."

After organizing countless layoffs, Jean had once again been laid off himself. It had happened twice before, in the 80s and 90s, back when circumstances were such that it did not devastate him or throw our lives too far off track. This time, however, he was crushed and disillusioned by how it was done: his entire life had been based on being a good corporate soldier, believing that the rewards would come, but there no longer seemed to be any reward for excellent performance or dedication. The quest for greater profits and reduced expenses had trumped the values to which we'd held for so long. Now employees were expendable for the sake of the shareholders. The corporate world we had once loved had lost its charm.

Unemployed and watching repeating footage on CNN of the World Trade Center attack, Jean was getting depressed. "What is life about? Where can we be safe?" he lamented. "I can't believe I brought a child into this insane world." Our wonderful South African nanny insisted on returning home immediately. "I wanted to stay here forever," she told us, "but now, after 9/11, I don't want to be so far from my family when the world is in such a terrible state."

I, too, was beginning to lose it, and we both knew it. I used to love my work. I thrived on it. I excelled at it. But it just wasn't fun any more. "I need help," I said to Jean one day. "The bookkeeper is retiring, and I have no idea what she is doing. Work with me until we can figure out our next step."

Jean, disillusioned by the thought of having to look for a new position, and tired of the corporate games in which human resource jobs became all about preventing lawsuits instead of building strong companies with talented people, took over finance and began to streamline and manage the operations of the company, relieving some of the pressure.

But it wasn't enough. One day, I yelled at him in a fit of frustration, "*You* try running a company without your long-term partner. I can't do it all!"

We had reached the tipping point. Life was no longer working. "Being super-mom is not all it's cracked up to be," I told Jean later, when I was calmer, but no less distraught. "We have been fed a bunch of lies about having it all. It just isn't possible."

"What do you want to do about it?"

"I'm not sure. The company is our main source of income right now; maybe we should grow it faster and then sell it? I just don't care much any more. I remember Virginia telling me how she didn't want to be fifty years old and running through the airport with her flipcharts to catch a plane. Well, I'm turning fifty next year, and I don't want to be running through the airport constantly, either." I was a professional businesswoman, and I was having a meltdown.

Then calamity struck—quite literally, and unexpectedly. As the airbags exploded, I wondered whether I was going to die. Careening into the center divide of the freeway, I jammed my foot on the brake, feeling the ankle twist in a shudder of pain. I felt my heart thump loudly in my chest as my thoughts ran rampant. *Please God, let me live.* I held my breath, waiting for another hit from the big-rig, as all fell silent. And then—knowing I was indeed alive—I vomited into the airbag.

Jean raced out of work to pick me up at a hospital in Sacramento, two hours north of where we lived, and took me to the emergency room closer to home to get an x-ray of my leg and ankle. Meanwhile, the babysitter had called Jean. "Zoé-Pascale is really sick," she said. "You need to take her to the doctor immediately."

"Drop me off," I told Jean. "I'll call Kirsten to come sit with me. Go take Zoé-Pascale to the doctor." Thirty minutes later, Jean called on the cell. "Guess what? Zoé-Pascale is upstairs." She'd been admitted to the pediatric ward with pneumonia. "At least you're both in the same hospital," he said, trying to lighten my mood. But I couldn't laugh. The whitewater raft we were riding had just hit the rapids, and one by one we were falling overboard.

Later, I hobbled into the pediatric ward, bruised and on crutches, with a swollen face. I could hear our daughter's screams as the nurses repeatedly attempted to find a vein to insert her IV.

"Stop, you're hurting her!" Jean finally yelled after observing a number of failed attempts.

I laid down on Zoé-Pascale's hospital bed, as Jean sang her the French lullaby, *Fais Do Do* (Go to sleep). I was happy that we were all together in the same room—alive, albeit not so well.

"What was the accident all about?" Jean asked me later that night.

"I don't know."

"These things don't just happen. Are you so desperate to get out of the situation?"

"I don't know. Am I?"

The next week, the phone rang. It was Jean's sister in South Africa. She called to tell us that her twelve-year-old daughter, our lovely niece, had been riding her bicycle and was hit and killed by a drunk driver in a speeding truck. We sat down in disbelief, sobbing over everything and anything. We had been miserable and yet our misery seemed mild compared to this news. Nonetheless, this was another wake-up call that life would not last forever, and that the present moment is all we have.

It was time. We needed a drastic change—a total shift in direction. We finally had to pay attention to the signs all around us: anger, illness, accidents, death, tragedies, money pressures, depression. Something had to give.

Chapter 8

Options

*If we don't change direction soon, we'll end up where we are
going.*

Professor Irwin Corey,
American comedian, satirist, and pantomimist (1914-)

WE BOTH AGREED THAT life as we now knew it was just not the
same as it had been. Yes, having a child was a major adjust-
ment and a huge expense, but it wasn't just the fact that we'd had
Zoé-Pascale. The world had changed, and so had we. We no longer
wanted our lives to revolve around work, but rather we craved wholeness, ease, and vitality. It felt like we were aboard a runaway train
that sooner or later would derail. Our options were to slow the train
down, get off the track, or crash and burn.

Over the previous two years, we had slaved and saved to pay off
the business debt incurred when Virginia died. In addition, we had

made a pact to pay off our credit card debt and save more money. We knew that unless we were free of debt, we couldn't even think of making any major changes in our lives. We had a beautiful home with a view and a hefty mortgage, and, after the stock market crash of 2001, had only about one-third of the retirement savings our financial advisor said we needed. Our two cars were paid off and we had a modest nest egg for emergencies and travel. We also needed to save for college and pay tuition at the private French school for Zoé-Pascale, an expenditure we felt was important.

We decided that a change of location was at the heart of the transformation we were seeking. Dusting off an old Microsoft Excel spreadsheet we had started a few years earlier, we reviewed eight cities in which we might want to live: Portland, Seattle, Boise, Santa Fe, Taos, Tucson, Asheville, and San Diego. Being rational, left-brained professionals, we examined each city against a set of ten criteria, including weather, cost of living, lifestyle, work opportunities, and family friendliness. We rated, ranked, weighted, and debated our top choices, but always found tradeoffs—such as too much rain or questionable schools—that made us feel uneasy.

Meanwhile, I was having nightmares of falling into dark holes and clinging to the sides screaming for help. I was anxious and depressed, and I wanted to throw everything away and just escape for a little while.

"This analytical process is not working," I said to a friend one day.

"Have you ever thought you might be using your brain too much? Try listening more to your intuition," she suggested.

It was then that something shifted, because over dinner one evening, seemingly out of nowhere, Jean suggested, "Why don't we go to France for a year?"

We both smiled.

"I feel so much more alive just thinking about it," I answered.

"Oh my God, we could do it, couldn't we?"

"I do believe if we want to do it, we can make it happen," he said.

We talked, and talked, and talked, attempting to convince ourselves that running away to France was a "normal" thing to do. Who in their right minds would give up their careers, their homes—everything they knew—to wander halfway across the world to experience a different way of living? However, none of the other places we had considered, though they seemed possible and doable, really called us; no city screamed, "Come here! Come live here!" Only the idea of a year or so in France was pulling at our heartstrings like a tightly tuned violin.

During the following days, we could barely talk about anything else. We felt unmistakably called to the sunflowers and smell of lavender; to the *garrigue* (low lying soft-leaved scrubland) and stone villages, to the Mediterranean, and to the wide, azure-blue sky. Unconsciously, we had been preparing for this adventure each summer we visited France. Not only would it be a change of place—it would be a change of pace.

Sure, some people would call the decision insane, irresponsible, and selfish; others would see it as an adventure of a lifetime. We knew that the choice was ours to make, no one else's. It was a choice between this and a continuing series of mid-life crises that could cost us dearly. It soon came down to the simple question: "If not now, when?"

༘ ༙ ༘ ༙

We knew that dealing with my business was the first major decision—and obstacle. We agreed that, when we returned from France, neither one of us wanted to resume running the company. At this stage, Jean was also ready to re-focus his career in his chosen field of clinical health psychology. Although others had done it, selling a niche company would be tough. It wasn't impossible, but it wouldn't be easy.

We filled a black-and-white engineer's notebook with tasks, research, and follow-throughs. Business, house, cars, residency permits, school: all items to be addressed. Finally, we were serious and passionate about something once again. Pushing ourselves toward a higher goal together brought Jean and me closer than ever. We beamed with happiness and glowed with ideas.

A month into our list building, however, Jean announced that he wasn't sure we should be selling the company and just cutting loose. He didn't know whether he could handle having his safety net cut once again, and at this point, there were still more questions than answers. Then there was the lurking thought that would pop up and suggest that we were doing this—giving it all up—simply because we couldn't cut it anymore. Because we were failing.

The next day we agreed to call in reinforcements, which, in Marin County, translates to seeing a therapist. A friend recommended a local counselor who quickly grasped our dilemma, our choices, our fears, and our vision, and helped us to look at things a bit more clearly.

"Suzanne's basically done," she told Jean in the no-nonsense manner that had initially drawn us to her. "She's gone from Virginia's death to Zoé's birth to turning fifty, all after fifteen years at the helm of the company. She's burnt out and desperately needs a major change. Her soul is dying. Another person might have an affair, or buy a new red Porsche convertible, but Suzanne has made it clear that she wants to run away together, as a family."

"Suzanne," she continued, turning to me, "Jean is in transition. He needs security and a clear destination, and can't just go off somewhere without a plan. To leave your current life with no definite goal in sight is not going to work for him. He wants a strategy and a likely outcome."

It was all true. I wanted—I *needed*—to cut loose, but Jean wanted to know what was coming next. On one hand, he loved adventure, travel, and learning; on the other, as a result of growing up in the developing world, torn apart by conflict, wars, violence, and tragedy, he understandably craved a sense of security.

It was as though the therapist had shone a laser beam into the dusty corners of our minds, verbalizing our dilemma so well that it sent shock waves through our system.

"The details you keep worrying about are just that, details," she went on. "Right now you need a clear vision you can both agree on to guide you. It is as if Suzanne sees a wide-open field. She wants the time and freedom to be open to any possibilities that might come her way. But a wide-open field with no particular goal is just too scary for Jean, so let's put a fence around the field. Let's build some parameters by exploring some options that are within bounds."

By the end of the first session, we had formed a mental picture to represent our dream. It was an open, green, grassy field overlooking a long valley with rolling hills and mountains, surrounded by an ancient low stone wall similar to those found all over the French countryside. The picture gave us a way to see past the details over which we'd been laboring, and focus instead on possibility. At the same time, it gave Jean the sense that we wouldn't wander too far afield in the process if we didn't want to. As ludicrous and pointless as it had sounded at first, the visual worked, and we began to feel confident that our dream was possible.

In sessions over the next few weeks, we tackled big questions, learned how to listen better to each other's fears, and began to understand what each of us would need to feel safe if we actually decided to go on this adventure—one that was becoming more real by the day.

Chapter 9

I'm Done

It's amazing what ordinary people can do
if they set out without preconceived notions.

CHARLES KETTERING,
American Inventor (1876-1958)

ONCE I HAD SAID, "I'm done" out loud, I began to feel like a new person. I told friends and family that I was done and eagerly awaited reactions, which ran the gamut from smiles to empathetic eyes to horrified looks.

It was so *freeing* to be done. I didn't want to keep up with the Joneses anymore. There was always someone who had more money, had more toys, was more beautiful, was more successful, and was having more fun. It seemed that everyone we knew was running faster, working harder, and making more money, and they all seemed to think it was worth it. But how did they really measure happiness? It felt liberating to realize that we didn't have to follow the script we thought we had to live by. Instead of looking outward at what other people had, we were beginning to focus inward.

We wanted time to sip our coffee out of real ceramic mugs, to read a newspaper and chat with a neighbor. We wanted to laugh with our friends as we cooked dishes prepared from farm-fresh ingredients, and finish a novel a week. We wanted to embrace each other and take a nap after lunch, or walk through the vineyards without fretting about missing a phone call. We wanted to let our hair down, pack a few pairs of blue jeans, and set out with a simple budget and money to travel. Money, prestige, beautiful clothes, and the latest gadgets were becoming less important by the day.

Had we gone over the edge? Why were we so different? Or were others in our situation just too scared to admit that their lives weren't working either, and that they actually craved the same things we did?

Now that we had our vision, we truly believed we could manifest it. First, we needed to focus on our options for the business. We realized we did not want to have to worry about the company while we were in France. Even if we hired a great manager to run things in our absence, we would still be involved and responsible. We had to sell.

Once that decision was made, the strategy became to divide and conquer. Jean would research, write the prospectus, establish the value, network, and prepare the company for the sale. He would move us and the staff out of our home offices, and set up the processes and systems in a new location to give potential buyers a clear picture of how the business fit together and operated. I would keep the company in good shape financially, get more clients and contracts, and network as much as possible.

We prayed, we toiled, we planned, we debated, we wrote out more to-dos in our black-and-white notebook, and we Feng Shui-ed the new office and our home. We were in this together, and if one of us fell into a deep hole of negative thoughts and despair, the other would hoist them out. The dream had become firmly planted in our psyche and we vowed to keep placing one foot in front of the other.

Nine months after we committed to the dream, a call came in. "I'm looking to buy or start a company," said a former client.

"Let's talk," I ventured, with a huge smile on my face. "I might have just the company for you."

Intuitively, it felt like the stars were aligned and this man had the ambition and talent to manage and grow the company. "This just might work," I told Jean. "It just might work!"

After four months of negotiations and working around the clock to provide every document required to close the deal, the sale was finalized.

"Are you okay with letting go?" Jean kept asking me.

"I'm more than okay with letting go. The company definitely needs a new kind of leader; I don't have it in me anymore."

Until we knew for sure that the business deal had closed, we didn't tell anyone that we were leaving for France. When we finally did, our colleagues and friends had a range of reactions:

"You're crazy to give up your company."

"What are you going to do over there?"

"What are you going to do when you return?"

"You're taking Zoé-Pascale with you?"

"This will be wonderful for you."

"You will get bored and be back in three months, I'm sure."

"Aren't you scared of not having income?"

Despite all the judgments (and thanks to the encouragement we received in equal measure), with every passing day, we became more certain that this was the right decision.

Our financial plan and budget were in place. We would use frequent flyer miles to get to France, and we had budgeted $85,000 of savings and funds from the sale of the business on which to live: $8,000 for a used car, $67,000 for all living and travel expenses while we were abroad, and $10,000 to retain the multitude of insurance policies that we wanted to keep. The Marin mortgage, house insurance, and property tax would be covered by renting out the house. When we returned from France, we knew we would still be receiving some income from the business to tide us over until we began working again. Not counting taxes and savings we would have put away if we were working, our overall expenses in France would be about 42% lower than what we needed to live on in the Bay Area for a year. If we followed our budget, the plan was feasible.

The garden in our dream picture suddenly seemed to grow new colors: rose pink, violet purple, golden yellow, and tea-cup white. We were committing to one path, one detour, one amazing adventure as a family. Occasionally, we still wondered whether the wiser choice was to put the money in the bank and keep working frenetically, continue to save for retirement and college, and uphold the lifestyle to which we had become accustomed. These thoughts, however, were rare and infrequent, and we gratefully squashed them like so many pesky ants, without a backward glance.

For every reason that moving to the south of France and living in a small village was a terrible idea, there was a reason that it was the perfect idea. The biggest positive was that we knew we were proactively making a crucial change in our lives. Also, we would be pursuing our family dream while our daughter was young and we were all in good health.

The most significant reason, though, was that our hearts were swelling with joy and we couldn't stop smiling at the thought of starting anew.

Chapter 10

Taking the Plunge

*Twenty years from now you will be more disappointed by the
things that you didn't do than by the ones you did do. So throw
off the bowlines. Sail away from the safe harbor. Catch the trade
winds in your sails. Explore. Dream. Discover.*

MARK TWAIN,
American author, humorist, satirist (1835-1910)

HAVING PUSHED BACK OUR departure date twice in order to
complete the sale of the business, we were determined to leave
California by the beginning of August and savor some of the French
summer.

Once the business was sold, we had two months to get it all
together. Jean attacked the long list he had made for our move: pass-
ports that wouldn't expire while we were away, financial statements,
birth certificates, police clearances, and important documents
translated into French by an approved translator.

I handled renting out the house, finding a storage unit, and keeping the business going during the transition to the new owner. Jean interviewed various moving companies, and we sorted, cleaned, tossed, and packed up the house.

Figuring out how to manage our money from overseas was challenging, but after a conversation with our money manager, we trusted that our investments would be in good hands. Our bookkeeper agreed to collect our mail and pay our bills until we could figure out another option. We did not have answers for everything; some matters would have to be solved once we were settled in France.

A major task to be completed together was applying for our residency permit at the French embassy. "Practice your introduction," Jean advised me, "and dress French—you know, wear high heels and drape a scarf around your neck. And bring a book to read. We may have to wait a long time."

Armed with a stack of documents we braced ourselves for the interrogation. The translations were reviewed with a nod here and there, and a few clarifying questions were asked. I smiled politely as Jean responded in fluent French. (We reasoned that they didn't have to know that my French was good enough only to order a meal or ask for directions to the library.) Four hours later, we were told we would receive our *carte de séjour* (residency permit) in the mail one week before our departure date.

Since we had bought our fixer-upper house twelve years earlier, we at least knew where we were going to sleep. The heating was a bit questionable and the tired kitchen was a throwback to the pre-dishwasher and garbage disposal era, with only a basic porcelain sink, a three-quarter size refrigerator, and a petite burner stove, but we were willing to forgo some earthly comforts in exchange for a new lease on life.

Zoé-Pascale, now five and a half, seemed at ease with, and excited by, the transition. She had visited the house in previous summers and could picture where we'd be living. She was as conversant as any

French six-year-old, having attended the *Lycée Français* in Marin since the age of three. She was the perfect age for traveling: strong on her feet, inquisitive, and curious. Most importantly, she wanted to be with us—her parents—more than anyone else in the world.

Prepared as she was, though, she was still full of questions. "Can I bring all my stuffed animals? I mean all of them? Which toys do I pack? Will I really be able to walk to school? Do you think I'll have a nice teacher? Can we go swimming in the river every day?"

We developed a plan for packing that included four categories: what to leave in storage, what to sell or donate, what to ship, and what to carry in our luggage.

Over the summer, Jean had hired the gardener to take the thirteen boxes to the Post Office in his pickup truck to be shipped to France. Eight hundred dollars and one dazed U.S. postal worker later, we were told the boxes would arrive in late September, two months after they were mailed.

Next, Jean looked at the measurements of our rental car. "These huge suitcases you bought aren't going to fit," he said, fiddling with the tape measure. "Time to rethink."

We exchanged the suitcases for six extra-large red duffel bags that we knew could be squished into the luggage compartment and back seat. Carry-on bags were filled with two laptop computers, two large monitors, and two docking stations. We'd buy a printer in France.

Unsure about what we were going to do on the back end of the adventure, we decided to lease out our house ourselves. We advertised online and in newsletters, and we spread the word to friends. We believed that there was someone out there who would love our house like we did, treat it like their own, take good care of it, and pay the rent on time.

Couples, families, career women with agents, and choosy renters ran in and out of our home during the series of open houses. Too big, too small, too much street noise, too much sun, and on and on. A month before we were scheduled to leave, we got a call.

"Hello, I am calling about your house for rent," the man said. "From the description, it sounds perfect. I am flying in from Barcelona—my wife, two boys, and I just spent the last year abroad."

We felt we had met a soul mate who would not only take care of our house, but who understood what we were doing. As contracts were signed and agreements were finalized, we knew we were in the home stretch.

"We are creating this," Jean said.

"Yes, we are," I agreed.

On the second Thursday in July, we finished packing up the office while the movers prepared the furniture to go to the new office in Monterey, a two hour car drive south. Watching the three men wrap blankets around the heavy wooden desks and bookshelves, I felt an equally heavy weight lift off my shoulders. I was truly ready to let go, and thrilled to say *au revoir* to all the files and books and boxes to which I'd clung for so long. That evening, we spread out a picnic dinner of pepperoni pizza and salad on the floor of the empty office while Zoé-Pascale watched a Cinderella DVD on the computer. By midnight, she was asleep on the industrial-grade green carpet and we were waiting to have the last brown cardboard box packed tightly into the red–and–green striped truck. The three-room office, which had been our second home for the last two years, was void of furniture and looked lonely and desolate, but we could only smile wearily, for our departure time was getting closer. Only one more packing session to go.

That weekend we boxed up the last of the house: all the things that were going into storage while we were gone. Kathy and Don, our dear friends of twenty-five years, drove two hours up from Salinas for the weekend to help pack. Kathy, who always dressed in purples and greens to complement her red hair, suggested we put on music and dance our way through the tasks as though we were in a remake of the movie *The Big Chill.* Singing Three Dog Night's "Joy to the World," we reached for the high notes with our own joy, wondering why we were leaving such good friends. In between choruses they told us about their year traveling the globe and how it was the best experience of their lives. Even now, twenty years later, Kathy vividly recalled hiking up the slopes of Nepal and lying in a field of flowers gazing at the luminous, oxygen-light sky.

Monday morning we woke early, ready for the movers, who were scheduled to arrive at 9 a.m. By 10:00, we had become anxious and started pacing the driveway, peering down the street, wondering where they were.

"Sorry," came the unwelcome call. "Our truck broke down and we don't have another one large enough. My friend can come with his big truck, but the price will be different." Jean fumed at their obvious scheme to jack up the price. After a few phone calls and exhausting all the negotiating skills we knew, we threw up our arms in desperation and gave in to the moving mafia. We had no choice—we were leaving the next day. The large truck finally arrived at 2 p.m., costing us double the price for a last-minute reservation.

I turned to Jean as the movers were carting away an old glass dining room table we had bought for our first condominium in San Francisco years before.

"I hate that table. Why are we storing it? Why didn't we sell everything?" I asked.

"I agree. Why didn't we just give it all away?" he said, wrapping me in a warm hug. "Stuff sure holds you down."

On the drive to the storage facility, we decided that one unit would be filled with the furniture, boxes, photo albums, important papers, and other valuable items that we wanted to keep. The other unit was for everything we now intended to sell upon our return, plus our car. It's an expensive decision to store things you don't even like, but it was a mistake we would have to live with.

As Zoé-Pascale saw her bicycle and bed being stored, she began to cry. "I want my things. I don't want to go."

We sat down in the shade and started to tell her stories about the village, to remind her of the place we were going to and the people she already knew there.

We painted a picture of the house in the center of the village, and the red tiled courtyard with a lilac tree, which we hoped we'd see bloom this year. The courtyard walls began to come alive for her, as she thought about sitting on the terrace watching the wild cats walk on the red tile roofs. Putting on our imaginary glasses, we walked with her to school, down the cobblestone streets, past the butcher, the pastry shop, the café, and the pottery workshop.

"Can I decorate my own room, and are you sure the postman will find the house to deliver my toys?" she asked. "And maybe we can get a dog, too? And when we get back, you promised that we would go get Sara and Fina."

"Yes, sweetheart," we said in unison. We looked at each other, thinking we would cross that bridge when we came to it. For now, Zoé-Pascale's two parakeets were on the farm of a pet shop owner, who'd promised he would take good care of them.

The next morning, before we left, Jean asked me, "What do you want out of this year?"

The words came tumbling out. "I want to slow down and find my passion again. I want to buy fresh vegetables and learn all their names, to experiment with cooking and painting, and improve my French. To take long walks, eat lunch slowly, and reconnect with the simple joys of living. I especially want to spend time with you and Zoé-Pascale. I want to be able to take her to school and pick her up on time, read to her, and travel as much as we can. Most of all, I want to get away from the rat race, the busyness we are always complaining about, and to find ourselves and each other again. I want us to be open to a new vision and clear priorities, and to know that this is the best thing we ever did in our lives—for ourselves, for each other, and for our daughter.

"What do you want out of it?" I asked Jean in return.

"I want us to rebalance ourselves and figure out the next half of our lives. As you say, with a young daughter, we now have to live to be a hundred. That's another fifty years to go—and we need to be rejuvenated, energized, and in charge of this next phase of life."

This was it. The day that felt like it would never arrive was suddenly upon us. Eighteen months after we first hatched the idea of going to France, eighteen months of arduous work and preparation, we were at the international terminal of SFO, standing in line with a hundred other travelers and business people, knowing our trip was not just a trip but a family dream, a leap of faith, a life-changing adventure during which we would reconnect and relearn what life was all about.

Part II

Transition

"Tell me one last thing," said Harry. "Is this real?
Or has this been happening inside my head?"
"Of course it is happening inside your head, Harry,
but why on earth should that mean that it is not real?"

J.K. ROWLING,
Harry Potter and the Deathly Hallows (2007)

Take yourself out of your comfort zone

Kites rise highest against the wind... not with it.

WINSTON CHURCHILL,
British politician and U.K. Prime Minister (1874-1965)

It is so easy to stay within a fifty-mile radius of your home, where you know everyone and everything, where daily routines are familiar, and where you run on automatic pilot. There is nothing wrong with living in your comfort zone, but once in a while—at least once or twice in your lifetime—we invite you to deliberately take yourself out of it. Challenge yourself in every aspect of your life. By stretching your limitations, you begin to see yourself in a new light. Take your entire family with you, and experience living outside your comfort zone together. The benefits of learning and growing together cannot be bought, only gained through experience.

There are endless choices regarding how to do this. One of the greatest challenges is to live in another culture for a month, six months, or a year. Perhaps you can volunteer to work together on an archaeological dig, build a house for Habitat for Humanity, or travel to distant lands.

You can also leave your comfort zone without straying too far from home. It may be as simple as engaging in a new activity, such as learning a foreign language, planting a garden, joining a chorus, or taking up a physical challenge with the entire family. If you live in a city, perhaps you can do a home exchange with a friend who lives in the country, or find some great family through HomeExchange.com. Exchange the gift of experiencing a uniquely different environment for free.

If you choose to venture outside of your comfort zone, remember that you aren't leaving your comfort zone forever (unless you want to)— just long enough to experience a change and open yourself up to the idea that anything is possible.

Chapter 11

Finding our Footing

*One doesn't discover new lands without consenting to lose sight
of the shore for a very long time.*

ANDRÉ GIDE,
French author, moralist, and humanist (1869-1951)

TWELVE YEARS EARLIER, WE had fallen under the spell of the
little village in the south of France that was to be our home
for the foreseeable future. We loved the tranquility, the beauty, the
lifestyle, and the people—all of which led us to buy our small village
house. It had been affordable at the time, but it still took every spare
penny we could scrape together.

The home we had bought with our hearts was one of the first
homes built in the village, in the 11th century, directly in the center of town. Like most homes of this era, it had begun its life as a
three-room stone *cave* (cellar). The second and third floors had been

added three hundred years ago, as families grew and more space was needed. We had bought it from a local family of four who had lived there for over thirty years. Having little extra money to pay for renovation, we ripped, molded, scraped, and painted during our summer jaunts until the house became habitable.

When at last the bones were cleaned and stripped, we painted our canvas with bright Provençal colors to match our moods and surroundings: a sunflower yellow kitchen, a lime-green-and-blue salon, and vines and flowers lining the bedroom walls. Our new grand *portail* was so blue that our neighbor told us we had put the sky on the door. We loved that image, and every year we touched it up to keep it as bright as the blue in the Provençal sky.

A few years back, we had hired professionals to build a much-needed new bathroom, enlarge our terrace with its view of the rooftops so that we could seat eight comfortably for dinner, and renovate the downstairs *cave* that I'd refused to go into because of the cobwebs, dead insects, and thick layers of dust. By the time we arrived for our year's sojourn, the three-room *cave* had been renovated into an office and guest suite. The upper floors were looking a little sad by comparison, but we wanted simplicity during our stay. We were happy to trade in our California kitchen, filled with appliances, for a basic place to prepare meals together.

Upon our arrival, we wanted to ease into the French way of living. We gave ourselves permission to take it slow for the first time in years and do whatever we felt like in the moment. I plunged into the romance novel that had been sitting by my bedside for six months. Jean put a final coat of white paint on the walls of the cave. We drove fifteen kilometers to swim in the sparkling blue Gard River, and ate leisurely lunches of warm goat cheese salad, with a carafe of wine and lemon sorbet for dessert.

〜〜〜〜

On our first Friday morning in France, my initial thought was to immediately visit our village *marché*. When we first came to our village, the *marché fermier* had been right outside our door on the *Place de la Mairie*, a square in front of the mayor's office. We woke up to the distinctive smell of fish and the sound of caffeine-hyped market vendors greeting each other, "*Bonjour, bonjour, ça va? Ça va bien.*" This was charming, but when the mayor decided to move the market to an open square near the school to allow additional vendors to sell their wares, we didn't miss the smell of fish one bit.

Everyone at the *marché* was enjoying the crystal clear day and soft sunshine peeking through the old poplar trees. One of the first people we encountered was Madame Laroche, the previous owner of our house. When we'd first bought the house, she and her husband had agreed to be the caretakers, water the plants, call the electrician in emergencies, clean the house before our arrival, and hold the key for guests while we were gone. When Zoé-Pascale was born, Madame Laroche immediately fell in love and claimed her as one of her own, naming herself Zoé-Pascale's French *Mamie* (grandmother), and volunteering to babysit whenever we needed her.

After exchanging three kisses on each cheek, we discussed what Zoé-Pascale would like for lunch when she visited Madame Laroche. The menu Zoé-Pascale dreamed up was nothing less than a starter, salad, entrée, cheese, and dessert. I secretly wondered whether she would expect similar five-course meals at home.

As we said *au revoir* to Madame Laroche, we ran into our well-dressed, retired German neighbor with beautiful green frame glasses, who spoke little French and no English. With a lot of kissing, smiling, nodding, and truncated sentences, we managed to converse. We talked about the soirée that night being organized by Laure, our affable and talented potter neighbor. All the neighbors in our *quartier* were invited to rendezvous in the small square to sing old French folk songs, play their accordions, guitars, and violins, and share in the season's latest Côte du Rhône and homemade dishes.

For the next two weeks, we slept late, sipped our cafés slowly, ate picnics under shady trees, and floated on the river staring up at the famous Roman aqueduct, the Pont du Gard. We sat on the terrace reading long-forgotten novels, sipped local red wine, took walks outside the village among the vineyards, and decompressed.

Chapter 12

Simple Routines

*All of us, from time to time, need a plunge into freedom and
novelty, after which routine and discipline will seem delightful
by contrast.*

André Maurois,
French Author (1885-1967)

WHEN WE BEGAN TO feel our tension melt away as the snow
melts from the mountains, we decided it was time to establish a simple routine—a rhythm to our day that would include Zoé-
Pascale's school schedule, part-time work, and creative projects. If
any activity felt too tortuous, complicated, or stressful, we resolved
that we just weren't going to do it.

However, even with our resolve to live simply, setting up our office, computers, and Internet was an unavoidable first challenge. We
intended to spend a few hours a day helping to facilitate the company's transition to the new management and completing assignments

with key clients. Jean also realized that he was finally going to have time to complete his Ph.D. in Health Psychology and Behavioral Medicine, something at which he had been chipping away slowly over the years. Plus, there was the book we wanted to write.

"C'est une catastrophe!" I yelled one day. Our French computer consultant had installed a new version of Windows on my computer—in French. At first it seemed like a good opportunity to practice the language, but when my computer started commanding me in a loud French voice with a snooty-sounding accent that I had to update my virus protection immediately, I knew it was time to change back to English.

As any newbies would do, we asked around for a great computer consultant. That's when we found Luc, a true godsend. He was a well-traveled, fifty-ish-year-old Frenchman with spiky grey hair who had lived in America for twenty years and who embodied the best of French and American savoir-faire. With his calm and persistent demeanor, he could tackle any nasty technical problem and wrestle it to the ground. He regaled us with stories of eating his first sloppy double-decker hamburger in America and his diametrically-opposed journeys to the vegetarian Ashrams in India. In between commands to the computer to reinstall my English-speaking Windows, he would laughingly tell us how he was always balancing his love of technology and his thirst for delving into the metaphysical with balance, nature and a good glass of red wine.

The next task was to sign Zoé-Pascale up for school. Before we left America, Jean had written ahead to the school and received a complete list of requirements: vaccinations, the *carte de séjour* we'd secured prior to our departure, and our *carnet de famille*.

The last item was new and intriguing to me. I asked Jean about it.

"The family history is recorded in the *carnet de famille* and handed to family members as a legal document," he explained. "It can go as far back as Napoleonic times, and is a critical document for many purposes within the French system."

Jean knew his family must have had a *carnet de famille* prior to settling in Africa, but it was long since lost. This was next to impossible to explain to the French bureaucrats. When they saw Jean's last name, it just made the situation worse.

"Well, you are clearly French, so you must bring it in, absolutely," the mayor's assistant told us sternly. "I must have it. *C'est la loi.*"

She then requested all the official documents we had already submitted, reminding us that all of them—including birth certificates—needed to have been issued within the past three months. Jean checked and double-checked to make sure he understood correctly. Couldn't we just use the birth certificates we had sitting in our files, he asked?

"No, it must have been issued in the past three months," she repeated.

This was *un grand problème* for Jean because all he had was a sliver of paper saying he was born in the remote Transkei region of South Africa, with no other details of his parents or family. Jean tried to explain that what she was asking was impossible—there were no computers at the time he was born, the town hall burned down with all its records (if there even was a record of his birth), and, to boot, the town itself no longer existed.

The sour bureaucrat was not pleased. "It is obligatory by law," she repeated. "We need your birth certificate dated no less than three months ago, and immediately. Plus I need a list of all of your vaccinations as well—not just your child's—from every doctor that ever vaccinated you, from childhood on."

I looked at Jean. "I think my pediatrician is dead."

"I never had one," he said, and shrugged.

"What can we do?" I asked later.

"I'm going to create a newly reconstructed *carnet de famille* on the computer, documenting my family history with all the details I have," Jean decided. "We will produce one in the best way we can, just like she said. We'll make a list of what we think our vaccinations were, date-stamp them to make them look official, and see what she says. The French love their date stamps," he added.

The next morning, after a long, sleepless night spent trying to document as much as we could, we walked back into the mayor's assistant's office and humbly presented a huge binder—our version of the *carnet de famille*, including family details, all medical and vaccination records in French, plus our bank and pay statements, and any other related documentation or translations we had.

Quickly leafing through it, she said briskly, "*Oui*, much better. See, I told you it can be done. Everything is in order now. Your daughter is allowed to enter *Cycle Primaire* (first grade)."

With the bureaucratic ordeal behind us and the school year approaching, we needed a vacation. With one week until school started, we headed off to the Alps, on the border between Switzerland and France. We went to the Valley of Abondance and the small village of Châtel, 45 minutes from Genève. Not quite prepared with the proper attire or hiking boots, as our boxes from the States hadn't arrived yet, we were nevertheless determined to hike the Swiss Alps. Zoé-Pascale and I donned our tennis shoes, Jean wore his leather sandals, and we all three had hats. Following the advice of our innkeeper, we joined a group of French hikers ascending the mountain on a gondola.

Loaded down with two fresh, hot baguettes, a large tranche of *fromage l'abondance*, sweet purple grapes, and bottles of Evian water, we jumped off the gondola and walked over to the nearby ski lift that would take us up to the top of the mountain, high enough to see Mont Blanc on a clear day.

"This way, Maman, this way, Papa. Look!" Zoé-Pascale yelled, pointing to three bulky black cows sitting on the path, with melon-shaped metal bells the size of softballs hanging from thick leather embroidered Swiss collars. Jean told us how he heard that in the summer, all the cows are free to wander the hillsides, eating the lanky, luscious grass during the day and returning to their mountain farms each night.

"I remember when I was a kid on my grandfather's farm," Jean recalled. "My brother, sister, and I used to bet each other that we could tip over a sleeping cow."

"Let's try!" yelled Zoé-Pascale.

"Are you sure about this?" I whispered to Jean.

"These cows are different from the bulls of the Camargue. They are used to people hiking on these trails," he said. "I think we can try it, or at least ring one of their bells."

As we passed a group of huge brown cows resting on the ground near the path, I whispered to Zoé-Pascale, "Okay, this is it. Here we go."

Creeping up slowly on tiptoe, I looked into the big black eyes of one of the beasts and reached out to her forehead, patting her softly.

"Ring her bell, ring her bell!" I heard Zoé-Pascale whispering behind me.

Reaching down on her neck, I grabbed the colossal bell and heard the sound I was waiting for: ding dong, ding dong.

"I did it!" I yelled.

"Tip her, Maman, tip her!" Zoé-Pascale encouraged.

Not sure I should try my luck further, I squared my shoulders and with all my force gave the muscular brown creature a push, knowing already I was no match for her.

The cow, curious about our presence, turned her huge head and winked at me as if to say, "What are you doing, silly human?"

"Okay, enough of this," I said, walking timidly backwards while keeping eye contact with my new friend. "I don't think this cow is going anywhere."

Jean rolled up in laughter at the sight of me trying to tip the cow, applauded our efforts, and suggested we continue down the path, pick some wild bluebell flowers, and let the cows relax in the sun.

"Look, Maman," Zoé-Pascale said, reading a sign up ahead. "That way is Italy, that way is Switzerland, and that way is France. We are standing in three countries at once. How is it possible?" Our first of many real-time geography lessons was taking place on a mountaintop in the Swiss Alps, where on a clear day you can—supposedly—see forever. What more could we ask for?

Sauntering down the winding footpaths, Zoé-Pascale and I sang our favorite songs from the "Sound of Music," laughing and skipping all the way down the mountain.

Chapter 13

La Rentrée

*Find something you're passionate about and keep tremendously
interested in it."*

Julia Child,
American Chef, Author, TV Personality (1912-2004)

On the first day of school, Zoé-Pascale, armed with her new
French pink daisy *cartable* (backpack), Jean, and I left our
house and walked three blocks down narrow cobblestone streets to
the village primary school. Along the way we waved *bonjour* to the
baker, the butcher, and the patron at the café. A group of parents
stood at the gate, kissing and waving to their kids.

The tradition of *la rentrée*—the reentry into the school year—
had begun. A season of its own, *la rentrée* lasts the entire month
of September as everyone settles back into school day schedules,
extracurricular activities, and the regular routine of work and fam-

ily time. Whether or not you are starting school, everyone wishes everyone else a *bon rentrée*: a happy return to routine after the long, relaxed summer days.

Within a few weeks, we adjusted to the rhythm of the school calendar. Twice a week, we returned to the school at noon to collect Zoé-Pascale for her two-hour lunch break, a luxury we hadn't expected. Suddenly we had time to see our daughter in the middle of the day, go on impromptu picnics, catch up on the morning's activities, eat on the terrace, or have lunch together in the café. At 2 p.m., we retraced our steps back to school for the afternoon drop-off, and were there again at 5 p.m. to pick her up. I was pleasantly surprised to learn that our exercise regimen was going to include eight rambles around the village each day.

Monday and Tuesday were full days, followed by Wednesday, which Zoé-Pascale had off. This meant that Tuesday night we could stay up a little later, read books, play cards, or watch a DVD. Wednesdays soon became filled with extracurricular activities and homework, but the midweek break seemed to energize Zoé-Pascale to dive back into her schoolwork and activities on Thursday and Friday, as well as a half-day on Saturday morning. School vacations consisted of two weeks each in October, December, February, and April, so there would be plenty of time to travel. With this in mind, school on Saturday morning didn't seem so bad.

Our routine firmly established, the next challenge was to find a ballet class for Zoé-Pascale. Upon the recommendation of the owner of the local grocery store, Jean and Zoé-Pascale headed out to visit Madame Lisette, a former prima ballerina from Paris who now taught classical ballet in the nearby village of Uzès. Arriving at her studio, they found a strong, disciplined woman in her early sixties, with the firm, ballet-trained body of a twenty-year-old.

"I'm sorry," she said, "I do not have a class for six-year-olds."

Zoé-Pascale burst into tears and whispered to Jean, "I want her;

can't she teach me alone?"

"Let's ask her," Jean suggested. Returning to the studio, they asked whether Madame Lisette might start a class with Zoé-Pascale by herself, until we could find other students her age to join her.

"If Zoé-Pascale loves ballet so much and wants me to teach her, I will do it," announced Madame Lisette.

I had traveled back to the U.S. to complete my last work assignment, and was anxious to hear how it had gone at ballet. Hearing that the *madame* came to the rescue of my heartbroken daughter, I cried with relief. It was all going to be okay.

A week later, I watched as Madame Lisette moved Zoé-Pascale's feet into the proper positions, lifted her chin, straightened her arms, and pointed her toes. This was a serious teacher: all discipline and no nonsense. I asked the woman who had recommended Madame Lisette what the experience of her two daughters had been.

"The first three years are challenging, demanding, and life-changing," she answered. "If Zoé-Pascale can stick it out, she will have the best posture and carriage, and enough skills to dance the rest of her life."

The French philosophy of teaching and learning was different from what we were used to in the states. One day I asked my French teacher to explain it to me.

"All activities, including extracurriculars, are taken seriously, studied, and practiced with high expectations," she explained. "Whether it is horseback riding, ballet, or karate, teachers are here to teach—not coddle the kids or develop their self-esteem. After all, the skill they are learning might become their career. Don't expect her to be nice, but what you'll get is a skillful, disciplined teacher who will work her students."

Was circus school going to be the same? I wondered. That was something else Zoé-Pascale wanted to do. How serious could a somersault be?

"My friend Renée is taking pony lessons. Can I take them, too?" Zoé-Pascale asked one day. After checking it out, we were surprised to find how reasonably priced the lessons were, compared to those in California. An abundance of *Clubs de Poney* throughout the area taught technique, form, grooming, and love for horses. It was a popular sport to pursue, but not for the faint-hearted. The commitment was for a year, and upon passing the exams, Zoé-Pascale would receive her *Prix de Galop I and II*.

In between choosing activities, we were also busy shopping for a small used car and debating whether to buy a TV. Jean and Zoé-Pascale wanted one, but I was bent on having freedom from mindless shows and news blaring at all hours, and I wanted to see how our days and evenings would be without it. So far I was winning—there was only a DVD player in the house, supplemented by Zoé-Pascale's newfound love for *Mickey Parade*, a weekly, 360-page Mickey Mouse comic book in French.

After researching options for a car, we settled on a three-year-old silver Ford Focus, the size of which was perfectly proportionate to the narrow roads and short buildings. It was so different from driving in California on fast freeways and wide, surfaced streets in our SUV, surrounded by tall billboards, strip malls, and skyscrapers. We had felt powerful and on top of the world then, and our new vehicle represented how we had scaled down in every way to blend in with our new surroundings.

"Just don't reverse into anything," Jean warned me, referring to the myriad hard-to-see, low-level poles next to roads. The French tend to keep their cars until the engine drops out, and practically every vehicle was riddled with dents and scrapes. However, it was tempting to keep ours looking new.

"Honey," I said a few days later when I came back from the store, "I'm happy to say I have broken our car in; it is now truly French. I dented it just the right amount, in all the right places."

"What? Didn't I tell you to be careful?"

"It was so low, it was impossible to see. I couldn't help it." I replied, trying to get him to break a smile. "It" referred to the cement post blocking the driveway to the *bureau de poste.*

After inspecting the damage and accepting with a big sigh that the car had been baptized, Jean told me about a curious incident he'd witnessed that day. Negotiating small roads and trying in vain to keep the car dent-free weren't the only traffic challenges in France.

On the way to the Grand Rue, Jean heard a commotion. Turning the corner, he saw a toy-like midnight blue Peugeot nose-to-nose with a boxy, carnelian red Renault on the narrow, one-lane street in the middle of the village. A Frenchwoman dressed in a long black summer dress with matching black sandals was pointing and talking with wild gestures, a look of disgust on her pretty face. Sitting in the red Renault was another woman, about forty, who refused to budge. A crowd had gathered around them.

"You are going the wrong way. They just changed the signs. Didn't you see them, Madame?" shouted the woman in the Peugeot.

"I am *not* going the wrong way. There are no signs," responded the woman in the Renault.

"Oh, but there is a sign," said a bystander. "I saw them put it up yesterday."

"Not on this end," said another bystander. "No signs, no!"

"I have as much right of way as you do," said the woman in the Renault.

As the argument raged on, the woman in the Renault took out a book and began to read, completely ignoring the other driver and the gathering crowd. The crowd burst into applause: this was going to be a good fight. The woman in the Peugeot decided to do the same, and took out a magazine.

By this time, a small traffic jam was in the making, and a few villagers began to attempt to convince the women to move their cars.

The bystanders took sides and were debating which way was more uphill or more downhill. If they figured out who was driving on the uphill incline, the right-of-way rule could be applied.

Suddenly, the street sweeper appeared in the distance, hurrying toward the scene. He was a short, stocky man in a brimmed street sweeper cap, overalls, and suspenders, with strong arms and a determined look on his face. He spent each day cleaning the streets with his long wood-handled broom and dustpan, always saying *bonjour* to any passersby before continuing to work furiously.

"*Pardonnez-moi, pardonnez-moi*," he said as he pushed his way through the crowd. "*Quel est le problème?*"

Each woman began to argue her side of the story and defend her right of way.

Scratching his head, the street sweeper said calmly, "*Un moment, s'il vous plaît*, I will return."

Before anyone knew what was happening, he ran off. The two women went back to their reading. The bystanders waited to see what would happen next. Two old men continued to argue over the grade of the incline.

A few minutes later, the street sweeper returned, dressed now in his policeman's uniform and cap. Radiating authority, he approached the two cars as if he was happening upon the scene for the first time.

"Now let's review the problem, *Mesdames?*" he said. "What has caused this situation? One at a time. You go first, *Madame*."

Jean described how the women seemed to cower into obedience to the authority of the uniform. Calmly and factually they stated their cases, their approximate arrival times, their belief in their right-of-way, and the other's lack of respect for traffic rules and civil behavior. The woman in the Peugeot took her time, describing in detail the new one-way sign that had just been put up the day before on the Grand Rue. The woman in the Renault said that no such sign existed on the far side of the Grand Rue, from which she came.

"*Oui,*" said the street-sweeper-turned-policeman forcefully. "*Vous avez vos raisons.* You both are right. The Mayor is implementing a new street sign system, but it is unfinished. This is simply a misunderstanding, and not so complicated that we can't resolve it together, *oui?* Do you agree?"

"*Oui, ce n'est pas grave,*" said both women in unison. (Yes, it is not very serious, it's not a problem.) That phrase—*Ce n'est past grave*—was the ultimate solution in solving a conflict. The policeman then orchestrated the movement of the cars in reverse until the street was cleared. No one was going to be allowed down the Grand Rue until the signs were fixed. Everyone had to go back the same way they came, so nobody won and nobody lost.

A slow murmuring among the bystanders could be heard as they continued on their routes. "*Ce n'est pas grave.*" "It is not serious." "Yes, this was the best solution."

On his way home an hour later, Jean walked by the place where the woman driving the Renault had said there was no sign. The street sweeper, after another change of uniform, was busily putting up the second "Do Not Enter" sign, officially inaugurating the Grand Rue as a one-way street. Jean complimented the street sweeper/policeman and told him he resolved the situation well.

"*Merci beaucoup,*" he responded. "By tomorrow morning at this time, the whole town will know that the Grand Rue is a one-way street. Gossip is the best form of communication in a small village like this."

Our *rentrée* was well underway, and all the road signs were pointing us in the right direction, toward a sense of well-being and general ease of living. Between the family-friendly school and work schedules, the convivial community culture, and the attitude that life should not be taken so seriously, we were beginning to soften. With gratitude, we were shedding our hardened souls and opening up to the possibilities of a different way to live.

Chapter 14

"Ce n'est pas Grave."

It is not enough to be busy; so are the ants.
The question is: what are we busy about?

Henry David Thoreau,
American author, poet, and philosopher (1817-1862)

A WOKEN BY THE MELODIC ringing of the 7 o'clock bells from the
clock tower and the early morning sunshine streaming in our
window, we rolled off our king-size bed, ready to start our project of
redecorating the bedroom. By the bed sat the 22-item to-do list that
we hoped to complete before the sun set. After dropping Zoé-Pascale at school, and wolfing down a café au lait and a hot croissant at
the local café, we headed for *Monsieur Bricolage* (Mr. Handiwork),
a well-known hardware store in France. We entered, glancing up at
the twenty-foot plaster effigy of *Monsieur Bricolage* himself. Soon
we met a friendly salesman dressed in a designer's version of a hard-

ware store worker's uniform: kelly-green poplin slacks, white shirt with green sleeves and pocket, and a green-and-white cap embroidered with the store's logo. He was carrying a measuring tape.

"Bonjour, je peux vous aider?" he asked.

Jean explained to this slimmer, shorter version of *Monsieur Bricolage* that we needed to strip old wallpaper, and wash and eventually paint the stone interior walls.

"Follow me," the salesman said as he explained our choices of environmentally friendly wallpaper remover and other cleaning supplies we'd need.

"I love hardware stores," Jean beamed, basking in the rows of possibilities surrounding him in each aisle.

"Allez-y!" I shouted, using my favorite new word for "hurry up." "Let's buy what we need. We have tons to do today." I pushed Jean down the aisle as his wandering eyes glazed over at all the hardware equipment. "We have to make progress on the bedroom."

Over the next three days, while Zoé-Pascale was at school, we scraped and scrubbed and peeled and rubbed while we sang along to the radio. Our conversation and occasional lyrics of, "Come on baby, rip it," or "I got it, I got it," floated through the windows and onto the street below. We did what we could to keep our motivation high as we endeavored to return the dirty old walls to their former greatness.

Every once in a while, a neighbor would hear us, walk underneath the window and yell *"Salut!"* or *"Bon courage!"* (Good luck!)

Arnaud, our closest neighbor, peeked in on his way home for lunch. He was in his late forties, single, and balding, with a thick Provençal accent and a constant 5 o'clock shadow. He lived in the same house his great-great-grandparents had over two hundred years ago. Currently, Arnaud was the groundskeeper at the nearby high-end campground; he loved to work outdoors. A gentle soul whose passion was to run marathons and whose running shoes showed miles—kilometers, really—of wear and tear, he stood silently in the doorway, watching for five minutes as we scraped, peeled, moaned, and sweated.

"*Qu' est-ce que tu veux faire?*" (What do you want to do?) he finally asked.

We showed him the container of wallpaper remover, and he began to speak in a fast, sing-songy accent that only Jean could understand. "No, no, tell them you need the heavy-duty remover. You are working much too hard. This is not sufficient. It will take you weeks to remove all this paper."

It was noon, and we knew *Mr. Bricolage* would be closed until 2:30 p.m. for the French lunch hour. After a quick shower, we hopped into our small vehicle and drove the main boulevard circling Uzès, parked along the curb, and sat down at a nearby outdoor café. The six tables set out on the sidewalk prominently displayed placards that said *Plat du Jour, Saumon et Riz.*

"I just want a quick salad," Jean said.

"Me, too," I responded, encouraging the waitress to come to our table so we could place our order.

"*J' arrive,*" she called out to us as she casually conversed with some other diners.

Trying to settle down, I yelled out to her, "We're in a hurry."

"No, you cannot eat fast," she said, finally approaching our table. "Please, you must eat your lunch slowly. What else do you have to do that can be more important than eating?" she lectured us sternly with a smile in her eyes. "Please, you must take your time and enjoy your lunch. That is why you are eating, right, for pleasure, yes? It is very important. Otherwise you have no life—*c'est vrai, oui?*"

We had been well trained to stuff down our lunches in five minutes at our desks. Looking around at the six little tables situated under the large poplar trees, set with tablecloths, polished glasses, and shining silverware, we saw no one in a rush but us. Lunch was meant to be a two-hour affair, where you could visit and share and discuss.

What could be more important than this life-enhancing ritual?

We laughed as the mirror was held up to us. We had come to France to embrace a simpler life, to rejuvenate and reinvent ourselves, and all we were doing was working even harder and feeling anxious about taking a long lunch. We were reverting to our obsessive-compulsive selves, living according to the American work ethic, and taking ourselves too seriously. We had been so conditioned to do, go, do more, and accomplish, that we no longer knew how to just *be*, and simply enjoy the process of life. But now the time had come, and we were willing to let go of the old ways and try to change. *Ce n'est pas grave*, as she said. The wallpaper and painting would just have to wait, because lunch was the priority. Taking time for lunch was a key to better living.

We certainly had a lot to learn about living the good life, *la bonne vie*, and enjoying everything about every day. The natural rhythm of life, like the seasons, had been lost to us. But no one says at the end of their life, "Wow, I wish I had spent more time at the office." Working hard and playing hard, no matter how much you like your job, is very different from living a balanced, healthy life where your calendar doesn't dictate your day.

Clinking our glasses of rosé in a high toast, we proposed that all of our lunches from now on would be long and luxurious. That we would taste our food and discuss our deepest thoughts—the chores could wait.

Hours later, returning to our favorite green-and-white *Mr. Bricolage*, we explained what we needed. *"Bien sûr,"* the salesman agreed. (Naturally.) "Heavy-duty wallpaper remover will do the job just fine."

Over the next few days we continued to rip, shred, peel, scrape, and break every fingernail we had. In between, we stopped for leisurely lunches and discussed what we were going to do with all the old, decrepit, dirty wallpaper strips, wooden planks, and assorted other pieces of junk that needed to be taken to the local dump. Using our hatchback as a pseudo-truck, Arnaud helped us pile in the old paper, rolls of broken linoleum, and pieces of dusty carpet. He helped stack the old wood planks on top of the car, tying them down with rope looped through the windows in a criss-cross fashion.

"That should do it," Jean finally said. "You drive, and I'll hang halfway out the window to help hold down the wood on top, so it doesn't fall off, just to be safe."

Suffocated by the dirt and dust, I squeezed myself into the driver's seat, which had been pushed forward to allow as much debris as possible to fit in the hatchback. With Jean hanging out the window, I drove at a speed of 25 km per hour (roughly 15 mph), waving at speeding cars to pass us. Fifteen minutes later, windblown and with splinters in his hands, Jean waved me over to the small dirt road set between a vineyard and an olive grove, which led up a steep hill to *la décharge* (the dump). Scattered on either side of the road were old refrigerators, broken chairs and tables, cardboard boxes, bottles, garbage cans, and indistinguishable metal objects.

Like warriors in battle, we drew up a plan.

"You drive very slowly up the hill. I'll stand on the back bumper and hold down everything on top of the car," Jean instructed.

"Are you sure this is a good idea?" I shouted through the window one last time

"Sure, it will be fine. Just go very, very slowly."

Accelerating at snail's pace up the incline, I hesitantly shifted gears from first to second and simultaneously pressed on the gas, suddenly jerking the car forward. With each bump I hit, I cringed, hearing wood scraping the paint on the car as the planks slid down off the back window. Determined but unsure of how to get to the top of the hill fast, I hunched further over the wheel, pressed on the gas, and bumped through a few unexpected potholes, bucking the car along.

Twisting in my seat to see what was going on behind me, I watched the last of the wooden planks with half-bent nails sliding off the sides and back of the car in a cascade of grime and dust. Wide-eyed and open-mouthed, I flew out of the car. Several yards back I found Jean, flat on his *derrière* in the dusty road. After a body check to make sure everything was intact, and a few dozen obscenities thrown out to the world in general, Jean burst into laughter at our calamity and ineptitude.

Concluding that the damage to his body was nothing compared to that of the scraped car, we looked out over the red, orange, and yellow vineyards and started laughing again.

That night, over fresh pasta pesto and a bottle of chilled Côte du Rhône, we reflected on our life in California. Though we enjoyed it, we had more often been apart than together, rushing from one thing to the next, throwing a quick kiss as we moved on to the next scheduled activity. Here, even the chores felt like an adventure that we shared together. Isn't that what being a family is all about?

There was also something about living in a house that was nearly a thousand years old—one that had been standing there for a very long time and would continue to do so for a very long time after we left. There was no hurry—the house was not going anywhere, and it would survive us. It imbued us with a far different sense of who we were in the scheme of things and in relation to the cosmos. As Zoé-Pascale said, quoting *The Lion King*, "It is not about you or about me; we are just one in a long line of descendants in the circle of life."

We had only just begun our journey, and already our mindset was shifting.

Constantly we reminded ourselves, *"Ce n'est pas grave."*

Chapter 15

A French Education

*I think, at a child's birth, if a mother could ask a fairy
godmother to endow it with the most useful gift,
that gift would be curiosity.*

ELEANOR ROOSEVELT

(1884-1962)

Zoé-PASCALE HAD BEEN going to school for three weeks when
she came home with a note in her *cahier de liaison*, a book that
was used to write notes back and forth between parents and teacher.
The note asked us to come to an all-parents' meeting. "Tomorrow
night," Madame wrote in the communication book, "we will meet
so that I can explain the curriculum and also your role as parents."

We had already seen some of the influence of the Professor (the
French word for a teacher at the primary school level is *le professeur*) in the precise list of school supplies the children needed for
the classroom: an exact brand of colored pencils, a ruler exactly 30

cm long (no less and no more), three distinct sizes of *cahiers* (note-books), and book covers.

The next night we nervously entered the *professeur's* classroom promptly at 6 p.m. with twenty-five other sets of parents. We sat at the tiny student desks, our knees bumping against the hard wood, eager to hear what the Madame had to say. With only a basic knowledge of French, I depended on Jean to take good notes so we could later discuss what I had missed.

Madame explained that the French educational philosophy is based on a national curriculum, emphasizing analytical thought and philosophical discourse, and promoting high academic expectations. Extracurricular activities take place through the *Centre Social* (Recreation Center), or through private after-school clubs and classes. However, our village had elected to hold school on Saturday mornings in order to include the arts in the curriculum. As a result of that decision, Madame said with a smile, "This year the children will experience courses in pottery, circus, choir, theatre, dance, music, and the Occitan language to stimulate the imagination and the creativity."

She said that she loved Occitan, which is the lost language of Provence, as well as a culture and a heritage beloved by the French Languedociens. After the French Revolution, when Paris decided to provide education to all children in one national language, regional languages such as Occitan were slowly being lost.

Among the novelties to which I'd need to grow accustomed was the school's bathroom: a big, unisex room with ten toilets lined up on one wall and ten urinals lined up on the other. In the middle was a big fountain that sprays out in a circle, so that ten children can wash their hands at the same time.

∪∨∪∨∪

We soon grew accustomed to the changes and the rhythm of walking back and forth to school four times a day. I was beginning to understand how the French remain slim.

"Vacation starts next Saturday, October 28," I announced to Zoé-Pascale and Jean. We planned to leave Friday night for vacation.

"Maman, I thought my teacher said we had school on Saturday," Zoé-Pascale said.

"She did?"

"Honey, did you get the calendar mixed up?" Jean inquired.

"Look, here it says, *Vacances, 28 Octobre au 6 Novembre.* That says to me that vacation starts on October 28 and ends on November 6. But it is weird that they give us Monday, November 6, as a holiday also."

"But maybe you should ask someone else," Jean suggested.

I walked over to Lorraine's one-room hat shop tucked in between two village homes. Displayed in her window were one-of-a-kind designs fit to wear to Ascot. Lorraine, an English milliner, and her family settled in the village a few years earlier. Her son was in Zoé-Pascale's class and, having a better grasp of the workings of the local school, had taken me under her wing.

"Lorraine," I said as I was greeted with a snuggle by her large, mixed-breed dog. "I think I might have made a mistake. Do vacations start on the day they are listed, or what? And when do they end?"

"I know, it is very confusing. I still get confused and sometimes dates change, so don't hold me to this. I think, however, that vacation starts the evening of the first day listed and ends the morning of the last day listed. In this case, vacation starts the evening of the 28th of *Octobre* and ends on the morning of the 6th, not the 7th, as you might think."

"I see. Well, *c'est la vie* for this *vacance*," I answered. Our reservations had been purchased and life was too short to worry about missing one day of school. Besides, for us, travel was a major part of Zoé-Pascale's education as well as our rejuvenation.

Except for the details, we loved the quarterly two-week vacation breaks in the fall, at Christmas, in February, in April, and then two months in the summer. Longer times off during the year, coupled with a shorter summer, seemed to make it easier on kids, teachers, and parents alike. Plus, not having school on Wednesdays assured that the kids would never get too tired. I never heard anyone say, "Thank God it's Friday."

Of course, things were working so well for us now because we weren't tied to 8-5 jobs like at home, but for those parents who did work, the villages provided inexpensive camps and daycare options. Taking care of the family in a quality manner was a key priority throughout all of France.

‿⌣‿⌣‿

As the school year began, it became evident that I was less and less able to help Zoé-Pascale with her homework. Reading to her in French with a bad Spanish accent (a remnant from the only other foreign language I'd learned) was detrimental, and my helping her with anything but basic spelling would probably do more harm than good. As a result, Jean took on the job of sitting down with Zoé-Pascale every day after school to review her homework.

Doing homework in any language is a mixture of anguish, angst, play, and the battle of wits. At their best, when Jean and Zoé-Pascale had energy and focus, Jean's unconditional love and patience held Zoé-Pascale's laser attention.

However, every now and again from the kitchen, I would hear Zoé-Pascale say, "You're *méchant* (mean)." But a hug and a few tears later, they would be on course again. I praised Jean for his persistence, patience, and love, and for being such a good homework champion. Once in a while, I'd be jealous of their time spent to-gether in intimate French conversations, memorizing a poem or rehearsing a scene for a class play. But after a week of supervising homework when Jean was traveling, I was more than grateful to let him take it over again.

Meanwhile, I was determined to ensure that Zoé-Pascale's English was up to par, and that she could read fluently in English as well as in French. Besides, my parents were constantly asking me, "Can she read English? Will she speak to us in English?"

My mother and father are first-generation children of Eastern European immigrants who were Americanized when it was *à la mode*, and never learned their own mother tongues. They had for-gotten that the whole world does not speak English, and as a result, were petrified that Zoé-Pascale would never talk to them again. Like many Americans, they are not used to the fact that most of the world speaks more than one language fluently, often as many as three or more.

Having brought hundreds of dollars worth of English phonics books with me to France, I set out a schedule to work through them with my daughter. But as time slipped by, we got busy and more in-terested in reading the *Harry Potter* and *Narnia* series, and I resort-ed to having Zoé-Pascale complete a great online phonics program on the Internet. Given the right environment, tools, and support, I knew her transition to English phonics would be easy, and my own anxiety about a daughter who spoke only French dissipated.

Then came the day when Zoé-Pascale discovered her French Disney comic books at the nearby *marché* in *Bagnols sur Cèze*, For one Euro, she had 300-plus pages of French *bande dessinée* (comic book—often called a BD) reading to last her a few hours.

One morning, I woke up at 8 a.m. and decided to read in bed for a while until Zoé-Pascale woke up and Jean brought me my coffee. (Yes, practically every morning I get *café au lait* in bed.) A few minutes later, my bundle of joy leapt onto the bed and said, "I want to read with you. I want to read my new comic book. This one is about Julius Caesar and Gaul. I also saw one about *Asterix* and *Obelisk*. I love Roman history!"

Reaching over the bed, she grabbed the book; we propped up some more pillows, and we both lay there, reading in total peace. I waited for her to ask me for help or get bored, but five minutes, then twenty passed in total bliss, set to the background music of Zoé-Pascale occasionally reading aloud a word or phrase in her perfect French.

I had a flashback to the time I drove across the country with my Dad, when I was nine years old. Each night we would stop at a motel, take a swim in the pool, eat dinner at a local diner, and buy a bar of Hershey's chocolate and a Coke to have later for dessert in the motel room. We'd get back to the room about 7:30 p.m., relax on the bed side by side, take out our books, and read until it was time to turn the lights out. A few words like "Pass the chocolate," or "Can I have a sip of Coke?" would be spoken, and then we returned to our books. It was a magical time in my life—a special trip, just my Dad and me.

Jean walked in with my café au lait, laughing and smiling at the two of us.

"You must be in heaven," he said to me.

Later, Zoé-Pascale piped up, "I finished that story. I want to read another."

"Okay," I said.

An hour later, I finally said, "It's time to get up; the day will be gone before we know it."

"But Maman, this is so great. I love to read in bed with you."

I could only smile, give her a big kiss and hug, and say, "You have just found a whole new world of reading."

"But you'll still read to me every night, right?"

"Of course, baby—think how many books in the world we get to read."

To our delight, Zoé-Pascale's love of reading grew so wildly that we began having to tell her to stop and eat, get dressed, or go to bed.

And reading wasn't the half of it. One day, she told us in all seriousness that she believed she was Cleopatra VII in another life, and that she spoke French because she also had helped Julius Caesar build Rome speaking Latin, which was not so different from French. It was becoming clear that spending this time in France, hiking through Roman ruins, canoeing under the Pont du Gard, reading about Julius Caesar in comic books and on statue inscriptions, walking the same roads as the Romans, and waving good morning to the people of the town was lighting up Zoé-Pascale's imagination. The intersection of her love of reading, a curiosity about ancient history (not to mention the luxury of being surrounded by it), and living in the midst of the most romantic language in the world had opened our daughter's mind to things that we would never have dreamed possible.

Chapter 16

Parlez-vous Français?

*I am always doing that which I can not do,
in order that I may learn how to do it.*

PABLO PICASSO,
the father of modern art (1881-1973)

BEFORE WE MOVED TO France, I had politely made my way during our short stays there using key phrases like *bonjour* and *merci beaucoup*, supplemented by help from Jean. No matter how hard I
tried, I could not distinguish between "*un*" and "*une*," and rolling my
R's was physiologically impossible. Learning to communicate that
year was the ultimate push out of my comfort zone.

"Just use your little tongue, the one on top of your throat...
move it up and down, fast," Jean would try to teach me. I never even
knew I had a second little tongue, and so the idea of using it was
baffling. Learning a language requires the ability to hear different

sounds and translate them into speech. For me, a visual learner, doing this was my biggest challenge yet.

"How do you spell that?" I would constantly ask Jean. "I need to see it to say it." I would fixate on a word I didn't understand, and stop listening to the rest of the conversation. I would fret over what I was missing, like a compulsive overeater. For example, Zoé-Pascale would tell me she had "*devoir*." From her actions I figured out she was referring to homework, but if it was homework, shouldn't the word be *travaille à la maison* (work at home)? I looked it up in the dictionary and saw that *devoir* meant "must or should do." *How did that become the word for homework?* I wondered.

"Why do you take everything so literally?" Jean asked. "Just listen to the sounds. What is the word saying to you? *Devoir*, must do. It's what the kids have to do at home, right?"

As difficult as it was for me, I loved the French language and had a deep desire to learn to speak it well. I wanted to immerse myself in conversations with locals, engage with Zoé-Pascale's French friends and their families, and not be so dependent on Jean.

I answered an ad placed by Maryse, a petite brunette divorcée with two teenagers, who taught French to foreigners. She was just what I needed: patient, understanding, refusing to speak English to me but allowing me to go on and on about whatever I wanted in French. I had a decent vocabulary; I just couldn't put a sentence together. I could speak in the present tense, but don't ask me about anything in the past, and forget about the future. I knew what I wanted to say, but I spoke with my dreadful California Spanish accent, making it extremely difficult for anyone to understand me. Maryse became my guide, my sounding board, and my ever-patient confidante and friend. Her patience, interest, and willingness to make sense out of my jumbled sentences were freeing.

"Honey, you are the only one I know who loves to take lessons but doesn't study or do any homework," Jean would say whenever I'd cry in frustration over my verbal inabilities. "Take time each night and memorize those verbs." I enjoyed sputtering out my thoughts to those who had the patience to converse, but memorizing just seemed a waste of time. Perhaps I expected that the different verb tenses would sink into my brain by osmosis. I was determined to practice out in the world, and would rather go to bed reading a Booker Prize novel than *501 French Verbs*. Maybe I wasn't exactly where I wanted to be, but my vocabulary was increasing. After all, I now used *devoir* frequently—and in fluent sentences.

And so, daily life became my classroom. Some days I would eagerly reach out to others to converse, and other days I would shy away. I could sense who would take the time to try to understand me, and avoided others whose thick Provençal accents or fast tongues would send me into a panic.

Once a friend from the States asked me, if it was so difficult to learn the language and make friends, why did I stay? The answer was that, not only was our life here worth it, but I loved the challenge. Like a baby who takes her first step only to hear her parents squeal with excitement and praise, I felt that an entire new world was opening up to me. Every time I had a one-, two-, or sometimes five-minute conversation in which I understood—and was understood by—the other person, my stomach would flip and my smile would widen. In that short exchange I would feel like that baby—proud and ever so pleased with myself.

One Sunday, upon returning home at dinner hour from a wonderful weekend, we decided to order the spicy, thin-crusted pizza well known along the Mediterranean while Zoé-Pascale finished *les devoirs*. With nothing in the refrigerator and the markets closed, pizza *emporter* seemed like the best option.

I walked out the gate and down the street to our neighborhood pizzeria, arriving at the counter alone. Reaching into my pocket, I realized I had forgotten to bring my reading glasses. Annoyed at my inability to read the fine print on the menu, I laid it down on the counter and explained to the young French Moroccan boy behind the counter the special type of pizza I wanted: one-fourth with cheese only for Zoé-Pascale, and the other three-quarters with assorted toppings. I was glad Jean hadn't accompanied me, as this was the kind of order that drives him nuts.

"Just order off the menu," he said. "You're not in California." I acknowledged it was a bit un-French, but necessary when the three of us shared a pizza. To ensure that the young boy wrote down the order correctly, I asked him to draw a circle to represent the pizza. I then pointed to the quarter piece and said, *"Seulement du fromage, et le reste avec champignons, poivrons, oignons, et artichauts"* (Only cheese, and the rest with mushrooms, peppers, onions, and artichoke.)

The shaved-headed boy contorted his eyebrows into a questionable grimace at my somewhat bizarre order. *"Seulement du fromage?"* he repeated in French.

"Oui," I responded confidently.

He continued to stare at me with a combination of confusion and resignation.

Ten minutes later, the pizza arrived piping hot at our door and we gathered around the patio table, anxious to dig in.

"Eckkk," Zoé-Pascale said, spitting out her first bite of pizza. "It tastes like fish."

"Impossible," I said. "I ordered just cheese. Try this other piece."

"Eckkk. There is fish in it."

"Impossible, you're imagining it," I said.

"Non, je refuse," she insisted. "There is definitely fish in it."

"It's plain pizza," I insisted back.

"Let me try some," Jean said. His expression immediately turned sour. "Oh yes, there is fish in it!"

"See? I told you," said Zoé-Pascale.

"What is wrong with the two of you? Let me taste it," I said.

Sure enough, I discovered they were right. "Do you think they got a piece of fish mixed in from another dish by accident?" I asked.

"Love of my life," Jean said, looking at me with a grimace. "What did you order?"

"I ordered *seulement fromage*. Just like she wanted."

As I repeated what I had said in my contorted French accent, Zoé-Pascale and Jean exploded into hysterical laughter.

"You said *saumon et fromage*—salmon, the fish, not *seulement!*" said Jean, still giggling. "You pronounce the *le* heavily; otherwise, it might sound like *saumon*. The boy behind the counter must have thought you were crazy, asking for a quarter of the pizza with salmon on it."

Suddenly the clerk's weird look made sense. "But," I said, trying to defend myself, "they sound exactly the same: *saumon* and *seulement*. How can any civilized person get it right?" And we started laughing all over again, but then I wanted to crawl under the table because of my mistake. I looked at Zoé-Pascale. "I'm so sorry, honey," I said. "I'm so sorry."

"Maman, it's okay," she said, "but next time, just say *que du fromage*—only cheese. From now on, you are banned from saying *seulement*, only *que* for you! *Que du fromage*, remember!"

"*Je voudrais que du fromage sur un quart*." I repeated over and over again, just to make sure I got it right.

The next day, I told the story to an English friend who, in my opinion, spoke excellent French. "You think that's bad?" she said, laughing. "Let me tell you a story."

On the way home from America two summers ago, she got off the plane in Marseilles, walked outside, looked up into the bright blue sky, commented on how bright the sun was, and then sniffed the air. Turning to her French friends who had picked her and her husband up at the airport, she *thought* she said, "*Sentez les pins*"— "smell the wonderful pines." But upon seeing her hosts' eyebrows rise in shock, she knew she had made a language mistake of the worst kind. Evidently she had said, *"Sentez le pénis"*—"smell the penis!"

Knowing I could easily make the same mistake, I thought, It's a good thing Zoé-Pascale didn't want pine nuts on her pizza.

The hardest part of not speaking the language well was the challenge of getting to know other people, especially women. I loved my friends back home, and missed our warm, intimate conversations about fashion, our kids, spirituality, hikes, and our lives in general. It just wasn't possible to have these types of conversations with the French women I met.

After discussing this (in French, of course) with Maryse, I learned that another layer to the difficulty I was having connecting with French women was that, unlike in California, where we seem to thrive on our intimate women friends, French women initially tend to see each other as threats, always wondering whether another might seduce her husband.

Living in a new culture requires so much more than learning a new language. It is the entire society, traditions, customs, and the way people look at the world that makes the experience exhilarating, intriguing, and intoxicating, but also exhausting and lonely. I found myself acting more timid, more shy, and less outspoken than I ever had before. Was I becoming an introvert?

Jean and I would discuss whether it was part of the rejuvenation process to be introspective and observe more. Maybe it was part of our healing. Maybe it had to do with age, or perhaps it was indeed my lack of close friends.

Jean, on the other hand, easily conversed with everyone from the postman to the potter next door, and was satisfied with building relationships slowly, over time. He adored the willingness of the French men to hug each other in greeting, complain about the latest strike, and argue politics in the café.

I was beginning to experience a torn, schizophrenic-like state as I struggled with the twin realities of not being able to assert my personality that was so connected with my native tongue, and the luxury of time and space to pull inward and find a new, creative me.

The French language became both my friend and my foe. I basked in the glory of having a simple conversation with Madame Laroche on the phone—a much more difficult task than speaking, for example, to Maryse—about her availability to babysit Zoé-Pascale. Jean and Zoé-Pascale would listen in, nodding their heads in encouragement and congratulating me as I hung up the phone.

ᴗᵛᴗᵛᴗ

My language lessons continued, not only with Maryse, but also in yoga class, where I began learning the names of every part of the body.

"There is one word I just can't get the hang of," I said to Maryse one Friday. "It sounds like *dendu ... tiend ... tadu ... tendu ... détendu ...*"

"*Tendu*," she laughed. "*Bien sûr.*" She slowly tightened her body to illustrate its meaning—to tighten, to stretch tall. "I think your yoga teacher was probably saying *détendu*—relax." A small difference in word, and a huge distinction in action. The next yoga class proved much better, as now I knew to relax whenever the teacher said the magic word, *détendu*.

At dinner I would announce my conversational accomplishments to Jean. "Can you believe it, I actually talked for a whole ten minutes with Marjorie when I went to pick Zoé-Pascale up at her house!" I was sure it was quite painful for Marjorie, but she was polite enough to engage me with empathy, rather than giving me one of those "I have no idea what the hell you are talking about" faces.

Over the next few months, I continued to enjoy my French conversations and was proud of every successful interaction. I was constantly amazed and jealous at how easy it had been for Jean to learn and communicate in multiple languages when he was a child in Africa, and how Zoé-Pascale spoke like a Provençal native. Sometimes I felt like I was paying Maryse to be my therapist or my friend—someone to just listen and talk to me with patience. We'd talk about everything and nothing. One day I asked her whether she knew how to knit. I had bought some gorgeous yarn and a pattern to make a shawl for Zoé-Pascale, but I needed help with understanding both the French pattern and what each word actually meant in the directions.

Over the next month, I'd bring my knitting along and we'd work on verb tense and pronouns in my sentences, reviewing both my knitting and my French vocabulary. Our meetings eventually gravitated to the *Bar du Marché* down at the bottom of the village. It didn't feel like work, and Maryse was becoming a friend, our conversations growing more and more personal. A shared café au lait was doing more for my French than *501 French Verbs* on the shelf at home.

One day, I picked Zoé-Pascale up from a birthday party at a friend's house on a nearby farm and suddenly found myself, without thinking, speaking in French to the jovial, down-to-earth mother. I was actually asking whether her son liked the gift and telling her that we had picked it out especially for him. She looked at me with wide eyes, responding to me and smiling. She knew I was getting over a hump in my progression toward rambling in almost-fluent French.

Zoé-Pascale decided that she was going to help me with my language lessons. Little did she know how difficult it was for me to understand her singsong Provençal accent. I would constantly have to say to her, "*Lentement, s'il te plait.*" (Slowly, please.) In her "trying to teach Maman" mode, she would review with me how to roll my R's and pronounce words correctly. She devised a thumb rating system: as she listened to me talk to other people, she'd smile and show a thumbs-up when I was doing well, a thumb to the side for *moyen* (so-so), and a thumbs-down for "Start again, Maman." Part of why I was so determined to speak fluently was for her, so as not to embarrass her. I wanted her to be proud of me and give me all thumbs-ups.

Interestingly enough, when Zoé-Pascale and Jean spoke together in French, I understood most of what they were saying. When I knew the context I could pick out the main themes and focus on comprehending the gist of the conversation. Every once in a while they would stop and include me, asking my opinion and giving me a chance to ask questions. Jean would turn to me in surprise and remind us both that I actually knew a lot more than I thought, assuring me that, with time, it would come together. However, I sensed that he wished it would happen faster, as he worried about me. Only half teasing, he would tell me he didn't understand how it could be so hard for anyone to learn a language. I would in turn respond with examples of my progress, accompanied by a sense of profound sadness.

Even for Jean and Zoé-Pascale, learning the language was as much about learning and understanding the culture, as the two are so intertwined. On days when Zoé-Pascale came home with a new *gros mot* (big bad slang word), she flaunted it with pride. It wasn't just the word, but the fact that she was becoming more like the kids around her and feeling part of something bigger than herself.

Slowly, by persevering through all my fears and aggravations, Jean's frustration and worry about me, and Zoé-Pascale's evaluations, I am proud to say, *Je parle Français un petit peu.*

Chapter 17

Thisane or Suzanne

Bread and water can so easily be toast and tea.

Author Unknown

My lessons in French culture and language culminated when I was admitted to a French hospital for a hysterectomy to remove fibroid tumors. I had put off the procedure for three years, never feeling I could take the time off from work to recuperate. In France, I no longer had that excuse. For seven days I would be sequestered in a private room with nothing but time to practice my French with doctors, nurses, and aides.

I checked into the private clinic the evening before the operation. In steel chairs attached three to a set, nine people sat holding little red plastic numbers taken from the red plastic number dispenser on the wall, waiting for their number to appear on a sign over our heads. It was a setup I was far more used to seeing at a deli or butcher than in a hospital.

"*Détendu,* relax," Jean repeated to me, my new favorite word coming to my rescue yet again.

I noticed that everyone else had tiny overnight bags placed neatly on their laps or under their seats. "They must not have gotten the checklist of what to bring to the hospital," I said to Jean, glancing at my medium-sized rolling suitcase. Where were the other patients' boxes of Kleenex, soft blankets, towels, and pillows (we all know what hospital linen feels like)? Where was the reading material to suit every possible mood they might experience? Where was their knitting, in case their hands get idle? Their iPods and DVD players? What about their Provençal tablemats to uplift the spirit? And their nightgowns, robes, slip-on slippers and six-packs of Evian?

Evidently, I was prepared and they weren't, we concluded, attempting to distract ourselves from the trepidation we were both feeling about my hospital stay.

Soon we were in the private room we had requested. In walked the surgeon, whose specialty was the *corps,* from the thigh to below the breast. He was a grey-haired, dignified Frenchman who was well respected in his field (translation: large ego). He would not speak English (I assumed he knew a bit), and focused solely on the task at hand. We exchanged quick pleasantries and he got right down to business.

"*Voulez-vous le plie de ventre en même temps?*" he asked. (Do you want your tummy tucked also?)

Without hesitation, I said, "*Oui.*" If I was going to have obligatory surgery and open up my stomach, I might as well get more for my money. The doctor then took out a big black marker, similar to the one that I used for writing on flipcharts at work, and drew what looked like an upside-down smile on my abdomen—his map to my new tight tummy, sans underlying melon-sized fibroids.

Not a minute later, he said, "*A demain, au revoir,*" and left the room.

With a surprised look, Jean whispered to me, "It sure is efficient here. Let's hope it's as effective."

A few minutes later, the *aide-soignant* (nurse's aide) brought in what would be my last meal for a week: one piece of paper-thin ham, dry toast, and plain yogurt. "Can we go out for dinner and come back?" I asked Jean.

Lovingly, he opened all the food containers for me and said, "If we follow the rules of presentation and take off the plastic, maybe it will all look more appetizing."

A few minutes later a nurse marched in and placed a bottle of disinfectant soap on the rolling table. She explained in French, "Wash yourself all over your body with this disinfectant. You must do this tonight and tomorrow morning before the surgery. Did you bring a glove?"

"Glove?" I asked, a bit baffled. Then I remembered Zoé-Pascale talking about how when she took a bath at a friend's house, they used a "washing glove:" two washcloths sewn together, forming a kind of mitt into which you put your hand. She had never seen one before.

After explaining that this was the one item that wasn't among my otherwise extensive repertoire (it wasn't listed, but was apparently a common sense item), the nurse, somewhat exasperated, brought in some throwaway washcloths for me to use. Once I was clean and disinfected, Zoé-Pascale and Jean left, and I was alone in my single hospital bed, in my single room on the third floor of a remote medical clinic in the south of France. I was scared—not so much of the operation, which I knew I needed, but of not awakening from the anesthesia and of being alone at night without my family. One last call home to say goodnight and throw kisses over the phone.

"Don't worry," Jean assured me, I'll be there when you wake up tomorrow afternoon."

The next day, I stared at the ceiling as the nurse wheeled me down the hall to the surgery. In an attempt to talk myself out of crying, I giggled at what I thought Jean would say if he was flat out on the gurney: "Is this any way to say goodbye to the world, staring at a sparkling white ceiling?"

Standing at the entrance to the surgery was a handsome distraction: my attractive, tall, male anesthesiologist with chiseled cheekbones and an aristocratic nose. Sensing my nervousness, he bent over to explain I would be breathing in a gas and slowly feel more and more tired, eventually moving into a dreamlike state in which I would feel and remember nothing, *rien*. Then he repeated that familiar, soothing word, *"Détendu, détendu."* I remember nothing more as I dozed into oblivion.

Later that afternoon, I woke up in a fog of morphine, with tubes exiting my body into bottles sitting on the floor, and a saline drip in my arm.

The doctor entered, declaring that the surgery was *"Impeccable, impeccable."* He checked my stomach, liked what he saw, and then proceeded to place a hefty sandbag right on top of my stomach, pinning me to the bed. I thought it rather inane and low-tech, but oh, did the pressure feel good.

Over the next couple of days and nights, I found out what painkillers would do to my French.

The first two evenings, the *aide-soignant* would poke her head into the room and yell out, "Suzanne." I would answer, *"Oui."* Ten minutes later, she would bring me a cup of hot tea, which I thought was so sweet of her. This continued for three nights in a row until finally I stopped her and asked,

"Quel arôme pour le thé?" (What flavor is the tea?)

"Tisane," she said, pronouncing the single S like a Z.

"Quoi?" (What?) To my drugged ears, I thought she was saying my name again, Suzanne.

"*Tisane*," she said again, "*Un thé special pour vous.*" (A special herbal tea for you.)

All this time, assuming I was responding to a friendly greeting in which the aide was calling me by name, I was in fact ordering some herbal tea, "*Tisane, oui.*"

One evening, a jovial blond nurse, who liked to practice her English with me, came into the room to check my blood pressure and ask how I was feeling. I answered using my new hospital vocabulary list that Maryse had given me. "*Oui, J'ai des douleurs.*" (Yes, I have pain.)

She looked at me and said, "*D'accord.*" (Okay.)

A few minutes later, she entered the room with a glass of water in a thin plastic cup. I looked at her with surprise and repeated, "*J'ai des douleurs!*" I have pain, pain, pain, pain!

She repeated, "*Oui, de l'eau.*" (Yes, I have brought you water.)

I concentrated hard, trying to say it more clearly. I knew the word, but my *r* just wouldn't roll.

"*Dou...leur.* Pain. It is pain, bad pain, *mal.*" I blasted. "I want drugs!"

"*Oui, de l'eau,*" she smiled sweetly, offering me the short plastic cup once again. By this time she began to see that something was wrong, studying my face, which was grimacing in distress. Finally she pointed to my stomach, and scrunched up her face in agony to mirror my own, as though we were two actors in an impromptu theatre class.

"*Bien sûr,*" she said finally. "*Vous avez des douleurs.*" Instead of immediately administering the drugs I so badly needed, she spent the next few minutes trying to teach me how to pronounce *douleur* correctly so that it didn't sound like *de l'eau*. Like many French people, she decided it was her duty to make sure I got my pronunciation correct first. When I did, the drugs would follow. I felt like Pavlov's dog, being rewarded with pain medication for a correct response.

Since I realized I was now in a hostage situation, I strove

to find the little tongue Jean had told me about, and blindly "RRRRRRRRRR"ed my heart out.

"*Non,*" she said, not "*r,*" but "*dou, dou, dou et après R, R, R.*"

I "*R, R, R*"ed until I burst out with my French pronunciation and sobbing uncontrollably. Finally, the well-meaning nurse realized that her day job had to take precedent.

Efficiency and effectiveness were two words that Jean and I use to summarize our experience with the French medical community. I knew the exact time the cleaning team would race through my room, sweeping away any dust particles and making the bed with military discipline. Save the impromptu French lessons, treatments were given precisely on schedule. The problem with this efficiency, however, was that the notion of bedside manner was left by the wayside. Conversations with doctors and nurses consisted of "*Avez-vous mal ou pas?*" (Are you feeling bad or not bad?)—that was it.

The surgeon came daily, shook my hand, smiled, felt my stomach, wrote something down (probably what I could eat the next day, which was boringly and repeatedly bouillon), and was off.

Would I have liked a bit more chit-chat and explanation? Sure. However, I stayed six nights in a private room, had a great surgeon, a competent nursing staff, and it all cost about one-quarter of what it would have in the states. I began to wonder whether the additional 75% paid for bedside manner, a little extra fluff of the pillow, the Kleenex box, the hospital supplies, the insurance gatekeeper, and better quality plastic cups were worth it. When it came down to it, I could bring my own cup. I became convinced that we have much to learn from the French healthcare system.

Recovering in the clinic, I had time to read two novels, listen to music, visit with some friends, and of course, watch a bit of French TV with Jean and Zoé-Pascale. The French actors spoke so fast, they were often difficult for me to follow; however, the cooking shows were an educational and entertaining relief. After six hours of having the best chefs in France dazzle me with a sampling of various dishes, I decided the key to making your meal look inviting—no matter whether it is an appetizer, a main course, or a dessert—is to put a mint leaf or a sprig of rosemary or tarragon on top of the dish. Just like that, *oh là là*, it looked so artistically French.

My final night at the hospital came. I was hoping for something more for my last meal than the usual Metamucil mixed in a broth and a small plain yogurt, but no such luck. Later that night, the *aide-soignant* stuck her head in and with the lilt in her voice sang out, "*Tisane?*" For a quick moment I thought I heard "Suzanne," and that she was coming in to say goodbye to me.

Part III

New Ways

*Every blade of grass has its angel that bends over it
and whispers, 'Grow, grow.'*

THE TALMUD

Place is important—but pace is even more important

Place is where the heart is.

Adapted from Pliny the Elder,
Roman Naturalist (23-79 A.D.)

Have you ever wanted to vacation or live somewhere else for a period of time, immersing yourself in an extraordinary environment or another culture? Why not go as soon as possible? Don't wait any longer! Many of us have a special place that seems to call to us. That feeling might come from hearing childhood stories of Ireland, reading about the charms of Italy, or seeing photos of the Eiffel Tower's twinkling lights on a rainy night in Paris. Maybe the first time you traveled after graduating from university or a classic film you saw years ago sparked curiosity about a particular place. Perhaps you want to return to the culture of your ancestors, to connect deeply with your roots, or to live closer to nature. Experiencing a place you've dreamed of—your "heart place"—will feed your soul and spirit. Plan for it, make it happen, and be open to the surprises that will occur as a result of your decision.

Coming from the fast-paced culture of the San Francisco bay area, we needed to slow down. We needed time to live simply, heal, rejuvenate, and be creative. Finding a place that allowed for a change of pace was vital to us. It's not just about escaping the daily grind, nor is it about living in the country, miles away from civilization—you can still be hooked up to e-mails and Blackberries 24/7, even in Northern China or Africa.

Fundamentally, committing to a change of pace is about shifting the rhythm of your day so that there is time to be with yourself, your loved ones, your creativity, and your work. It's about being in tune with your body, mind, and spirit. It's about being conscious enough to prevent technical intrusions and shift back to a natural human rhythm that is so intrinsically linked to joie de vivre.

Many people are able to alter these rhythms without changing locale. It's possible, but the results may not be as profound and lasting. One activity may simply replace another. Life's demands alter only slightly, and the frenetic pace of living may continue. Changing both place and pace, even if only for a short respite, creates a dramatic shift within one's being down to the cellular level, and it is from here that one experiences heightened awareness and the ability to focus on what is truly important.

Healthy Living

The best six doctors anywhere
And no one can deny it
Are sunshine, water, rest, and air
Exercise and diet.
These six will gladly you attend
If only you are willing
Your mind they'll ease
Your will they'll mend
And charge you not a shilling.

NURSERY RHYME QUOTED BY WAYNE FIELDS,
What the River Knows (1990)

Chapter 18

Café Life and the Two-Hour Lunch

No time like the present.

DELARIVIER MANLEY,
English author (1663-1724)

I F THERE IS AN activity that sums up how life in France is different from that in America and the other Anglo countries, it is that, in France, all doings revolve around mealtime and "café time." It is the shopping for seasonal fresh foods in the local markets, and the actual sitting down at a table for thirty minutes to several hours for each and every meal.

In winter in France, our family dined in our large country kitchen, sitting at the long wooden table covered with a green Provençal tablecloth. As soon as the weather obliged us, we were outside on the terrace.

It all begins out in the many farmers' markets throughout the region. On Fridays after school drop-off, we head to the local *marché* to pick up fresh vegetables and fruits, a roasted chicken, homemade goat cheese and lavender honey, olives marinated with fresh chopped basil, and fresh pink salmon cut to order *sans arrêt* (without bones). On Wednesdays, I wander the Uzès *Marché Bio* (organic) while Zoé-Pascale is at ballet, and on Saturdays I pick up a few specialties at the *Grand Marché à Uzès*. All market shopping is accompanied by an obligatory stop at the café, and meeting up with friends and neighbors for an exchange of three kisses and the latest news. Between market trips, I bring my straw basket when I pick up Zoé-Pascale at school so that I can pop into the half-size supermarket in the village. En route, of course, are also the *boucherie* and the *boulangerie*. There is never the excuse that I don't have something to cook.

But it's not just the food that makes mealtimes so different—it is the rhythm of mealtime and café time. In France, eating is a public affair, whereas in America, it is very private. Here, there are rules and hours and etiquette for each meal. In America, people eat wherever, whenever: in the car, at the desk, in front of the TV. In France, eating somewhere other than the dining room table is sacrilegious and shameful. On more than one occasion, we were caught by a neighbor walking down the street munching on an apple or baguette. With a look of scorn, they shake their fingers at us and say, *"Mais mangez à la table?"* (Don't you know you should be eating at the table?) Over time, we learned to do our munching and crunching at the table. On the rare occasions when we were out and about and only had time to grab a banana or a piece of baguette, we felt like thieves in the night, hoping nobody would see us.

With a café on every corner (at the very least), we found ourselves sitting down daily for a café crème, a small espresso in a short petite ceramic cup, or a cold drink on hot days. Whether it was to take a few minutes to read the paper, warm ourselves up in the sun, people-watch or converse, the café always beckoned to us. Like many residents of the area, we had our favorite haunts, and soon came to silently know the other regulars: the divorced florist, the unemployed men who play *boule*, the German couple who live in the village, and other familiar faces. The cafés we loved soon became second homes, and their owner/proprietors became part of our world. Sure, we love our Starbucks non-fat lattes, and yet moments spent sitting in an intimate outdoor café watching the world go by are among the most relaxing, indulgent, and special times of the day.

I asked Maryse the question that many Americans wonder about: how French people eat such big meals and stay so thin. She told us that there is a rule of thumb for eating at home, and a different one for eating out at a restaurant.

"When you eat at home, you eat baguette, small meals of fresh vegetables, a small piece of meat, and a salad. Desert is left for special occasions and Sunday lunch, and you drink only water, wine, or an espresso *sans* milk. When you go to a restaurant, you enjoy your meal and eat whatever you want: a starter, an entrée, a starch, vegetable, and a dessert. We eat well and we love our food, but our portions are suitable for people, not giants."

Twice a week Zoé-Pascale ate a five-course meal at the *cantine* at school. The *cantine* tables were covered in pretty patterned French Provençal tablecloths, and the students always eat with a set of proper silverware—no plastic knives and forks. To our delight, she was beginning to insist on drinking water at mealtime.

Eating in France reminded me of a lecture I once heard from a rabbi, entitled "How Friday night Shabbat dinner can save your child's life." *How is that possible?* I had thought as I listened intently to his talk. Yes, dinner together was important, but life-saving?

However, our daily ritual of eating lunch and dinner together around the table in France started me thinking about the notion of the sacred family dinner. Growing up in Los Angeles in the 1950s and 1960s, my dad, a furniture salesman, worked every evening during the week except for Wednesday, which became our Shabbat. Mom would cook a full meal of his favorite consommé or bean soup, meatloaf with a beautiful slice of egg in the center, a green salad, and a wiggly red Jell-O mold.

Wednesday night dinner was held in the dining room instead of at the kitchen table, where we girls ate when Dad wasn't home. We sat at the long oak table with chairs covered in green-and-gold velvet to match the wallpaper. My two older sisters and I fought over who got to sit next to dad; being the youngest, I usually got one of the coveted seats. Dinner was lively, with my sisters and me talking about our day and enjoying the warm feeling of everyone being together. To this day, when I think back to Wednesday night dinners, I get a feeling of being wrapped in love by my family. For Jean, Sunday lunch at his grandfather's farm evoked similar feelings of security, family, love, and special moments of childhood.

In California, when we both worked non-stop and traveled regularly, we tried to carve out weekend nights for our family dinnertime together. I remember one night when Zoé-Pascale was fifteen months old, sitting in her high chair at the dinner table. All of a sudden, I saw her look directly at me, directly at Jean, and finally at my visiting mother-in-law. Within a few seconds, she raised her grubby little hands and arms high into the air, telepathically influencing the three adults to do the same, all laughing together. It seemed as though she had somehow learned that dinnertime is a special time when everyone tries to be present, converse, and really connect with each other.

During our year in France, we started a new ritual: we would go around the table and say what we were grateful for that day. "I'm grateful that Maman walked me to school," Zoé-Pascale would say. "I'm grateful that my work was easy," "I'm grateful for a play date." Soon, her gratitudes morphed into a global, "I'm grateful for everything!"

One day, Jean shared that he was grateful that he was able to resolve a conflict with a client. As she often does, our daughter said, "I don't understand what you are saying. I don't get what a conflict is."

"Okay," Jean said, "let's act it out."

Jean assigned himself and me the roles of two people in conflict. Zoé-Pascale would play the role of the judge, which she loved, as she was in the stage of childhood during which many things are "not fair." For the next twenty minutes, we ate and acted, laughed, and created a phenomenally rich learning experience for all of us.

In France, we were able to enjoy Friday night family dinner—that crucial time that kids know is theirs; an anchor that they can use to keep them grounded—almost every night. The ritual of lighting candles, sharing the day's ups and downs, and learning valuable lessons may indeed save our child's life—who knows? For now, it simply makes us feel that we are part of a family who cares, and part of a bigger universe we discuss and reflect upon. Best of all, this way of living is portable—a custom we can carry with us from place to place, wherever we are in the world.

Chapter 19

Shifting Priorities

How we spend our days is, of course, how we spend our lives.

ANNIE DILLARD,
Pulitzer prize-winning American author (1934-)

L IFE WAS TAKING ON a rhythm of its own, based solely on Zoé-Pascale's school calendar and our desire to flow with the day without spending hours on administrative trivia. We'd read an article that said all that is needed are three and one-half hours of focused time per day to accomplish what most do in a full eight-hour work day. Following this advice, we spent three and one-half hours a day on work. We'd wake up around 7-7:30 a.m., read before breakfast, eat at the table with Zoé-Pascale, and then get her off to school for the 9 a.m. start time. After drop-off, we'd take a four-kilometer country walk or go to a French yoga class, followed by a stop at a local café for an espresso or *café au lait*. Ey 11 a.m., we would be ready to hunker down in front of our compuzers, me focusing on my writing and Jean on his research. The fact that the school day ended at 5 p.m. gave us more uninterrupted time to get things accomplished than we had when we picked her up at 3 o'clock in America.

Our evenings (at least on school nights) involved a few minutes of downtime, a healthy snack of cucumbers or fruit, homework, and then dinner: a healthy affair involving the five courses to which Zoé-Pascale had become accustomed, always including dessert of creamy yogurt, apples and honey, a piece of dark chocolate, or fresh raspberries. Our evenings were ours. No television and a silent phone allowed us to focus on each other. Jean played the CD from a musical we'd seen in Vienna, and we danced in circles in our tiny living room.

One day, after speaking to our dear friends in San Francisco, I was reminded how wired life in the Bay Area could be, and how people—especially those in the business world—were expected to be available 24/7.

"I don't know how I feel about going back to a life like that," I said to Jean.

"We definitely have to be clear and strong about our priorities if we go back to a place that values work, work, and work above everything else," he said. "Or we have to know it may be only temporary until we can move to the place that will support how we want to live our life," Jean responded.

The French as a society embrace family and lifestyle as their number one priority. They balance productive work with rejuvenating breaks. They are conservative with debt and don't expect to have a new car every two years. If they want a swimming pool and can't afford it, they build it themselves with the help of a few friends. They recycle everything, buy from the local farmers, and are willing to wait to remodel the kitchen. They love their sports, travel feverishly, and engage in philosophical discussions over long, leisurely meals. As a result, they don't seem to be stressed over finances the same way we are.

"I love San Francisco," my friend Craig said during a visit, "but I can't say I have any type of feeling of a community among our neighbors. In fact, we are the only people who have lived in our neighborhood longer than ten years. We live so close together, but no one knows each other and no one says good morning. I truly don't know why."

Our village, on the other hand, was one big community. Our neighbors have lived in their homes for most—if not all—of their lives. Every day that we walk Zoé-Pascale to school, we say *bonjour* to at least five people, and stop to kiss a few on the cheek as well. The thought of living in a place where people don't say good morning and chit-chat as a matter of course began to seem odd. Our priorities were shifting.

While in France, we met some wonderful transplanted ex-pat families from England who gathered together for holidays and bike rides and exchanged tips on how to get things done in France. Their family life was in the south of France while their work was back in England and via the internet. The kids were global, bilingual, and living the good life. Then there was Astrid and Brian an English/Irish couple who stimulated our minds with great conversation from food to politics. As half-year residents, they immerse themselves in a nature-based simpler life, and then return to friends, family, and the excitement of London in the winter months.

Was that the answer, we asked ourselves: two places, two lives? Would that make life easier or more complicated? Would it be harder to build community, or more rewarding? The more we talked, the more we realized just how many ways there are to live in this world, and that each person—each family—has to find out what suits them best.

Chapter 20

Cuisiner la Vie

All children are artists. The problem is how to remain an artist
once (s)he grows up.

PABLO PICASSO,
Father of Modern Art (1881-1973)

T HE FAMOUS MARCHÉ AUX TRUFFLES (truffle market) is held
every January in Uzès, and professionals and amateurs alike
gather to sell their truffles for 1,000 euros a kilo. Restaurateurs from
around the globe, amateur chefs from throughout France, tourists,
and locals show up en masse to buy and then freeze their yearly
stock of exorbitantly priced truffles. It's a once-a-year opportunity
to buy in at the ground floor, for the bargain price of about $1,600 a
kilogram. This translates to about 30 euros ($50) for what looks like
a clump of mud a little bigger than a golf ball. Not much to look at,
but flavorful as a glorious barbecue cooked over an open fire.

New Ways

During the event, the Sunday lunch menus across Uzès and nearby villages triple their usual prices and offer entrees with smoky, musty truffle: omelettes with sprinkles of the evocative perfume-smelling truffle, goat cheeses with chocolate truffles, and truffle-splashed aperitifs. Every restaurant is full of intergenerational Sunday strollers plunking down 25-50 euros per person for a special truffle meal.

In the center of the grand square of Uzès, surrounded by the leafless January poplar trees, a makeshift faux forest was built up with sand, dirt, and the miniature oak trees under which the knobby little dirt-ball truffles are known to grow. Wrapped in winter coats, fur hats, cashmere scarves, suede boots, and leather gloves, crowds gather around to watch the simulated truffle hunts by the dogs and the infamous truffle pig.

"Try it out; see whether your dog can sniff out the truffles!" yelled the announcer. The event organizers had hidden special Perigord French black truffles, which grow naturally in the woodlands, among the imported oaks.

"Let's see if Pantoufle can do it," I cried to Jean and Zoé-Pascale.

Pantoufle, meaning "slipper" in French, was the newest member of our family: an apricot miniature French poodle who was now accompanying us everywhere we went, as she hated to be left home alone.

"She hasn't been practicing," Jean observed. "But who knows, maybe she has the knack."

"Here, let's let her sniff our truffle. That way she might remember what to smell and look for," I said, offering the teensy nugget we'd purchased to Pantoufle for a whiff.

"Fine, but don't let her eat it," Jean replied, a bit disgusted at the thought of our fuzzy puppy slobbering on his precious truffle.

"Last chance, sign up your truffle-hunting dog!" the announcer warned.

"Okay, I'm going. Come on, Pantoufle," I said, pulling my newly trained truffle hound behind me to the gate. "Smell this one more time and let's show them what we're made of. Besides, if you do well, maybe this is my next career."

"Look, Papa, I can't believe it! Maman is really taking Pantoufle to hunt the truffles. Bravo!" Zoé-Pascale cheered.

Inside the ring in front of the crowds, I stood with Pantoufle as she crept up to the first miniature oak tree, sniffed, wiggled her nose, shook her tail, and then peed right on the spot where there could have been a truffle. Okay, I thought, every dog, even a female, has to mark its territory.

Next tree. Sniff, sniff, and with a glance up at me, another squat with leg half-raised. It was a new form of artistic performance for the crowd! I let her guide me to the third tree, where she slowly but encouragingly began to paw the dirt and dig a little bit, but soon turned to look at me as if to say "sorry," and peed once again. The audience, who had been silent up to now, burst into laughter.

"Maman, I think she smells something," Zoé-Pascale called from across the enclosure.

"Okay, one more tree," I said to Pantoufle. "You can do it."

This time, Pantoufle was taking the lead. Sniff, sniff went her little brown nose, followed by a wiggle of her squatty tail and a shake of her bear-like winter hair. She stopped to look out at the crowd as though she knew they were watching, and began to circle the tiny brown oak tree, sniffing each leaf.

After one-and-a-half laps around the tree, she stopped. Tentatively, she began to dig with her right paw, then her left, then with both paws, faster and faster, the dry sand spraying up and under her legs as she pushed her nose along the ground.

"Oh my ... she found a truffle!" I shouted, quite surprised. "She found a truffle! I can't believe it!"

The crowd applauded their approval. "Bravo!" the announcer

said rapidly. "With a bit more training, you will have yourself a truffle-hunting dog!"

"Papa, can we train Pantoufle?" asked Zoé-Pascale. "Or maybe we should get a pig. Pigs love truffles, too. That would be fun."

Our neighbor Mr. Boucher, a short, round native of the area in his sixties who wore a plaid wool winter cap all year, was standing near Jean and Zoé-Pascale as I approached.

"Honey, I've got a pig you can try, but let me tell you, those guys are really mean," he told her. "They almost bit my hand off when I was holding a truffle they found, because they wanted to eat it. I'd stick with your hairy little dog here. She looks like she has potential." Jean translated for me from his heavy Provençal accent.

"*Merci beaucoup,*" I whispered to him, happy not to have to dissuade Zoé-Pascale from adding to the menagerie. Stoking the embers in my mind of my back-up career as a truffle hunter, I said, "Let's go home and make a dish with our truffle."

Since we had begun to settle into French country living, the concepts of food and cooking had completely shifted for us. No longer were we asking each other what to pick up for dinner or what we could quickly microwave. The questions instead became, what was in season that we should try cooking, or what new ingredient or recipe did we want to experiment with from the various magazine articles I'd been cutting out?

"Just picture a grating of musty truffle on some roasted garlicky meat," Jean dreamt on the way home, "or with an *aubergine* casserole, or imagine truffle with a homemade olive *tapenade* spread on warm raisin-and-wheat bread, served with steamed vegetables." Our mouths were watering, imagining the possibilities of unique flavors that existed in our meager purchases.

A few weeks later at the *pâtisserie*, Jean and I ran into Tristan, the chef of our favorite three-star Michelin restaurant located under the clock tower, and his wife, Amelie. They let us know that they were holding a cooking class and we were welcome to join if we liked. We accepted immediately.

At the appointed day and time, we entered the well-stocked, compact kitchen set in an old stone village house, the bottom half and garden of which had been converted into an elegant but relaxing restaurant. Tristan and Amelie lived in the upper half with their three daughters.

Once the group of eight students was assembled, Tristan displayed the menu we would be preparing. The primary ingredient for the lunch was going to be asparagus—green and white, fat and skinny, long and short, domestic and picked in the wild. We'd be making an asparagus-type mousse garnished with three tips of asparagus, *roquette* greens (Jean calls them "weeds"), special shiitake mushrooms, mini tomatoes, fresh parmesan cheese, and a sprinkle of *huile de noisette*. Each ingredient had been neatly laid out in bowls around the rectangular preparation table.

"First, *c'est très important* to peel the asparagus," Tristan informed us.

"Have you ever peeled asparagus?" Jean asked me. "That's what's been wrong all these years," he said, laughing.

With further instruction, part of the group completed the asparagus mousse, while the rest of us were told to lightly blanch the green tips of the asparagus, and place them on top of the mousse under the *roquette* greens and shaved cheeses. Simultaneously, we peeled the white asparagus, cooking them with additional spices that magically resulted in a delicious white sauce that would go with the main course of white fish. Not wasting one inch of the organic asparagus, we mixed the white tips with a tomato-and-onion sauce that was simmering on the gas stove.

The experience was like a ballet being orchestrated with utter precision while the eager ballerinas were being instructed on the choreography and technique. Tristan informed us that fish should be cooked only on one side, on top of the stove, skin side down; that way, the juices stay in and the fish cooks through perfectly. As he checked the temperature, he had us build a beautiful foundation of onion, tomatoes, and white asparagus tips in the center of the golden dinner plates, which had been specially made by a local potter. On each plate, we arranged a browned piece of fish, removing the skin as we laid it out, drizzled the white asparagus sauce over the fish, and added a final splash of hazelnuts.

"Can you believe we actually did this?" I said to Jean. "I feel like I'm painting an original landscape. I think this is how you can learn to love to cook."

Tristan had started our desserts earlier that morning by laying out some fresh pastry dough. Under his instruction, we baked the dough and heated fresh strawberries, straining them so the juice was separated from the berries. Our next step was to decorate the crusty pastry cookie with the berry sauce, creating our own artistic rendition of the famous French red poppy. To emphasize the petals, we added a homemade cream made from mascarpone, milk, powdered sugar, and vanilla beans soaked in rum. The zest of a lemon was drawn as an overlay, and the dish was finished off with a drizzle of strawberry juice. Knowing that we had to wait until after the meal to dive into those sweet beauties, we couldn't resist licking the stirring spoons for *un peu de goût* (a little taste).

As we sat down to our private lunch, Amelie brought out three different wines: a gold-medal white from Vacqueras, a rosé from Lirac, and a sweet white from a neighboring vintner. As we savored course after course of our own creation, we talked about the textures and flavors of the food, and the challenges of cooking like a seasoned French chef.

"It's all in the ingredients and your love for them," Tristan told us. "The technique can be learned. Go home and try something new this week! Asparagus are in abundance and can be bought at the local market on Friday for two euros a kilo. Or go hunting for the thin wild ones in the fields. You won't get them any fresher."

I took Tristan's advice and bought two kilos of a variety of green and white asparagus at the *marché*, in addition to traipsing through the nearby woods, looking for wild thin asparagus. At home, peeling each stalk by hand, I hummed along to the radio until I had a triangular pile of "nude" asparagus.

Since I did not have an asparagus cooker (who knew there was such a thing?), I followed Tristan's instructions and carefully placed the asparagus into the boiling pan of water, with the tips hanging over the edge. "Three minutes for the stalks, or until pliable with a fork, and then gently push the tips into the boiling water for the last 30 seconds." The result: a perfectly evenly cooked asparagus from tip to toe. Drizzled with extra-virgin olive oil from a local grower, accompanied by a warm baguette, goat cheese, and a tomato salad, we sat down that evening to eat my simple, fresh meal in sublime contentment. Raising her water glass high into the air, Zoé-Pascale said, "A toast to *cuisiner la vie*."

Sensuality

Sensual pleasures are like soap bubbles, sparkling, effervescent.
The pleasures of intellect are calm, beautiful, sublime,
ever enduring and climbing upward to the borders
of the unseen world.

JOHN AUGHEY,
Author (1828-1911)

Chapter 21

The Woman in Blue

Without leaps of imagination, or dreaming,
we lose the excitement of possibilities.
Dreaming, after all, is a form of planning.

GLORIA STEINEM,
American feminist icon, author, and publisher (1934-)

A S MUCH AS WE loved our village's local market on Fridays, nothing could beat the melodic sounds and cool Saturday morning
air that hung over *la Marché d' Uzès*. Stretching throughout the center of the village, the Uzès outdoor market is one of the biggest in the
region, with vendors selling an array of produce, fish, poultry, meats,
cheeses, olives, nuts, fabrics, pottery, clothes, purses, CDs, tablecloths,
soaps, and many other specialties of the region. I nudged Jean to wake
up, kissing him on the neck. "It's market day!" I sang out. I knew that
if we were on the road by nine, we'd have time for a café crème and a
freshly baked croissant before serious shopping began.

As we left our small village to drive the four kilometers to Uzès, we passed the wine cooperative and fields of vines, budding with clusters of green and ruby grapes. Rolling down the windows and poking our heads out of our petite silver car, we inhaled the aroma of lavender in the air and knew it would be a great day.

The market vendors overflowed from the Roman arcades surrounding the *Place aux Herbes*, the center square, where the round, double-tiered fountain sprayed water into a stone basin into which kids happily dipped their pudgy fingers. The vendors' folding tables and colorful wares lined the eight narrow cobblestone streets that extended from the center square like spokes on a wheel. Lush poplar trees shaded the tables, with beams of light filtering through their massive branches. In places where there were fewer trees, the vendors had put up tent umbrellas to shade themselves and the food they were selling from the warm morning sun. Backed up in a circle against the fountain were stalls filled with red, white, and coffee-colored onions, handpicked lettuce, long French green beans, and bright red tomatoes piled high on wooden crates. A blackboard tablet reading, "*Tomates* 2.50 euros/kg" was perched between the crates.

Next was the table displaying the olives. Twenty-plus sturdy brown baskets, lined in plastic, were pushed up against each other like a checkerboard, precariously balancing small clay plates of olives for tasting. We stared at the glistening sea of green and brown. Our favorites were the khaki-green olives filled with red pimentos mixed with small pieces of carrot soaked in vinaigrette. We sampled the wrinkled black olives, savoring the strong taste of vinegar and garlic and nodded to Olivier, the appropriately named vendor of Provençal olives, "*C'est bon.*"

"This one is specially flavored," Olivier told us. "You must taste; it is my newest treat."

"*Bien sûr*," Jean replied.

This was such a contrast from the cans of black olives my mother used to buy when I was a child. My sisters and I would slip the identical, factory-prepared orbs on our fingertips, pretending to be witches with black fingernails. Until recently in America, a small selection of gourmet olives could be found only in high-end food markets for a very high price. Watching Zoé-Pascale, at age six, select her weekly stash of olives, her palate as distinguished as that of an adult, we wondered what other surprises were in store for us in terms of her experience.

In between the baskets of olives sat the famous bottles of Provençal olive oil, light green and extra-virgin. The slim bottles, wrapped like presents, decorated Olivier's table in various sizes: small, medium, and large bottles, plus grand tin cans to last you all winter long.

On this particular Saturday, after weaving our way through some of the food vendors' tables, we arrived at the *Café d'Esplanade* across the street from the monument built to honor those who had lost their lives in WWI. We'd first seen the monument that summer long ago when we had fallen in love with the area around Uzès, and had been stunned to see Jean's name—J. P. Roux—carved on the statue. We didn't know whether the name belonged to a long-lost relative of Jean's or was a relic from a past lifetime, but we had taken it as a sign that we were in the right place.

We loved this café, not only because it was one of the best spots for people-watching, but because it had the finest café crème in the village. We settled ourselves in the sturdy brown-and-black rattan chairs arranged around the small, square marble tables, drinking our café and eating piping hot croissants from the bakery next door. Looking out at the market-goers, I spotted a woman carrying a basket.

"*Regardez,*" I pointed her out to Jean. "That woman has a fabulous basket." It was so different from the beige straw baskets everyone else carried. Jean glanced over at her. She was a striking woman with a radiant glow and a smile that revealed straight, gleaming white teeth framed by pink lips. Dark tortoise shell sunglasses and a floppy blue straw hat hid what I imagined were twinkling blue eyes.

The woman moved with grace and speed through the crowds, her flowing blue gauze dress swirling around her. Intrigued by her movements and casual, yet elegant outfit, I turned to Jean and asked, "How do Frenchwomen have so much style? Is it in their genes?" She reminded me of how I saw myself dressed in my fantasies: a dreamy linen dress wrapped around my calves as I walked with a hat hung over my left eye: sophisticated, charming, and a bit eccentric. And yet, here I was in knee-length shorts and black leather sandals—like most Americans, choosing comfort over style.

I continued to watch the woman glide through the crowd as though she were parting the Red Sea. Stopping to buy some fresh goat cheese nearby, we could hear her clear Parisian accent as she asked the farmer selling the goat cheese for *un petit goût*, a small taste of the round flat cake sprinkled with Provençal herbs. I nudged Jean.

"What is she saying? I can only make out a few words."

He bent over and listened. After a minute he turned to me and said, "She said she just arrived for the long weekend from Paris. She teaches art at the university and is planning on painting and picnicking over the next few days. They are talking about a goat cheese recipe now."

I watched her wave to the vendor. *"Au revoir, à bientôt!"* she said, slipping her purchases into the lovely basket. Hanging onto her floppy hat, she dance-walked through the crowds as the friendly vendor politely echoed after her, *"Au revoir!"*

"Jean, I have to meet this woman," I said with certainty.

"But why?"

"She seems so extraordinary, and besides, I want to know where she bought that great basket."

Secretly, I was somewhat embarrassed by my outfit and reluctant to introduce myself; on the other hand, I felt that she had something to share with me. A past life synergy experience, perhaps, or just an intuitive feeling that we would click easily.

"Okay, go," he replied, briefly looking up from his newspaper and glancing over at Zoé-Pascale, who was busy reading her new *Mickey Parade* comic book. "*Bon courage.*"

I ran after the woman, calling out, "*Bonjour, bonjour! Où avez-vous acheté le panier?*" (Where did you buy your basket?)

But the market crowds got larger and the woman was swallowed up without hearing me. I wanted to follow her, but realized that Jean and I hadn't made specific plans on where to meet at lunchtime.

On many market days, Jean would tag along as I wandered through each alley and stopped at every stall to admire the fruits, vegetables, olives, tablecloths, and soaps from Marseille. Though he never complained of the crowds, the time came when we realized that for both of us to enjoy the market, we would have to follow in the footsteps of the French: while the women shop, the men sit in the café, reading the newspaper and sipping a glass of dry white wine or a coffee. Wherever we looked, from ten to noon, there were men, sitting in cafés visiting, enjoying the glorious, bright-blue morning.

I returned to Jean, made lunch plans quickly, and kissed him and Zoé-Pascale goodbye once again. "*A tout à l'heure!*" I called out, and skipped off to find my new friend. Had anyone seen her? Did they know which way she went?

I stopped at a stand filled with rolls of cloth printed with colorful Provençal patterns: yellow lemons, lavender bunches, red poppies, and sunflowers scattered over a brightly colored background. I was reminded of a day we'd spent on a mountaintop in Les Baux. Looking down into the valley below, I nudged Jean. "Look, if you frame a piece of the landscape with your fingers, you can see where the artists find their inspiration."

After purchasing a two-meter length of vinyl blue cloth sprinkled with drawings of grapes and olives for the patio table, I turned into the center of town, slowing down to listen to the jazz ensemble, wearing white panama hats and dark sunglasses, performing in the impasse. I had learned that they'd been playing in the same spot for years, and spend the winter months producing new music and CDs. In France, it is fairly easy for musicians to get help from the government to begin their careers, and to be paid unemployment benefits when they are not working. It is the part of French society and culture that is loved by the British and Americans, but is not supported in our own countries.

Temporarily distracted from my mission to find the woman with the basket, I stopped to purchase a melon, a kilo of apricots and peaches, two ripe avocados, and farm-fresh tomatoes. Two more stops at the chicken man and the *boulangerie* for our Saturday evening meal. With each stop, I told myself that I would find her. It was meant to be.

But first, it was time to lighten my load. Hustling through the crowds, I found Jean right where I'd left him, halfway through the *Le Monde* newspaper and sipping a glass of white wine while Zoé-Pascale drank her *jus de pomme* and played with her Cinderella sticker book.

He looked up with a relaxed smile. "What did you buy, love?" But before I could answer, he added, "By the way, the woman you were looking for went that way."

I plopped my purchases next to him and threw them both a kiss. "*A bientôt,*" I yelled, scurrying around the shoppers in the direction he pointed. This time, I wasn't going to be deterred.

As I rounded the corner toward an arched doorway surrounding the center courtyard, there she stood, surrounded by a stunning array of baskets. Straw baskets of all sizes, colors, and shapes were stacked on folding tables and hanging from hooks: sunflower yellow, kelly green, sky blue, bordeaux red, lavender, traditional beige, and polka-dot, with either straw or leather handles.

I had seen other basket stalls, but nothing like this. It took up the space of at least four stalls, with rows of baskets in varying colors and patterns piled on long tables: square, rectangular, and round. At the edges of the stall were long metal poles two stories high, with even more merchandise hanging from hooks: red, green, blue, yellow, rose, plaid, striped, short and long handles, briefcase-style, floppy, round, and square. As I stood there, transfixed by the rainbow, the woman smiled at me and nodded.

"*Oui*, I can tell, you are also a lover of baskets. The vibrant colors make your heart sing and the leather handles add the perfect touch, no?"

Butterflies flitted around my stomach as she came closer and whispered, "It is so important that women understand the magic of the baskets, don't you think? Once you understand, they will always bring you happiness, *C'est vrai, n'est-ce pas?*"

What she was saying about the baskets was resonating with me at such a deep level that all I could do was look at her. She smiled and said, "Yes, it is true. *Bien sûr.*"

From time to time, I've had these types of interactions with other strangers, in which we immediately connect, if only for a short time. It's always a sign to me that I am opening up again. The exhaustion, depression, and dark dreams of the past few years were fading away. My smile grew wider as she continued to explain (something I was finding the French love to do: share their opinions about everything).

"Baskets are a part of women's history," she said. "We have used them since the beginning of time, not only as functional objects, but also as objects of beauty. Each time you carry a basket, you are reliving history and showing others how beautiful life can be. It is never a chore to shop with a basket, but a glorious and exquisite experience filled with delight."

I nodded, silently urging her to continue.

"*A bientôt,*" she then said with a smile, a musical tone in her voice. "I have to paint this afternoon. I hope to see you in the market next week, carrying a beautiful basket."

"*Merci beaucoup, vous êtes très gentille.*"

She glided away and disappeared into the crowd before I could say another word.

I was moved. She transformed food shopping, an otherwise mundane errand, into a pleasurable activity by toting her purchases in a beautiful basket. Back home, I found grocery shopping a chore, having to pack and lug my purchases in thin plastic bags that were impossible to pry open, brown paper bags that had to be doubled so they didn't fall apart, or floppy recyclable sacks that toppled over.

As I studied the people walking by, I realized that most of the men and women carried straw baskets full of fresh, delectable foods on their shoulders or in their hands. The basket was another expression of the attention the French paid, not only to preparing food, but to purchasing locally grown produce and then carrying it home in the perfect receptacle.

That day I bought not only the magical blue-and-yellow plaid basket that attracted me in the first place, but three others, including a child-sized green one for Zoé-Pascale. I wanted to own these charmed containers and to experience the sense of tradition of which my wise new acquaintance had spoken.

As the clock tower struck noon, I realized it was time to meet Jean and Zoé-Pascale for lunch at the café *Le Temps Perdu.* Jean had reserved our favorite table so we would be assured a seat facing the street, shaded by poplars. Once we ordered our lunch of fresh goat cheese salad, *pomme frites,* and a carafe of wine, Jean looked up into the branches of the large, leafy tree, and took the opportunity to fill us in on what he'd learned about them that morning.

"Napoleon," he explained. "Napoleon ordered that all the farmers plant large trees along the side of the roads to beautify the country and to provide shade for the soldiers as they marched through France. Today, we have Napoleon to thank for all this glorious shade."

We talked about how this was yet another display of French attention to detail and quality of life. Not only did they plant trees alongside the roads, but when it came time to make decisions about cutting down trees to make the roads bigger, the magnificence of the foliage always won out. It reminded us of Emerson and Thoreau and other great thinkers who, in the nineteenth century, influenced the U.S. government to establish national and state parks that would be available for everyone to use. In retrospect, these great men had tremendous foresight for future generations and for the protection of the planet.

Jean and Zoé-Pascale were drawn to the brightly colored baskets I had bought, and I told them the story—the search for the woman, and the pot of gold I found at the end of the literal rainbow. I told them about the magic of baskets, and how it was possible to infuse small, everyday tasks with a bit of enjoyment.

That day was not just the start of our basket collection, but the reminder to put extra joy into our lives in simple, elegant ways.

Chapter 22

Barefoot, Topless, and Pregnant

If you think you can, you can.
And if you think you can't, you're right.

HENRY FORD,
American Industrialist (1867-1947)

CARRYING OUR BEACH CHAIRS, umbrella, and towels, we sauntered down a trampled, pine-tree shaded path, jumped over a fallen branch, traversed a dry river ravine, and finally arrived at a little-known beach we had fallen in love with many years before. Plopping ourselves down at the river's edge, we dug a hole for the umbrella so that it would be just high enough for adequate shade, but low enough not to be blown over by the dry mistral winds responsible for the blue cloudless skies and glorious sunshine. We were early—one of the first families on the beach—so we had our pick of spots. Zoé-Pascale immediately ran to the river, poked her toe in, and shouted, "*C'est parfait!*"

Low in the water, halfway to the other shore, an oblong-shaped rocky island protruded from the river.

"Can we swim to the island and catch a tadpole?" Zoé-Pascale yelled.

"Play for a few minutes, and then we will go swimming," Jean responded.

I asked him, "Do you remember the summer I was pregnant with Zoé-Pascale and we came to this beach?"

"Absolutely," he said smiling. "The last time we were alone *sans enfant.*"

I thought back to that time, when my tummy was bulging and my boobs were huge. I wore my lapis blue tankini and looked like a tan penguin waddling down the beach. Back home in California, I would have been too self-conscious to wear a two piece while I was pregnant, but this was France—it was hot, and I didn't care.

One Sunday that summer, an entire family—mom, dad, grandma, grandpa, a teenage daughter, a school-age daughter and son, and a toddler—were picnicking on the beach nearby where we sat. Like typical French picnickers, they had brought a table and chairs down to the river's edge, along with an umbrella, a basket full of food, a huge apple pie, heavy plastic picnic plates and matching silverware, bottles and bottles of water and wine, and of course, the family dog. We watched them for a while as we ate our meager picnic of bread, cheese, and fruit—what we thought to be a proper French picnic. It looked like they had brought their entire kitchen to the beach.

When their lunch was finished—two-and-a-half hours later—they laid out their towels and beach chairs and began to settle in for the afternoon. Nonchalantly, first mom, then grandma, then the two daughters took off their tops and laid down on the towels to soak in the glorious sun. Grandma looked pretty good for her age in a modest one-piece bathing suit, but once she pulled down the top, it was easier to tell how old she was. She didn't care. It was sunny, and grandma was going to enjoy the moment. Grandpa, dad, and brother went right on fiddling with fishing poles and bait while the woman sunbathed.

Later, Mom tossed aside her top and walked down to the water to take a swim. She yelled for her daughters to join her, and they too threw aside their tops and dove into the water, laughing and splashing happily. The men came down to the water's edge and bantered with the women about the big fish that got away. Canoes floated by, their skippers waving joyously. Once in a while, a foreign tourist in a canoe gawked just a second too long, smiling embarrassedly or giggling at the unfamiliar sight.

That day I debated with myself about sunbathing topless. Was it risky or risqué? What would I feel like if I bared not only my big stomach for the world to see, but my big boobs as well? It wasn't the way I was raised, but I *was* in France, and no one back home would know. Still, it was a big leap, and I didn't feel ready.

"I would have thought that growing up in California would have made you less puritanical," said Jean. "Are you that embarrassed to show off your stomach? It is so beautiful, don't you realize it?"

It was easier for Jean. He grew up among Europeans and Africans, in a family that was much more liberal and comfortable with the human body. He thought it was silly that men and boys in America wore big, baggy swimming shorts. "They are uncomfortable, do nothing for the physique, weigh you down, and you can't swim or tan properly," he said. In France, he was happy to wear Speedos like the other French men, though our visiting American friends did not always feel the same. When our friends Patrick and Sally came to stay one summer, we all went swimming at the public pool. At the reception desk, the clerk glanced down at Patrick in his long, oversized swim trunks and promptly informed him that he couldn't go in the water unless he wore a Speedo.

"*C'est obligatoire.* No exceptions. You can rent one if you don't have one," she added.

Jean assured Patrick that this was very natural in France and that he shouldn't be embarrassed, but Patrick wouldn't hear of it. "If you laugh, I will kill you," he warned Jean as they entered the changing room with a tiny, midnight-black Speedo dangling from his index finger.

When Patrick was finally ready, he had Sally stand guard and scope out a clear path to the pool. Then he flew out of the dressing room, scrambled through the foot washing pool, and dove into the water like a bullet. Sally, watching her crazed husband, was laughing so hard she was crying.

It seems like France pushes everyone's comfort zone just a little bit.

The borders of my own comfort zone were expanded the day that Margaux, an artisan who had recently moved from Paris to our village to enjoy a simpler life, invited us on a picnic with her family the week following my introduction to topless bathing. We happily accepted, but I didn't know what to wear. I had my more fashionable tankini, but since I was pregnant, I thought I should wear the black one-piece.

We met Margaux and her family—husband, mother, sister, brother-in-law, nieces, two school-age children, and two dogs—as we parked our cars on the side of the road near the beach. We gathered the wine and dessert we had brought, along with our beach gear and chairs, and set off down the path to the sunny, stony beach at the river. I noticed that Margaux's picnic was packed in four different-colored baskets, each covered with beautiful matching cotton napkins to conceal the items inside.

After choosing a spot that was safe from the wind and where the table could be balanced well, we settled in. The children tore off their cover-ups and ran into the water, wearing only their bottoms.

The dogs followed the kids into the water while the women laid out the picnic, consisting of *foie gras*, baguettes, *saucisses*, *salades*, melons, strawberries, fresh cream, assorted cheeses, and the *tartes de pommes* we had brought. Soon we were laughing, talking, and eating.

At one point, I asked Margaux tentatively, "How do French women really feel about topless sunbathing?"

Margaux laughed. "It's natural. The sun is here to enjoy, and wearing a top is so cumbersome. Besides, we don't like strap lines—they take away the beauty of the shoulder in a sundress, no?

"Look at the children," she continued. "Children are born natural. When they become teenagers, sometimes they choose to wear tops, but other times not. It is natural, the way God intended us, and we feel proud of what he gave us to enjoy."

"I know, but it seems embarrassing for everyone to see your breasts," I said cautiously. "I mean, don't the men gawk?"

"Oh no, the men just enjoy our beauty," Margaux said. "Our bodies are admired. No one judges if you wear a top or not. It is very irrelevant, don't you think? It is also not so much what you wear or not, but whether your behavior is appropriate," she went on. "If you act inappropriate or perverted about something natural, you are probably a *toc-toc* (coo-coo person) anyway." She shook her head and laughed at what should have been obvious to us Americans.

At that, the men left to go for a swim. Now, alone with Margaux and the women alone, I seized my chance to ask more questions and get their real perspective. "How do I get the confidence to sunbathe without my top?" I ventured, pretending I was joking.

"Start here," she said. "Lie down on your stomach and then slowly turn over. Roll down your bathing suit so that your baby can feel all of the sun. It will feel good and freeing for you and the baby will love the warm sun."

The kids were playing at the water's edge, and the men were

gone. I decided now was the time to take a little risk. After all, it wasn't like I was doing anything illegal.

"Okay," I said to Margaux, who quickly untied the neck of my bathing suit top before I could protest. She smiled as I laid down on my beach towel. My swollen boobs burst free into the sunshine. They were so big that it had actually hurt to have them squashed inside the swimsuit. I rolled the top of my suit farther and farther down—all the way to my bikini line. I splashed lotion on myself quickly before anyone could see me touch my breasts, and then hid myself under my big hat, pretending I was not there. With my face hidden, I realized how wonderful the warm sun felt on my body, just as Margaux had said.

Ten minutes later, Jean called to me from the water, "Come in and take a swim. The water is great."

Now what to do? I wondered. Roll my bathing suit top back up, or keep it down? I sat up and decided it was now or never. Could I walk to the water's edge with my pregnant breasts swinging in the air? Before any more mental negotiations could take place, I stood up and looked around. Not too far away, five women were sitting topless, chatting. A couple was playing beach tennis in the river; the woman was topless. Margaux wandered towards her topless mother at the edge of the river, laughing and splashing water on the kids. I wanted to feel as free and comfortable as the rest of the women, but I just couldn't.

Next time, I promised myself. It's all about taking baby steps. This just wasn't the day.

Later that week, Jean and I went to the beach alone, and I decided to test my nerve once again. I wore my bikini to make it easier, resolving to sunbathe *sans* top. And so I did. Reading my book, sipping water, and feeling the sun on my body felt like a little bit of heaven. Suddenly, before I realized what I was doing, I stood up, walked down to the river, and dove into the water. It was ecstasy.

Feeling the silky cool water against my breasts and stomach as I swam to the nearby rock, I knew that, self-conscious or not, I wasn't going back to wearing a top—except perhaps when my parents came to visit.

The whole experience was a good reminder of how often we live by values and rules that we are afraid to push against or even examine, even if they no longer hold meaning for us. How often are we held back by old habits and patterns from trying something new? I became certain that if we were able to stay open to new experiences, our time in France would guide us to the ideas and vision of what our future might hold.

"Come on, Maman!" Zoé-Pascale shouted now. "Let's swim to the island." I smiled at my daughter and, without a second thought, jumped up *sans* top to join my family in the cool, refreshing water of the river.

Chapter 23

Peek-a-Boo

Sex appeal is fifty percent what you've got
and fifty percent what people think you've got.

SOPHIA LOREN,
Award-winning Italian film actress (1934-)

EVERY DAY, ALONG WITH millions of other women, I put on a bra—usually beige, but sometimes black. It's sensible, satisfactory, and comfortable. Soon after moving to France, I became more and more tantalized by all the French women with assorted colored bra straps peeking out of their sundresses and T-shirts. There were clear ones that the young girls were wearing with tank tops, gingham check with lace worn by the grocer's wife, the neighbor's green ivory, a friend's purple with roses, the elegant black seen at night, or the silky pink under a rose-colored dress. Rarely, if ever, did I spy a plain white bra strap.

Even the insurance agent, I noticed one day, was wearing a red sleeveless dress with a matching fire-engine red bra strap slipping down her arm, as if to say, "Aren't I beautiful?" Indeed, I thought, that strap really does have something to say.

I was used to buying my staple Wacoal beige bra at Nordstrom's once a year. It is a comfortable one to wear under white T-shirts or suits—no imagination, and definitely no mystery. Intrigued to find out more about Frenchwomen and their lingerie, I began my own investigation.

I discovered that Frenchwomen spend nearly twenty percent of their annual clothing budget on lingerie. In the U.S., the average clothing budget is $1,759 a year. Twenty percent of that means that an average American woman should be spending $350 a year on lingerie. I personally am falling way below the average. *Why is that,* I wondered? Perhaps it was because I was a product of the 1970s, when women were burning their bras to promote female liberation, putting comfort above meeting confined and narrow social expectations of beauty. But now, thirty years later, I wanted something more from my lingerie, something these French women secretly knew and loved.

My various interviews proved my hunch—every Frenchwoman believed with her heart and soul that wearing a beautiful lace or satin bra with matching underwear was the essence of looking and feeling good. It isn't about the man (although some say it is), but about how the woman herself feels wearing cool silk on her warm skin, or a demi-cup that reveals her cleavage glistening in the summer heat. In fact, the bra was invented in 1889 by a Frenchwoman, Herminie Cadolle, who cut the midriff off her corset to allow for more waist movement.

My research continued at the local mini-department store in Uzès. I tried on a selection of mid-priced bras—black and white lace, pink satin, and purple and blue flowers—and decided upon all three. After all, I did have a lingerie budget of $350.

Over the next week, I wore each bra under a coordinating T-shirt, tank, or summer dress, taking time to match the bra with the color top. I felt different somehow—more put together, more elegant, more French. Next, I picked up a few colored bras at the local *marché* for a mere five euros apiece. Soon, however, I found out that you *do* get what you pay for: the *marché* bras were fun, but vexatious and ill-fitting. A ten-euro experiment, I told myself.

I stared in the windows of the two French lingerie stores in town, drooling over the beautifully designed Chantall and Aubade bras displayed in the window, with the book *L'Art d'Aimer* (Lessons in Seduction) tucked close by. A white lace bra with green leaves, plum cherries, an orange-and-white gingham bow, and straps edged in black jumped out at me. I loved that bra! It made me feel jubilant and impish, and I was only looking in the window!

Opening the door, I boldly walked in and asked to try it on. I slipped into the dressing room, wiggled into the bra, and realized it was a demi-cup—something I don't usually wear. But wow, did it look flirtatious and whimsical! It held me firm while showing off my upper half, and oh, how soft it felt against my skin. I turned and twisted in the mirror, seeing if I could run for the bus (not that I ever ran for the bus), dance, and jump without my boobs falling out, and daring the bra to say, "You shouldn't buy me."

Did I dare? At 75 euros (approximately $100), it was going to put a big dent in the lingerie budget, but it just had to be mine.

For the next six months, I pranced around wearing my economical, moderate, and expensive bras in turn, loving every minute. Jean loved it too, and admitted that the *très cher* bra was the most beautiful on me. *So the investment does pay off*, I thought, keeping that in mind for the next shopping spree.

When I'd bought my white-laced demi-cup with green leaves and ruby-red cherries, the woman shopkeeper had politely asked whether I would like to have matching underwear. I figured that my Victoria's Secret three-for-$10 underwear had done just fine up to now, and I'd pass. However, as my lingerie investigation continued, I soon came to find out that the French would no sooner wear underwear that didn't match the bra than wear two different color shoes. It was simply unheard of.

Did it really make a difference if you wore matching underwear? Was it really more important to feel elegant and sexy than to be sensible? Evidently, the British thought so, ever since *Bridget Jones*. One report stated that the British are now spending more than the French, Germans, Italians, and Spanish on lingerie, and definitely more than the Americans.

I'd tried wearing a thong but could never get the hang of it, even though I read recently that it is not the breast that is getting the most attention these days but the *fesses*, or buttock. Returning to my favorite lingerie store during their January winter sale, when the coveted 75-euro bras were on sale for 50% off, I wondered whether now was the time to indulge in matching underwear. A leopard-print silk bra trimmed with beige lace was waiting for me in my size. The saleswoman smiled as she proudly brought me the matching *sous vêtements*, also on sale.

"*C'est bon marché.*" (It is a good price.) Yes, I thought, *I have to have it.* Instead of wrapping up the package, I told the saleswoman I wanted to wear the garments. "*Bien sûr,*" she said with a smile that insinuated, "You must be meeting a special man."

Walking out of the store and down the street in my leopard lingerie, I concentrated on how it felt: soft, silky, playful, and sexy. I swayed to miss a dog and danced around a tree, whistling a song I had heard on the radio. I then realized I was smiling at everyone I met. *Bonjour, Monsieur. Bonjour, Madame.* They smiled back, and I wondered whether they could possibly know *my* secret.

Art and Creativity

The key question isn't "What fosters creativity?" But it is why in God's name isn't everyone creative? Where was the human potential lost? How was it crippled? I think therefore a good question might be not why do people create? But why do people not create or innovate? We have got to abandon that sense of amazement in the face of creativity, as if it were a miracle if anybody created anything."

ABRAHAM MASLOW,
American Psychologist, (1908-1970)

Chapter 24

The Other Side of the Brain

Creativity requires the courage to let go of certainties.

ERICH FROMM,

Social Psychologist (1900-1980)

JEAN AND I SIGNED up for a weeklong sculpture class in an effort to reclaim the creative parts of ourselves that had gone dormant. Every day from 2-5 p.m., we walked down the street to the village's *atelier*. The building, which had once been the town's bar, had a grand view of Uzès and overlooked the village. The bar moved down to the *Place du Marché*, and the large space with the twelve-foot ceilings became a working studio for both novices and resident artists. Inside were chest-high natural wood tables with high stools for leaning and sitting, makeshift wooden shelves topped with pottery in various stages of completion, three potter's wheels, and artist's tools in odd-size plastic containers caked with clay. Boxes of finished pieces made by the schoolchildren were piled along the old bar on the eastern wall.

"*Bienvenue,*" the teacher welcomed us as we walked into the class promptly at 2 p.m. "*Je m'appelle Monique.*" Covered in a red-clay-bespattered apron was Monique, our teacher. She was somewhere in her early forties with a smiling, scrubbed face, no make-up, twinkling blue eyes, and fuzzy blonde hair. Seated along the tall worktables were four of our new classmates, ready to make their mark as artists.

In her perfect Parisian accent, our teacher began to explain that we were going to first make mini-masks to learn how to create expressions in clay: a smile, a frown, a grimace, joy, sadness, and laughter.

"Sounds easy," I whispered to Jean.

Fifteen minutes later, Jean was laughing loudly at my mini-masks. "Your smile is crooked and your sad face looks like a clown. I think you spoke too soon." He was so right.

For the next three hours, we worked on our faces. Propping a small hand mirror against a tall Evian water bottle, I scowled, laughed, frowned, and made funny faces as though I were two years old again. Trying not to get distracted by the lines in my face or the need to pluck my eyebrows, I concentrated on the expression itself.

"Watch this," I said to Jean, pulling a scowl to show my point. "They are right about how frowning causes lines. Look what happens to my face when I frown, yet when I smile, my eyes actually twinkle." I was learning about much more than sculpture.

The next day at 2 p.m., we reentered the *atelier,* ready for something bigger.

"Today, we will sculpt a head and face that looks like you." Monique informed us. "First, pound a ball of clay together. After that, you will shape the eyes, eyebrows, nose, mouth, ears, and hair."

Following her instructions, we spent the next three hours in our own worlds, pounding, molding, smoothing, ripping, and fighting with the clay, trying to mold it into something that resembled our inner selves. The sound of the fan whirling in the background was interrupted every so often with a question to the teacher.

"How do I do a mouth?" "How do I do the eyes so they don't look like a bird ate them out?" "How do I make curly hair?"

Since I was in a French pottery class and still hadn't mastered the language, I resorted to a lot of pointing and show-and-tell. Monique was sweet enough to teach me the vocabulary of the face in French in addition to showing me how to sculpt each part. I learned that the word for "eyes," as in "both eyes," is *les yeux,* and one eye is *un oeil. Why in the world would the French have two words for the same thing?* I characteristically wondered, though I was becoming more used to the many subtleties of the language.

At 5 p.m., with our clay heads finally coming to life, we were feeling euphoric. I decided to add some sophisticated elegance to my head: a *chignon* to my *cheveux* (a bun to my hair), and big pearl earrings around the neck. Jean's head had the kind of curls one might see on an African man, and flat eyes, where mine bulged a bit.

By the end of the second day, we'd come to know the rest of the group: Noemie, a French mom; Simone, a Swiss-American; Anais, a Belgian retiree who loved to laugh; and Amaury, who looked like a bearded goat chewing on an old tobacco stick. The only time he stopped chewing the stick was at the end of class, when he would pop his unlit pipe into his mouth, ready to light up the minute he was outside.

Our hands were dry with the red clay, our fingernails broken and beyond repair, and our spirits high as kites. We were artists.

"The last step," she instructed us, "is to cut your head in half and hollow out the inside."

"What does she mean, cut it in half?" I said to Jean. "It will get destroyed."

"Just watch her," he replied. "I think we have to do that so it won't break in the kiln."

Fifteen minutes later, we had anxiously sliced our heads in half, hollowed out the insides, and put them back together again. Monique then suggested we think about what we wanted to do for our "big" project, which would take several days to complete. She suggested we look through magazines and books to see whether anything inspired us, and passed out a variety of examples for the class to look at.

Jean toyed with the idea of copying Praxiteles' Greek god Hermes. "I love the Venus de Milo," I said to the teacher, "Do you think you could teach me how to do a statue like her?"

"We can try," she answered, not wanting to discourage her eager students. "It will be your own version of Venus de Milo, but just as capable of dispensing love and beauty. It is wonderful that you all have such excitement in your hearts for sculpture. This is critical to being an artist."

That night after dinner, I leafed through some magazines and sat with a pencil and paper, trying to figure out what I wanted to sculpt. What feeling did I want my piece to represent? What was important for me to create? I wrote down some key words: calm, peaceful, joyful, beautiful, loving, and happy. I began to picture my statue as it encompassed these feelings. Meanwhile, Jean was making sketches of his own.

"Why do all your drawings look so very African?" I asked.

"I don't know. Part of my sub-Saharan history, I guess," he answered. "This Provençal red clay is making me want to focus on primitive art. I'm just letting my hands do the work."

The next afternoon, we all walked into class armed with photos, magazine cutouts, and pictures of what we wanted to create. Sitting in our usual spots on our high stools, we began to move our fingers in unison—almost as though the entire class was creating one David.

The teacher walked behind us, helping to move legs into position, explaining why a statue on one leg would not hold up well, and pointing out that Amaury had to create a head big enough to hold a pipe in its mouth.

Jean hovered over his ball of clay, forming another version of his African male, with knees bent and hugged against his chest, muscular calves, and huge flat feet with perfectly formed toes and toenails—a work of art that the entire class admired.

Inspired by my desire to create a statue of a serene, peaceful woman—the one I was striving to be—I began to sculpt and, following Jean's example, let my fingers do what they wanted. Slowly, the clay was molded into a woman in a yoga-like position with a little girl sitting on her lap. I adorned them each with a string of large pearls (which ultimately would be painted yellow) and matching pearl bracelets. On each ear, I placed large round earrings and, resting on top of the woman's head, a wide-brimmed straw hat with a silk band and a flower on the side. (The hat also served to hide some of the less-than-perfect facial features.)

I took the liberty of providing the woman with a boob lift, so that her breasts stood out straight and firm just like I always wanted, muscular arms, and finely shaped thighs. Her back was straight and her buttocks round and tight. She looked as though she had been doing yoga for years and was the precise image of what I looked like in my dreams. The little girl, her hair pulled up high on her head, sat silently on her Maman's lap, wrapped in love and adoration.

At the end of the week, we lined up our creations and examined them in detail.

"Suzanne, your sculpture is so peaceful and tranquil," someone commented. I nodded with a big smile, thinking to myself, *and this is how I'm finally beginning to feel inside.*

The comments continued down the table. "How did you do the

hair like that?" "Look at those great eyebrows." "Wow, *bijou* (jewelry)." "I love it." "I love that pipe, Amaury." "Anais, your Venus is beautiful."

We raised glasses of wine to toast our first full-body sculptures, convinced there was no end to our talents. An entire new world of creativity had been opened up to us.

We were hooked! "Now what?" we asked each other. Another pottery class? A drawing class? Since we lived in a potters' village, we decided to sign up for the year-long weekly class, in which we could do either pottery or sculpture. Anais and Amaury continued along with us, and we were joined by a few other newcomers.

We started with small bowls and eventually created a huge round vessel that would become a receptacle for computer cables. Together, Jean and I made a set of ten plates using the old-fashioned method of molding, patting, and shaping them to perfection, and stenciling upon them bunches of grapes, pears, apples, cherries, and more grapes. Growing a bit bored after awhile with creating china, we moved back into figure sculpting. Jean continued with his African theme, this time focusing on an African woman with plump, sagging breasts.

"And whose boobs are those?" I asked him, laughing.

"In my dreams," he responded, giving me a peck on the cheek.

I continued with another sculpture of a woman in a big straw hat, her elbows bent and hands palms up, as though she was waiting for an offering. And of course, she wore what had become my signature necklace, bracelet, and hat.

It was as though the right, intuitive side of our brains were not only allowing us to play and create, but were actually working through us, bringing messages of truth about who we wanted to be, and who we were becoming.

Chapter 25

En Plein Air

*The highest prize we can receive for creative work is the joy of
being creative. Creative effort spent for any other reason than
the joy of being in that light filled space, love, god, whatever we
want to call it, is lacking in integrity.*

MARIANNE WILLIAMSON,
spiritual activist, author, speaker (1952-)

NEXT IT WAS ON to painting. Our neighbor David and his wife
Linda were organizing a painting week for guests at their villa. They were young entrepreneurs from England who rented out
their grand home to vacationers, providing bike trips, painting, and
cooking classes as part of the package. There was room in the current class—did I want to join?

"Yes, yes, yes." I said. "Sign me up."

For years, I had been dabbling in painting by copying my favorite Provençal artist, Lèon Zanella, out on the terrace. His vibrant
colors and abstract landscapes inspired me. I loved his trees that

looked like lollipops, and the way he made the landscape sing.

I was still a bit of an amateur at painting *en plein air*. Twelve years earlier—the year we'd bought our house—we had seen a postcard of the Pont du Gard and knew we had to visit to see what this place really looked like. We thought the photograph may have been doctored to look so incredibly beautiful, and we decided to go see for ourselves. We packed a great picnic of fresh strawberries, *chevré*, baguettes, and juicy tomatoes, and set off on our trip. We were determined not only to find the Pont du Gard, but we also wanted a chance to take our newly purchased canvases and paints and follow the footsteps of Van Gogh along the Provençal landscape.

By noon, we had sketched the breathtaking architectural wonder. With utter delight, we began to add color to our canvases to capture the beauty of the scene as best we could. Very soon we were surrounded by a group of energetic ten-year-old school kids who wanted to know all about our paintings.

"Oh, they are very beautiful," the children said. "Are you famous painters?"

"Would you sell the paintings?"

"Oh, my *maman* would really like that one. Would you give it to me?" one freckly boy innocently asked in his sweet voice.

We offered them strawberries and water and they smiled, truly believing that they had met two famous artists. Eventually, their teacher called them back to their school bus and they ran off happily. Their excitement was contagious. We were feeling on top of the world and thrilled with our creative endeavors.

Eager now to recapture that euphoric feeling, I joined the small group and our art teacher, Sara, at the Pont du Gard.

"Pick your spot," Sara said.

Staring at some tall trees across the walking path, I saw the picture I wanted to paint. Shadows were everywhere and I knew it would be a challenge, but if not now, when?

I began to paint and soon became engrossed. For three hours, I was one with my trees. The shadows kept moving, and I kept moving with them. The sun changed, but I didn't care. I was alone with my painting.

Like the schoolchildren years before, tourists came up behind me to see my work. Out of the corner of my eye, I watched them nod in admiration, secretly wondering whether they could do the same thing. I wanted to shout, "Of course you can. It's fantastic. Come paint!"

The next day the class went to a nearby château. It was a bright, sunny day, and the sky was that perfect color blue found only in Provence. What to paint? The old château itself, the doors and windows, the garden with its pool, or the chairs and umbrellas in the garden? Finally settling in on my view, I began to draw, but it just wasn't working. I called the teacher over and she gave me a bit of advice on how to draw the chairs more easily, without so much detail. Drawing was not my forte, and I was happy to accept the model she gave me.

This was the start I needed. Soon the tables and chairs were drawn in, followed by the umbrellas and garden. After I added a dark shade of olive green to the bottom of the trees, followed by khaki and lime green at the top, the sun began to shine between the leaves of my painting. The umbrella became a soft vanilla with a chocolate brown base, and the tables sat at sharp angles in the middle of the garden. The chairs stood out in a fine teak wood color with sunflower yellow cushions. On the ground lay a carpet of gray French petite *caillou* (pebbles) so characteristic of France. Flowerbeds surrounded by a low stone wall sat in the foreground of the painting, close-laced with shiny pink roses, violet and golden pansies, and rosemary.

Stepping back from my painting, I was mesmerized. *I did it*, I thought. It actually looked like what I saw. I decided to take a short break and look around at the other artists' work. Yes, the professionals on vacation produced work that was quite good and realistic, but I was amazed at what the newer artists like myself were painting. Each painting felt inspired, artistic, and delighted. Was there something to painting *en plein air* that Matisse and others knew, and that I was just learning?

Jean, Zoé-Pascale, and I would be traveling to Prague and Vienna the following week. I decided that was the perfect opportunity to continue my drawing and painting. I bought little books for all of us, and packed pencils and watercolors, which are easy to use, although not my favorite medium. On our trip, whenever we saw something beautiful we wanted to draw—a church, a village from afar, a plaza, a vineyard—we stopped and sketched. Later on, we took out the watercolors and painted in our scenes.

Falling in love with painting *en plein air*, I created a portable art studio packed into a yellow-and-green plaid straw basket: assorted acrylic paints, brushes, plastic cups, and folding easels. In the late afternoons, I would sit on the patio table and work on one of my Zanella-inspired paintings. Sometimes Zoé-Pascale would join me, sketching out her landscape and filling it in with her favorite colors. On lazy afternoons we would pack a picnic, take the art basket and head out to a mountaintop, into the vineyards or to the river, and allow ourselves the time to create. This was not about being productive or making income; it was about being courageous, letting go of judgments, and being in love with life.

Claiming the creative part of ourselves was helping us to appreciate who we were in totality. We were learning that we weren't just our professions, our careers, or even parents. We were discovering yet another aspect of our wholeness, one that allowed for more simple joy in our lives.

Travel and Adventure

En Voyage (The Voyage)

Pour partir là-bas, je prends ma valise.
Je pars pour aller en croisière pour les grandes vacances.
…Je pars, je pars pour une grande vacance.
Je mets dans ma valise le soleil, la pluie, le vent, et la lune,
ma maison, mon jardin et ma chambre,
la chambre de mes parents et la famille.
…Je sens la mer, je goûte les glaces, je vois les dauphins et les poissons,
les autres bateaux nous disent bonjour, et quand je dors, je rêve de la mer.

To leave to go over there, I take my suitcase,
I leave to go on a cruise for the great holidays.
…I leave; I leave for a great vacation.
I pack in my suitcase, the sun, the rain, the wind, and the moon,
my house, my garden and my room,
the room of my parents and my family.
…I smell the sea, I taste the ice cream, I see the dolphins and the fish,
the other boats say hello to us,
and when I sleep, I dream of the sea.

By Zoé-Pascale de Saxe Roux, age 7

Chapter 26

Reading, Writing, Arithmetic, and Travel

You lose sight of things...
and when you travel, everything balances out.

DARANNA GIDEL,
Author (1948-)

DURING OUR DREAMING PHASE back in the States, we often discussed the idea of taking a "gap" year, like that rite of passage
of so many college graduates, to travel abroad and explore the world.
After talking to others our age who had done this with their children,
and doing extensive research, we decided the best option was to find
a home base in a different culture and travel from there. Hence our
decision to live in our adopted French village and travel, during Zoé-
Pascale's school breaks, throughout Europe and Africa. In addition to
her curriculum of reading, writing, and arithmetic, we felt grateful for
the opportunity to teach her about our global village.

By October, the colors across Europe had become a rainbow of ruby red, deep yellow, and burnt orange foliage, and the sun shone undauntedly in the afternoons, warming up the earth. Strolling through the fourteenth-century lanes of Prague, we watched the sophisticated Eastern European women in their three-inch heels wobbling and teetering confidently between the cobblestones on the intricately designed streets. "How do they do it?" we wondered. They looked as sophisticated and elegant as the royalty who had majestically promenaded down these narrow stone streets before them. We deduced that it must be a skill one acquires at a very young age in this part of the world.

In addition to watching the women defy physics and gravity, we were equally entertained by twisting our necks like cranes to look up at the mysterious gargoyles, stone statues, and intricately carved sculptures that decorated each edifice.

"That looks like a wedding cake," Zoé-Pascale would shout. "And look at those dancing lady statues! They are so beautiful."

Walking along the Vitava River with its thirteen bridges, we felt we'd been transported back to the Renaissance, when Baroque artists made their livings adorning buildings with eccentric golden decorations. Architecture, art, and beauty were so intertwined here. Prague was like one massive museum.

Thirty statues of saints protected the Charles Bridge, which was built in the fourteenth century as a major trade route from western to eastern Europe. The saints escorted us from the old city to the cathedral at Prague Castle on the other side. The stone bridge is rumored to have been built with egg yolks mixed into the mortar to make it extra strong. The fact that it has survived numerous floods over the last five hundred years made us wonder whether it was something more than a myth.

"This looks like Cinderella's castle," Zoé-Pascale said, pointing to the entrance to the Charles Bridge.

"It absolutely does. Fantasyland must have been conceived here," I agreed.

"Look over there." She pointed to a side wall plastered with old communist posters. "That looks like those Russian dolls I have," she said, referring to her set of Russian nesting dolls—a series of beautifully-painted figures in descending sizes, one fitting neatly inside the next. "Why do the dolls in the poster have teeth like a shark?" she asked.

"From middle ages to communism," Jean said. "I guess this is as good a place as any to explain World War II, communism, and the holocaust, all at once.

"Once upon a time ..." he began and, over the next several minutes, attempted to summarize that horrendous part of human history in a way Zoé-Pascale might understand.

Zoé-Pascale summarized, "So there are bad countries and good countries, and sometimes one doesn't like what another one does, or they want to control each other. There are bad leaders and good leaders. Sometimes people fight and kill each other. That's not very nice. But now the countries are friends again, so that's good."

"Well, I guess that's one way to look at it," I remarked, grateful for her clear and simple six-year-old summation.

Crossing the city, we stopped to enjoy jazz musicians playing a mélange of New Orleans jazz and smooth contemporary Eastern European sounds. It reminded me of the music from the *Fiddler on the Roof*. Zoé-Pascale, with her dancing soul, swayed to the music with abandon.

"Let's tip the musicians," she said at the end of the song. Farther along the bridge, she asked, "Can I have some more money? I want to give some to the beggars. There are so many, and they are kind of praying, so we should give them all money."

Some of the beggars were, in fact, on their knees and prone on the ground, as if in deep, silent prayer. Every few yards, raggedly-clothed men would slowly lift their sun-spotted foreheads a few inches off the ground and nod, as though to say, "Thank you." Women wrapped in greasy wool shawls, with babies feeding at their breasts, stared at us with vacant eyes and waited to see whether we would put money in their palms. For Zoé-Pascale, it turned into a game as she ran from one beggar to the next, dispensing change.

"Zoé-Pascale, we have to choose how and whom to help, as there are so many people and creatures in need."

"I want to help them all," she answered. "I choose all of them!"

I wanted to tell her that what she wanted to do was the right thing—the only choice—and yet my hardened adult heart was wondering whether these beggars couldn't get some type of job. As a compromise, I suggested we help those who seemed willing to help themselves.

"Okay, if I must choose, then I want to give to everyone who does something for me," Zoé-Pascale decided. "I won't give to the beggars who are lying down, but I will give to the singer, the musician, and the dancing monkey. I think they all work hard for their money. And maybe God will give some money to the rest."

All of a sudden, *giving* took on a new meaning. Who among all the beggars was really worthy of a big tip? Who tried harder, smiled wider, sang with delight, and beamed with happiness as passersby applauded their private shows? We were like angels, picking whom to reward and whom to skip. Not such an easy task.

From the Charles Bridge, we took a bus and then walked uphill to the fabulous Prague Castle. Zoé-Pascale took on the character of Rapunzel as we ascended 287 tiny stone steps leading in a spiral formation up to the bell tower, with its massive, eighteen-ton bell tolls. It was said that nobody knew how to lift such heavy objects up to tower until the princess created an effective pulley out of her hair. After the bell was installed, she destroyed the machine so that nobody would know the working principle. For hours after hearing that story, Zoé-Pascale played with her hair, trying to reinvent the ancient pulley system.

Pagans, Christians, and Jews had resided peacefully side by side for centuries in Prague. Back in the old town, we wandered through parts of the original twelfth-century Jewish quarter, where the oldest thirteenth-century Jewish synagogue in Europe is also located. Speeding through history, we could sense the expansion of the highly cultured Jewish life of the sixteenth century, when three additional synagogues were added, along with an intricately designed Jewish center with heavily carved oak doors. By the mid-nineteenth century, all of this beauty had succumbed to a ghetto.

"This is where thousands of souls perished during World War II," we said to Zoé-Pascale. "Eighty thousand Jewish people were slaughtered by the Nazis or forced to leave the country for concentration camps. Only about six thousand Jewish people now remain here."

"Why would someone want to kill so many people?" she asked.

We did our best to explain the concepts of ego, power, and lack of tolerance that have perpetuated the horror of war to this day.

"Look at that statue," Zoé-Pascale said, moving on. "It's a headless man with another man on top."

"And so it is," Jean agreed, launching into a children's version of the story of Kafka and existentialism. As we studied the bronze statue, we talked a bit longer about the tendency of humans to create such beauty and, simultaneously, practice such hatred and cruelty. How is that possible? What is this life truly about? What is our purpose on this planet? Why are we here at this time? Aren't these the same questions Prague's most famous son would have asked?

Zoé-Pascale, who had been busy following a squirrel, jerked us out of our deep thoughts. "There are many very old buildings here, lots of dead buried people, beggars, sculptures, old history, and the Prague Castle that I like. But I'm hungry, so can we go eat now?"

"I know just the place!" I said. "Let's go the square and get that delicious dark brown bread and *saucisse* with mustard."

"I'll race you," she said, and off we went.

From Prague, we took a train to Vienna. I had told Jean and Zoé-Pascale that I absolutely had to show them Mozart's home, thinking back fondly to my travels in Austria after graduate school.

After hours of walking down the streets looking at nothing but government and business buildings, then watching an actor dressed as Mozart hand out leaflets for that evening's concert, Jean said, "Now what exactly did you want to show us in this city?"

I had wondered the same thing since we'd arrived in Vienna earlier that day, and soon realized that I had made a mistake. It was Salzburg, not Vienna, that I wanted them to experience. Not the place where Mozart lived, but where he was *born*. Embracing our newfound mentality of *Ce n'est pas grave*, Jean laughed good-humoredly and said, "Oh, there must be a reason we are here. We are exactly where we are meant to be." He suggested taking the train to Baden-Baden the next day to swim in their famous thermal pools. "Then we can take a boat trip down the Danube. Zoé-Pascale will love it, and the fall colors will be like floating through a painting."

That evening, we attended a German musical, *Romeo and Julia, das musicale*, a modern version of Romeo and Juliet. We sank into the plush red velvet seats in the old theatre and were swept away as the actors in their costumes of dark blues, purples, and deep violets for the Montagues, and burgundy reds and smooth oranges for the Capulets, sang and danced to unforgettable upbeat music. Though Zoé-Pascale and I don't know any German, we were both crying when Romeo and Julia lay dying on the stone table as the rest of the cast sang to their love.

‿˘‿˘‿

A few days later, before leaving Vienna to return to Prague for our flight, I urged Jean to fit in a last-minute visit to Sigmund Freud's house. "You have to see it. We have time, and I know the route to the train station," I assured him. I had the morning schedule planned: eat a quick breakfast, walk to Freud's house, take a few photos, and then catch the bus to the train station.

"Eleven o'clock and here we are, just on time," I said to Jean as we settled onto the bus behind the Austrian driver, with our three rolling suitcases and a daypack crammed in the corner.

After a few minutes, though, I realized the passing scenery didn't look at all familiar.

"Sir, is this the way to the *gare*, the train station?" I questioned the driver in Franglais, a mixture of French and English, hoping he would understand my question.

"*Nein*," he told me in his thick Austrian accent. "You need to take the bus on the other side of the street."

"Get off the bus, now!" I shouted to Zoé-Pascale and Jean.

Ten minutes later, we silently settled on the double-length bus heading toward the train station, glowering at each other and not speaking. It was obvious to both of us we weren't going to make it in time to catch the train, which meant we wouldn't make it to Prague to catch our plane. This meant we wouldn't get to Marseille to meet the taxi waiting for us, which meant we wouldn't get home when we thought we would, which meant that Zoé-Pascale would miss her return to school, and so forth.

I could see Jean's mind reeling, weighing our options. I didn't think he'd be mad long, but was surprised by his prolonged deathly silence.

"What are we going to do?" Zoé-Pascale cried, breaking the tension.

We both realized that we could be angry and point fingers later, but for now we had to solve *une grande probleme*, immediately.

"One thing your *Maman* and I are good at is figuring out how to solve a problem," Jean soothed her. "So let's put our heads together. Our choices are to get another train, a plane, or a bus."

"Or a taxi," I added.

"Yes, a plane," Zoé-Pascale piped up.

"Or a rental car," Jean said.

Jumping off the bus, we rolled our suitcases up to the train station window. "You booked the last train for the day to Prague," the station agent informed us. "You'll have to come back tomorrow to catch the next one."

Jostling our way through the double swinging doors of the station, Jean beelined for the rental car stalls. "Is it possible to rent a car and drop it in Prague?" he inquired.

"Sure, but it will cost you 500 euro plus a 300-euro drop-off fee. You might want to check the airline office on the square," the attendant suggested.

Still glaring at each other, we turned and dragged our suitcases to the airline offices. The woman behind the counter acknowledged that it was possible to fly to Prague, but that a one-way ticket would cost three times what we paid for a round trip ticket from Marseille. So much for Plan B—on to Plan C!

Jean left to talk to a burly man in a gray parka with a day-old beard standing next to the taxi stand.

"Look," I said, pointing at a nearby sign. Across the street was a Starbucks Coffee, something we had not seen in six months. Hoping that it would smooth out the situation, Zoé-Pascale and I hustled over for lattes and hot chocolate while Jean bargained with the taxi driver. As we exited, Jean was beaming and waving at us to run.

"Hurry! I just negotiated a 400-euro trip to the Prague airport!" It was about a four-hour drive. If we hustled, we'd have an hour to spare.

"I can't believe we did it," I whispered as we scurried into the back seat holding tight to the comfort of our Starbucks lattes.

Smiling at the *coup de grace*, Jean answered, "Yes, we did it. Well, for a price."

Two hours later, as we hit the Austrian-Czech border, Jean heard the driver cuss under his breath in Turkish and call a friend on his mobile phone.

"I don't have the toll card for the Czech freeways, and my GPS system stopped at the Austrian border," he told us. "How do I get to Prague?"

As the driver weaved off and on the freeway without the GPS to guide him, he and Jean pointed, grunted, and communicated in a mixture of Turkish, French, Dutch, and German, interpreting the Czech signage and the route to Prague. Zoé-Pascale and I were in the back seat holding hands tightly, pretending to read our books while eavesdropping on the men's conversation. We giggled as the agitated driver shed his jacket, sweater, and shirt, leaving him sitting in his sleeveless graying undershirt.

"Ah, an airport!" he finally yelled, spotting a sign with a small airplane on it. A few miles down the road, we looped around the entranceway to an airport that was big enough to hold about ten small Cessnas. Evidently, this was *not* the Prague International Airport.

Back on the freeway in heavy traffic, our half-naked Turkish driver was sweating, swearing, and hunched over the steering wheel, frantically searching for the sign to the Prague International Airport.

"This way, this way," Jean yelled as they approached a steep turnoff with a painted sign that indicated the International Airport.

Five minutes later, we bounced out of the taxi with a worried glance at a 970-euro charge on the taxi meter. Fortunately, our exasperated driver said, "No, I said four hundred, and my word is my word and my honor."

"Take fifty more and have a nice dinner," Jean yelled as we dashed into the airport with our luggage flying behind us.

Minutes later, panting heavily and yelling, *"Attendez, Attendez!"* in Franglais, we reached the entrance just as the flight attendant was pushing the clunky thick steel door closed.

"Quickly, come in, hurry, we are ready to depart," she said sternly to us.

Snapping our seat belts in place, I leaned over and said to Jean, "An expensive traveling miscalculation."

"Yeah, but we solved the problem," Zoé-Pascale stated. "And it was genius!"

We all settled in, feeling strangely gratified. We realized that this is what travel does to us: it tests our resolve, forces us to be flexible, pulls upon our inner resources—and sometimes our bank accounts. As the comedian Dave Barry says, "that's the wonderful thing about family travel: it provides you with experiences that will remain locked forever in the scar tissue of your mind."

To this day, Zoé-Pascale still tells the story of climbing the steps of the beautiful Prague castle, dancing on the St. Charles Bridge, and her joyride with the sweaty Turkish taxi driver from Vienna to Prague. Thinking back to that trip, we are always reminded of Kafka's writings and his endless search for meaning and purpose. Like so many of our generation, our small family was on its own existential search in a new kind of world. The intimacy of travel—with all the trials and tribulations that succeeded in bringing us closer—afforded us a far broader perspective of our intriguing, complex world.

Chapter 27

Bic Pens and Tea

Certainly, travel is more than the seeing of sights,
it is a change that goes on, deep and permanent,
in the ideas of living.

MIRIAM BEARD,
American Historian (1876-1958)

IN FEBRUARY, THE COLD, howling mistral winds pushed us to venture across the Mediterranean to Morocco, where the weather is
warmer, the land is barren and rocky, and the call to prayer is heard
five times a day.

With a six-year-old in tow and the strong anti-American tidal
wave stimulated by the Bush presidency we sought out protection
from prying eyes and pickpockets with n a secure, walled resort.
We also wanted to be able to venture out, take a tour, hire a taxi, and
explore safely. Searching the Internet, we happened upon a French
all-inclusive resort with a kids' club for Zoé-Pascale—an added

benefit for everyone.

There had been a time when Morocco was seen as a backpackers' haven for cheap travel with minimal comfort. However, with the French occupying Morocco in the first half of the century, famous Moroccan riads (houses with beautiful inside gardens) were constructed, and were soon followed by ritzy destination resorts squeezed between the ancient Bedouin villages and modern, congested apartments.

After settling in at the resort, we dropped Zoé-Pascale off at the mini-club, which was led by two college students. The *moniteurs* (camp counselors) told us that they would be going on a field trip to visit a nearby Bedouin village where the kids would learn up close how the locals lived. Always security-conscious, Jean said, "I'm not so sure I want her out of the compound traipsing about Marrakesh."

I was usually less apt to think of all the things that could go wrong, focusing instead on the adventure she would have with the other kids. Admittedly, also on my mind was the fact that Jean and I could have a good part of the day alone to relax without a charming, chattering child begging to go swimming or for something to drink. To confirm my feelings that they would be well taken care of, I bent over to the mom of another little girl Zoé-Pascale was playing with and asked her whether she thought it was safe. "Yes," she said. "I think it is okay."

Meanwhile, Zoé-Pascale and her new best friend, Chantelle, were skipping around the play area singing in French, "We're going on a *sortie*; we're going on a *sortie*." How could we resist?

Relaxing on the sunny lounge chairs next to the crescent-shaped swimming pool after a game of tennis, we opened up our vacation novels, newly purchased from the used bookstore in Uzès, and drifted away.

"You sure Zoé-Pascale is okay?" Jean asked.

"Don't worry, relax," I replied. "Read while you can." Glancing over, I added, "You are so overly protective. She will be fine."

Following my lead, Jean slowly began to let the warm sun penetrate his skin and soothe his nerves, and dove deep into an adventure of modern conspiracy and medieval passion surrounding the true Holy Grail.

As the sun rose high in the sky, we heard the ringing of the bell signaling lunch being served at the terrace dining room. I wrapped myself in my blue-and-yellow flowered sarong and sandals, Jean slipped on a shirt and shorts, and we headed over to the buffet lunch of salads, chicken, and couscous.

"*Bonjour,*" said the slim mom to whom I had spoken earlier, dressed in capris and a T-shirt. "Join us for lunch and we can talk while the children are out on their *sortie.*"

Over the leisurely lunch and café we chatted (actually, they did most of the talking with Jean in French while I listened) about our lives, their home in the north of France, and the bar and café they owned in Brittany. Once in a while, Jean would turn to me to make sure I hadn't drifted off or become overwhelmed with the French conversation. I had actually pushed past the point of frustration and was beginning to see it as a game I was playing with myself, called "how much can I comprehend?" The object was simply to not lose the thread of the conversation in an attempt to grasp all the details.

"I wonder when the kids will be home," Jean said with a worried expression, as the mid-afternoon cocktail hour approached. "They should have been back by now."

"I'm a bit worried, too," Jeanette, the other mom, admitted.

"It's okay, I'm sure," I assured them, shifting into the optimistic idealist persona I often took on, repressing my own anxiety in order to offset Jean's. It was a talent I had inherited that was useful in times such as this. I remember my mom shifting into Pollyanna mode whenever I had an asthma attack as a kid. My dad would hold me, tears running down his face as I hung my head out the car window gasping for air. Meanwhile Mom, who never cried, would repeatedly tell us everything would be fine as she drove furiously to the hospital.

Having received genes from both parents, I found myself able to focus on the positive when others were getting nervous, but later, in private, I'd grapple with the guilt and let the tears run wild. For now, positive thinking and action were required as Jean dreamt up scenarios of snakes and wild dogs. His childhood traumas and life-and-death situations in Africa had predisposed him to look for potential problems. He once told me that the saying "I got up on the wrong side of the bed" was taken literally in his home country. If you weren't aware and awake to your surroundings you could very well step into a dangerous situation: a snake in a boot, a baboon jumping on you from a tree on the way home from school, or the shooting quills of a vicious porcupine. Understandably, Jean tended to be overly cautious and keenly observant.

I headed off to check with the resort's director, and returned to report what he said: that the children should have been back by now, but he would send out one of his guides to see where they might be.

"That's just great," Jean said, "a scout." He turned quickly to the other dad. "Shall we go after them?"

"*Oui*, let's find out exactly where they are supposed to be. We'll grab some scooters and see if we can find them."

The wrinkled bartender, trying to soothe the worried parents, interrupted in a loud voice, "*Ne vous inquiètez pas—nous sommes au Maroc, Mon Dieu!*" (Not to worry—we are in Morocco, my God!)

"Look at that dark thunder cloud moving over the sky," Jean uttered quietly.

Staring up at the menacing black sky, I squeezed Jean's arm to get his attention at the same moment a sinister lightning bolt flashed its jagged line and lit up the sky. Torrents of rain poured down like a waterfall.

"Get inside," Jean yelled, as a sudden, inch-deep desert flash flood swept under our feet.

As the director approached the dining room armed with buckets and tarps, we yelled out, "Where's the scout? Where are our kids? They should have been back hours ago."

"*Ne vous inquiètez pas.* They aren't far. Just stuck in the rain, I'm sure," he replied to no one's satisfaction.

A few more frantic parents huddled together. "I would call the police, but I heard they won't come out in the storm," someone said. A timid young mother with long black hair cried silently in the corner. As we continued to debate the pros and cons of riding a scooter in the mud and storm, or starting off on our search by foot, we heard the faint sound of a farm tractor approaching, and what sounded like kids yelling.

"I think that's them!" I screamed, sprinting to the front gate, drenched and barefoot, having thrown off my waterlogged leather sandals minutes before.

The cacophony of sounds got louder as the tractor slowly edged its way up to the resort's entrance and out bounced eight wet, muddy kids, laughing, joking, and shouting.

"I went on a trip to an Arab village," Zoé-Pascale chirped. "Guess what? The Madame served us hot mint tea in small glasses, and homemade flat baked bread, and we sat on the dirt floor. Can you believe it? Their house has a dirt floor, and the chickens and cows live next door!" She continued excitedly, "And I played with the goats, and the family even had little kittens. Walking back, it started to rain so hard, the *moniteurs* hitch-hiked and waved down the tractor. I have never had so much fun. I love Morocco! Oh, and guess what, I got to drive the tractor!"

With her safe in our arms, our fluttering hearts finally slowed down. "She's okay, she's okay."

Once the panic subsided, we were struck by the notion that Zoé-Pascale had eaten outside the resort, which we had been advised not to do. As we began to lay out contingency plans in the event she got sick, Zoé-Pascale interrupted us.

"Papa, Maman, I loved my field trip. Can I go again tomorrow?"

"I think tomorrow we all go together." Jean winked at me. "We missed you too much."

The next day, with Zoé-Pascale apparently feeling healthy as a horse and very happy with her previous day's exciting excursion, we decided to visit the *souk*, or Arab market, of Marrakech for a different experience—and to keep her safely under our wings. As a precaution, we donned scarves on our heads as we had been advised, hoping to hide Zoé-Pascale's long copper curls and my highlighted *coiffure*. A French friend had also told us that it was better to speak French in public rather than English, in light of the Iraq calamity and the anti-Anglo sentiment.

"Also, to be safe," Jean advised as a final precaution, "If anyone asks, we're from South Africa."

Approaching the *souk* by foot, we squeezed by horse-drawn carriages waiting for tourists; donkey carts pulled by skinny pack animals with fruit hovering precariously over the sides of the wagons; buses packed with women in high-necked loose robes with their heads covered carrying plastic red-and-blue plaid plastic bags stuffed with merchandise; taxi drivers shouting for fares; Arab men with flowing white, brown, and black robes; and a pulsating and pushing crowd. Desert palm trees lined the main walkway, which opened onto the grand square of the *souk*. The *souk*, the largest traditional market in Morocco—and also the busiest square on the entire continent of Africa—is an ancient labyrinth of stalls, stores, craftspeople, and places to eat, reminiscent of Aladdin's colorful mystery world.

Entering the *souk*, we were accosted by the disparate smells and sounds of over five thousand two-by-two-meter alcoves with tin roofs. Hunched on their heels, dejected old men in tattered robes, barefoot boys, clingy shy girls, and sad-faced women crafted objects out of iron, leather, and silk. Stall after stall was jammed with various wares: Berber jewelry, pottery, spices, antiques, leather slippers, iron lamps, and mirrors.

The claustrophobic nature of the winding alleys was made worse by the sludgy puddles and the dreary, wet sky still dripping rain. Pushing our way through the unbelievable sea of pedestrians, bicycles, motorbikes, and donkey carts along the narrow passageway, our eyes stung from the smoke of the welders and the cigarettes of the Arab men working the stalls. Old sewage, rancid in places, converged into tiny, potholed, muddy alleys that stretched forever, like a vast underground city from an alien world.

"In here, in here," the vendors called as we passed each stall, vying for our attention.

"Look at those children working. They're my age!" Zoé-Pascale said to us, pointing at some kids pounding at the raw leather. "Why aren't they in school?"

"Kids here often have to work to make money for food," Jean responded. "If they are lucky, their parents will send them to study instead of to work."

"It's true," I added. "Children are urged to go to school by the government, but many parents are afraid to educate their children for fear they will leave them for better jobs and greener pastures in Europe. I heard we can help the children here by giving them pens, pencils, and paper to use at school, rather than money."

"Then let's go buy some," Zoé-Pascale replied, staring at the kids working in the stalls.

As we walked by the next stall, a shy little girl with dark brown eyes and strappy sandals on her feet peeked out from her mother's skirt and showed us a child's gold silk belly-dancing costume hanging on a hook. Her face beamed as she thrust it in our hands, and we exclaimed how beautiful it was.

Before we knew it, her father and brother shoved their way in front of her and the little girl returned to her hiding place behind her mother's skirt.

"You like? You buy!" the father exclaimed. "Here, give me money. It costs 200 dirham. You want, you want, you want?" The sounds echoed in my ears as we were pushed further and further into the store. Was the little girl a pawn in this game? Did she even belong to this family, we wondered?

"Okay, I'll give you 100 dirham," I murmured, thinking even that was way too much money for the shoddy, home-sewn costume.

"No! You think I can live on that? You crazy woman."

I love to bargain and negotiate, but when someone starts calling me names and gets aggressive, I do what any self-respecting woman would do: I go elsewhere to shop.

"No, you keep the costume. You are *méchant* (mean)," I said, picking up Zoé-Pascale's way with words.

Zoé-Pascale, peeking out from behind *my* skirt at this point, said, "Let's go, Maman. I don't want to buy anything here."

We turned to walk out of the crowded stall. An old, wrinkly-faced man quietly ensconced on a stool began to fondle the curls hanging out of Zoé-Pascale's scarf.

"No!" I cried, slapping his hand. "Stop it! Don't touch her!" And we ran out of the store, practically knocking down the mannequin blocking the entrance.

"I love to shop, but this is too much, even for me," I confided to Jean. "Let's get some air in the open square."

Spotting a forlorn-looking Arab woman squatting on a carton, Zoé-Pascale observed, "There are some pens. Let's buy them."

"Good idea," I said, buying two dozen ten-cent blue Bic pens.

Holding the pens close to her chest, Zoé-Pascale set out to find the kids who looked to be in most need.

Spotting the pens, a young group of shabbily dressed Moroccan boys and girls suddenly darted up to Zoé-Pascale, pulling at her arms and grabbing at the Bics.

"*Moi, moi !*" they yelled. (Me, me!)

"Get away from me! *Allez, Arête!*" (Go away, stop it!) she screamed, throwing the pens at them.

Jean shooed the kids away. "*Allez!*"

Zoé-Pascale stared at them as they ran away. "Why weren't they nice? I wanted to give them the pens anyway."

"Honey, unlike you, they have learned that the only way they will get something is to fight for it, so they just did what was natural. They are just trying to survive," Jean explained.

"I don't like that. It's very *méchant*," she said in her usual Franglais.

"You've just seen another way of living, honey. When children don't have as much as you do, they have to fight for their lives and for every scrap of food every day."

"Okay, but I don't want to live here," she said, swallowing her tears.

"Do you think bringing her here was too much?" I asked Jean with concern.

"No, it is all part of her education and ours, to learn about different cultures and our world. She's had experiences and seen things that she will not easily forget. I believe it will give her a new perspective and gratitude for everything we have."

Winding our way through the snake charmers playing their flutes and the monkeys chained to their owners, I whispered to Jean, "Maybe Zoé-Pascale would like to hold a snake or a monkey?"

"*Oui, oui!*" she responded, dancing over to a snake charmer. To my horror, the snake danced up Zoé-Pascale's arm and slithered its slimy silver body around her shoulder as she froze in place, half smiling and half in shock.

"This is so weird!" she screamed. "Oh look, Maman, a monkey wants to climb on your shoulder."

"*Merde!*" Before I knew what was happening, another sneaky man dressed in a red robe and large straw hat had thrown a brown spider monkey onto my shoulder, while his cousin propelled a second one onto my head.

"Off, off!" I screamed, shaking my body violently. "Jean, get them off!"

"Money, money," the vendor repeated.

Through teary eyes, I begged Jean, "Just give them some money and get these animals off my head!"

After receiving a wad of notes, the owner called off the monkeys and slowly walked away to the next unsuspecting customer.

"The snake charmer and the monkeys," said Zoé-Pascale. "This is the best part of the *souk*."

Having had enough of crowds, the next day we joined a caravan of jeeps to trek into the rugged Atlas Mountains, the range that separates the Mediterranean and Atlantic coastlines from the Sahara desert. We imagined the lines of jeeps as a modern-day caravan of camels crossing the Sahara to ensure security from aggressive Bedouins.

Jean was determined to see the Berber people. The word Berber shares the same roots as "barbarian," and he was intrigued by their ability to have kept a culture and identity separate from the rest of the world for over three thousand years.

"They are mysterious people," Jean told us, "the oldest known people historically, as far as records show, in the North Africa region." He went on to explain that over the centuries, the Berbers have been in conflict with every dynasty and controlling force that has come into the area, but have found a way to preserve their heritage, customs, and language by hiding in desert regions in the Sahara and in the Atlas Mountains.

The journey snaked up the steep mountains, stopping in muddy towns still soaked from the previous day's rainstorm. Clay-and-straw huts were built one on top of another along the hillside. To protect themselves from the bitter winds and the heat of summer, the Berbers dug their homes into the earth, with sleeping accommodations and storage underground.

In harmony with the sun, the Berbers get up at sunrise and go to bed at sundown all year round. They wake at 6 a.m. and have a bit of olive oil for breakfast before heading off to work in the steep, terraced fields while the sun is still low in the sky. A mid-morning meal is followed by rest, chores, or spinning crafts in the cool shade. Dinner is at 5 p.m. and bedtime soon follows. We wondered which aspect of this daily existence kept them so youthful and vital, contributing to their average life span of 85 years.

As we traversed treacherous roads, slipping, sliding, and dipping into potholes, we began to feel like we were in a blender, and joked with the handsome gay couple from Paris in the row in front of us about the benefits of a good chiropractor versus a French kinetherapist.

Having heard Zoé-Pascale recount the story of the children and the ten-cent Bic pens, the couple decided to see whether the Berber children would accost a grown man as well. At our next stop, Maurice, the forty-year-old designer dressed in faded Calvin Klein blue jeans, brown Cole Haan loafers, a yellow Polo sweater, and Louis Vuitton sunglasses, casually stepped outside the Land Rover. Standing on the side of the road, he thrust his hands into the air and shook a dozen No. 2 pencils and as many sturdy Bic pens. Within seconds, a distant schoolyard full of children dressed in castoff clothes, pink skirts, blue sweaters, orange hats, and striped tights caught sight of our new friend and ran toward him, pushing, pulling, and shoving each other to get to the pens.

"Mon dieu ... Oh my god, they're going to jump me!" he shouted, throwing down the pencils and splattering his fine leather loafers with mud as he ran for the jeep. Laughing hysterically, we rooted him on as he dove into the Land Rover and slammed the door shut just in time.

"Honey, I guess it wasn't you. They just love those pens!" I said to Zoé-Pascale. By the end of the trip, our new friends invited us to come visit them in Paris. Maurice, having bonded deeply with Zoé-Pascale, could not wait for her to come see him and his *atelier*. Zoé-Pascale told him how she really wanted a Louis XIV dress and he said, "*Pas de problème, mademoiselle.*" (Not a problem.)

Our experiences in Morocco opened our minds even further, bringing to life the enormous breadth of ways human beings live, work, play, pray, and survive. Photos are fantastic for visualizing, books and articles allow us to understand the history and people from afar, movies bring us even closer to that reality, and music gives us a visceral experience of what moves other cultures. However, traveling allows for a deep soul connection to our fellow global citizens. We see the lines in an old women's face as she smiles up at us, hear the cacophony of sounds in a town square, and take in the smells of fried onions and burning incense. Travel etches the world into our skin and our psyches like a sharp grey drawing pencil might. The sensory experiences of travel—particularly the ones that are challenging, difficult, or especially emotional—are forever available to be called up at a moment's notice, constantly being applied in different contexts and lending themselves to new and ever-expanding views of the world.

Chapter 28

Where Are We Going Next?

One's destination is never a place,
but a new way of seeing things.

Henry Miller,
American Novelist and Painter (1891-1980)

J EAN HAD A MEETING scheduled in Switzerland at the same time as Zoé-Pascale's next school vacation. We decided to take advantage of the beautiful colors of autumn (not to mention the lack of crowds in the off-season), and extend our trip by driving through Tuscany on our way home. Passing through a two-kilometer tunnel from Switzerland into Italy, we found ourselves in pitch-darkness. Glancing up from my knitting, I slipped my sunglasses down my nose and looked up over them at Jean to ask why the tunnel's lighting might be out. Just then, the left front wheel dipped dramatically and we heard a loud crunch. The back left wheel echoed the motion and sound, after which the car began wobbling through the tunnel at top speed.

"What the heck was that?" I yelled.

"I don't know, but I'm not stopping," Jean yelled back. "Cars will strike us from behind in the dark and we will be killed. I think something cut the tires—I'm going to drive on the rims as far as we can. I'm not getting stuck in a dark tunnel or on an Italian mountain bypass miles away from help."

Lurching, wiggling, and weaving, Jean hung on to the steering wheel and slowly aimed—literally—for the light at end of the long tunnel, and the next town ten kilometers beyond. Sitting on the edge of my seat with my nose inches away from the windshield, I anxiously scrutinized the road. "Five more kilometers." I shouted. "Keep going." At 12:30 p.m., we hobbled on buckled rims into a gas station at the foot of the Italian Alps.

"*Mon Dieu*," said the attendant. "You are lucky to be here. It is lunchtime, however, and the mechanic is eating and will return at 2:30. Go next door and have lunch. Relax, eat."

Grateful to be off the isolated mountain pass and near civilization, we headed over to the workingman's café. Opening up the double doors and stepping into the coat-check area, we sniffed at the air as the scent of rosemary and lamb floated by. "This is just what we need," whispered Jean as the proprietor greeted us with a warm smile and a wave to an open wooden booth in the corner.

"I saw your car hobble by," he said. "What happened?" Shedding our coats and relaxing into the booth, we told him our story.

"Oh yes," he said after hearing our tale, "they are working on the tunnel and there are many ditches with metal plates covering them. Maybe a cover came off and you fell in a ditch. But now you are here. Eat, drink, and wait," he said.

Three hours later, we were the sole remnants of the lunch crowd. By now our meal of salad, the *plat du jour* (lamb with rose-

mary), cheese, and dessert had been cleared and replaced with a carafe of wine, a jug of water, and Zoé-Pascale's schoolbooks. Jean had
spoken to the mechanic who promised to notify us of the scope of
needed repairs—and how long they would take—within the hour.
In better humor and with full stomachs, we weighed our options:
walk around the parking lot ten times, read a book, play cards, or
finish all of Zoé-Pascale's *devoir* for the vacation. We decided this
was a serious *devoir*—"must-do"—moment.

"Maman, Papa, this is kind of like what happened in Vienna
when we missed the train," Zoé-Pascale observed. "I guess we still
have to learn to go with the flow, like you said. But why do we always
have to learn that lesson, and why do I always have to end up doing
devoir?"

"Has she got our number, or what?" I smiled to Jean.

Several hours and 600 euros later, our car dilemma was solved
and we drove to a small hotel in Aosta, a Roman town built in 25
B.C. The next morning, after a breakfast of croissant, baguette, com-
fiture, *café au lait* and *chocolat chaud*, we set off for Florence, stopping
at a take-out restaurant set up off the freeway for travelers.

"I'm starving," Zoé-Pascale said as I finished paying for the
sandwiches. "How long does it take for them to make one?"

As I leaned over to listen to her over the din of the crowd, I felt
a bump against my shoulder and twisted around to see that it was
just a young man brushing by me. Instinctually, I shifted to grab
my red leather purse backpack, and I could tell immediately that
something wasn't right.

"Oh, no. Someone stole my wallet!"

I ran over to the guy who had bumped me, jabbing my hands
into his coat pockets. "You took my wallet. Give it back!"

"Not me, Madame, you are mistaken," he said with his hands
raised.

Jean rushed over, whispering, "They are so good, I'm sure he passed it to someone else."

Chastising myself for putting my wallet in a brightly colored purse on my back, I cursed the young man, who was repeatedly claiming his innocence. We finally let go of him, and the store manager explained that the police would not come out even if we had caught the thief. In fact, the manager and bystanders actually seemed to delight in the entertaining misfortune of the stupid *Americanos*. It was our fault that we were not more careful, they told us over and over.

We spent the next hour calling credit card companies and canceling our cards, after which we finally hit the road, grateful that Jean had some separate cards we could use for the rest of the trip. Before we'd even reached Tuscany, we had shelled out for the car repairs, lost all the contents of my wallet, and were in the hole for well over a thousand euros. Jean sighed, surrendering to the calamities we had endured in the previous twenty-four hours.

"We have to remember that even though we are living here, life is not perfect, and there are plenty of people who want to take advantage of others," Jean said. "We travel to explore other ways of life, and we want to believe everyone is honest and pleased to see us. This makes us vulnerable."

Finally, tired to the bone and emotionally drained, we approached our reserved hotel in Tuscany. As we drew closer to the property, I read out loud the sign, "Closed for the season."

"Impossible," I said to Jean, bursting into tears for the umpteenth time that day. "We have a definite reservation. Now this, after everything else."

"Maman, don't worry, remember this is all part of the traveling lesson. You told me that yourself," Zoé-Pascale said soothingly.

We knocked on the hotel's door and tried to explain the situation to the clerk, showing him the printout of our confirmed reservation.

"Well, we know you reserved, but we decided to close the hotel tomorrow," he explained casually. We demanded to see the owner,

who appeared after a half-hour wait. We showed the confirmed reservation again, explained that we were very tired, had come a long
way with a young child, and were looking forward to the stay in his
excellent hotel. He stared at us blankly. "Okay, you can sleep for
half-price in the lobby on the couches if you can find nothing else
today," he said. "But I have already drained the pool and cleaned the
rooms, and my restaurant is closed for the season."

"Imbecile," I muttered under my breath as I stormed out. Clearly, this trip was not meant to go well.

"Okay, these are the trials and tribulations of travel," Jean said
again to Zoé-Pascale, letting me hold the anger for both of us. "Let's
see what we can do to figure out our next steps."

A few miles further on, we arrived in the town of San Gimi-
gnano and spotted an old restored hotel with windows facing the
rolling hills of the valley below.

"I wonder how much this will eat through our budget?" I said.

"At this point, let's just get a room anywhere!" Jean replied.

"*Oui, bien sur.* Of course we have a room, and with a view for the
young lady," the front desk person replied in a friendly fashion.

"Maman, it is beautiful. Can we stay a long time?"

A quote I had recently read by Susan Heller, a writer and culture reporter for the *New York Times*, kept wandering through my
head: "When preparing to travel, lay out all your clothes and all
your money. Then take half the clothes and twice the money." That
was definitely proving true during our short stay in Italy.

Having finally settled into our comfortable but over-budget room
on the terrace, I was beginning to shed my aggravation and despair. In
emergencies like this, finding a sweet hotel with a room with a view
and a bed piled high with comforters was just what we all needed.
Jean uncorked a bottle of Chianti he had picked up in the lobby and
suggested we all sit out on the balcony and enjoy the view.

"Let's draw," I said, already in better spirits and falling in love with the vast rolling vineyards curving over and about the hillsides. A few minutes later, the three of us had started to sketch the orange, golden, green, and burgundy scene surrounding us. In the background stood church steeples, tall and straight, tolling their bells as if to say hello to the weary travelers.

"I've never seen anything so gorgeous in my life," Jean said, breathing in the crisp autumn air. "Of all the places we have been, this might be the most stunning." He gave Zoé-Pascale a few tips on her sketch, and then left her to her own devices.

"Why don't the teachers make us look at real things when we draw in school?" she asked.

Good question! We wondered as well. How great it was to see our daughter discover the idea of drawing what is in front of her eyes, versus what is in her imagination. Could this art lesson have happened in Marin, California? Or even in France? Maybe, maybe not, but what we know for sure was that our travels allowed it to happen in Italy, at that precise moment of golden splendor of an autumn sunset in Tuscany, after a long and arduous journey.

Chapter 29

Global Kids

*The biggest adventure you can ever take
is to live the life of your dreams.*

Oprah Winfrey,
American television host, producer, philanthropist (1954-)

Jean and I dreamed of a week in Paris at Easter time, imagining walking the streets of Paris as free souls as we had done in our twenties. We soon discovered, however, that touring Paris with a child is a very different experience.

We had never really noticed before, but outside of every metro, in every park, and near every toilet is a carousel. More often than we may have liked, we found ourselves sitting on green metal chairs, getting dizzy watching the merry-go-rounds go round.

Ascending to the top of the Eiffel Tower, Zoé-Pascale confidently announced it was completed in 1985, as she had been told by Carmen

San Diego, a cartoon detective. Nothing could change her mind, as she had heard it from the source. She did eventually acquiesce later and admitted that the painting of the Eiffel Tower was probably finished in 1985, but the Tower itself was built a bit earlier. We realized she probably didn't comprehend the difference between 1885 and 1985—really, what is a century to a six-and-a-half-year-old?

Visiting Maurice at his studio, Zoé-Pascale was surprised with a burgundy velveteen Louis IV dress with puffed sleeves, a cinched waist, and a full bouncing skirt down to the floor. Zoé-Pascale promptly stripped down to her underwear and insisted on wearing the dress as we walked through the streets of Paris.

"Is there a parade?" we heard another little girl whisper as she saw Zoé-Pascale walk by. "Is she a real princess?" At that moment, Zoé-Pascale was indeed a reincarnation of one of the little princesses of Versailles. We strutted along behind her like two proud peacocks.

One morning at the Louvre, Zoé-Pascale gazed at the Mona Lisa. "She is beautiful, but how do her eyes follow me wherever I move?" she asked. "Oh, and I need to go to the toilette."

Pushing our way through the crowds along another long hallway and down a flight of stairs, we found the toilette, decorated with fabrications of Venus de Milo. "How beautiful," Zoé-Pascale exclaimed as she walked into the stall. Listening in, I heard her singsong voice say, "Scooby Doo, we now have to solve the mystery of the missing painting. I know Mona Lisa is quite pretty. Maybe her eyes can tell us which direction to go? And maybe Venus can use her wings to fly overhead and see if there is anything suspicious."

Aha! I thought, laughing to myself. *All this history and culture has made some of an impact if the Mona Lisa and Venus de Milo have joined Zoé-Pascale's posse of imaginary friends.*

After the Louvre, we meandered over to the stately Luxembourg Gardens and plopped down into two of the green slatted iron chairs placed randomly throughout Paris. Zoé-Pascale sprawled out on the ground and began to dig for ancient artifacts. The gardens were full of students, retirees, the unemployed, tourists—the entire world lazing about, just as it should be in Paris. We imagined Sartre and Simone de Beauvoir sitting in these same chairs, philosophizing about life. We thought about the conversation Kafka would have had with Sartre: What is life all about? How should we live our lives? How do we enhance the quality of our lives? I'm not sure Sartre had the same worries we did; nonetheless, we felt his presence, like an angel hovering over us.

For a different view of the city's history, I urged Zoé-Pascale and Jean to accompany me on a tour of the city's sewers at the *Musée des Egouts de Paris*. Not one of the most popular tourist walks, but an unforgettable one. Following fifty years of planning, 2,100 km of sewers were built beneath the city between 1850 and 1920. The sewer system includes 26,000 manhole covers and over 800 *égoutiers* (sewer workers). It is thought to be the most efficient system in the world, even though its technology has not been updated in over a century.

Among the many facts Zoé-Pascale was intrigued to learn (while barely tolerating the smell), was that if we dropped a key or ring into the toilet, a call to the Sewer Department would likely have it found and returned within an hour.

After the sewer, we returned to the city's art, deciding to take in the works of the impressionists—Monet, Pissarro, Cézanne, and Manet—up close at the Orsay Museum.

"Charlotte from the book *Charlotte in Paris* lived next door to Monet and was best friends with Manet's daughter Julie," Zoé-Pascale informed us. "I know all about them. They loved to paint *en plein air*—like you, *Maman*. Are these paintings real, mommy? We can get so close, we can almost touch them."

"Yes, they are real," I replied, wondering whether they actually were the originals, since we were allowed to stand as little as two inches from each painting.

Outside the museum, we passed by a forest-green sculpted ceramic drinking fountain, tall and round, with three dancing ladies holding hands back to back.

"Cool," Zoé-Pascale said. "I'm thirsty. But *Maman, Papa, ça ne marche pas.*" (It doesn't work.)

Standing nearby was an elderly Frenchman out for his stroll. He leaned over and said, "Let me tell you the story about these fountains." He went on to casually inform us that originally there had been three hundred of these Wallace water fountains, donated to the city by a gentleman named Wallace in the late 1800s. The story was that he went into a bar and asked for a glass of water, which the waiter told him would cost the same as a mug of beer. Appalled at the thought of having to pay for water, Wallace decided to do something about it. Evidently the water in Paris was not suited for drinking at that time (after all, the sewers were just being built), so good drinking water was scarce. As a gift to the city, Wallace designed and built these beautiful forest green sculptured water fountains—most of which still stand today, albeit without water.

From that point on, every time we spotted a Wallace fountain in the city, we would run up to it and test to see whether any water was still spouting. To Zoé-Pascale's dismay, we could only ever look at the beautiful work of art, but couldn't drink its fresh, free, clean water. History does repeat itself, we realized, as we walked into the nearby store and paid two euros fifty for a small bottle of water suitable for drinking. Where are the Wallaces of the world when you need them?

⌣ˇ⌣ˇ⌣

A few months later, at Christmas time, we decided to visit Jean's family and explore a bit more of Southern Africa. With Zoé-Pascale's schoolbag full of *devoir* (we couldn't avoid having her miss a few school days this time), we set off.

Situated on a tiny beach hamlet near East London was the home of Ouma, Jean's mom. The Wild Coast is one of South Africa's undiscovered jewels, where the natural rugged beauty of the landscape has been left to nature. The N2—the main road along the coast—is ten kilometers inland, with off-roads leading to bays, beaches, and hamlets filled with summer cottages and campgrounds. There are no long stretches of beach apartments and resorts spoiling the gorgeous natural coastline. The wide-open countryside reminded us of the northern California coast: rolling hills topped with rugged brush interspersed with low-lying grasses constantly blowing in the wind. The winter rains keep the area a vibrant green.

The Indian Ocean is warm, and delightful to swim in. Along the shoreline are endless white beaches with rocky outcroppings for fishing, bays for swimming, rivers for frolicking, and wild surf where dolphins and whales are frequently spotted. Waterfront summer cottages are located along several rivers that flow from inland out to sea, which ebb and flow with the Indian Ocean tides, creating lagoons and mud flats to explore when the tide is low.

Shortly after we arrived, Retha, Jean's sister, suggested a hike. Taking off on the first 10-km leg of a potential 50-km hike, we walked the beach and followed in the footsteps of the strandlopers—little white birds with black beaks that walk swiftly along the sand, combing for food, just as the ancient Khoisan people had done on these same beaches.

"Let's go," I said, picking up the pace, eager to exercise my legs. The long beaches, beautiful, bays and assortment of seashells were just what we needed to keep Zoé-Pascale and her seven-year-old cousin, Heinrich, busy.

Several days later, riding in the back of Jean's sister's *bakkie* (smallish truck, pronounced "buckey"), we ventured out to the game reserves in the Limpopo region, the northernmost province in

South Africa on the Botswana border. An amatuer bow-and-arrow hunter, his sister had reserved stilted tent cabins for us high on the cliffs of a private bow hunting reserve.

Once we were settled into our accommodations, which included a kitchen, a dining area, a campfire big enough for twenty people, and a maid to clean up, we piled back into the *bakkie* and headed off through the reserve.

"Ahead, ahead!" Retha yelled. "Look, don't move." Moving stealthily along in the distance was none other than a family of giraffes. To the right was an ostrich, and to the left, a few gazelles. For the next few hours we crept along and watched the African countryside come alive before our eyes.

"Tomorrow we will walk through the game reserve," Retha said with a big grin. "We will have to be careful, but it is such a different experience."

Early the next morning, more of Jean's siblings and their children joined us on the reserve, and we set off down the animal trail.

"What do you have in that cute little purse?" I asked Retha, wondering why she would carry such a thing through the African bush.

Pulling out a huge pistol from the fancy little bag, she smiled and said, "Oh, just for protection, mostly from the lions." Observing my shock, she continued, "Oh, don't worry—the gun is only for emergencies. I don't like to shoot them unless it is in self-defense, like when an elephant or ostrich stampedes or tries to attack us. I first shoot into the air and try to scare them off."

"A *what* stampedes us?" I asked, taken aback. Suddenly our little stroll along the nature trail took on a whole new meaning, as I realized that lions and elephants were out hiking with us. "What did I get into?" I asked Jean.

"This is Africa. You are with the best. Remember, we grew up here. We know this land. Enjoy."

Walking between Retha and Jean, I stomped the ground and waved my walking stick, swishing away any snakes that might be hiding in the grass. I was taking no chances.

"I want a game farm when I grow up," announced Zoé-Pascale. "Everyone here can work on it for me."

"Zoé-Pascale, you know you will need to become a veterinarian or a zoologist if you want to own a game farm," Jean told her.

"Not a problem. I will become a veterinarian. Can I start studying now?"

"This is the beginning, honey. You *are* starting now."

⌣⌄⌣⌄

En route home from our exotic adventure in South Africa, Zoé-Pascale asked, "Where are we going to visit next? I want to go see Rome and the Coliseum. I also want to visit Mt. Olympus where Zeus was born and travel to Norway on the longest day of the year. I read about it, and I can stay up all night dancing around the campfire. Oh yeah," she added, "and don't forget the Great Wall of China."

Being in Africa with Jean's family was a reminder of how much more global the world has become. Our families lived on three different continents, and we were living on a fourth. Our child was not of one culture, but several. We knew that experiencing each of these environments at a young age would forever shape her interests and passions, and deepen her respect for the diverse people and cultures of the world. This was one gift that she would have forever—one that could never be taken away.

Part IV

Life Lessons and Moving Forward

We keep moving forward, opening new doors, and doing new things, because we're curious and curiosity keeps leading us down new paths.

Walt Disney,
Film producer, inventor, creator of fantasy (1901-1966)

Do Now What You Have Always Wanted To Do

All our dreams can come true—
if we have the courage to pursue them.

WALT DISNEY (1901-1966)

Have you ever wanted to travel the world, live by the beach, write a book, start a business, go back to school, raise horses, or just have time to garden and cook with fresh, homegrown, organic vegetables? At any age— but especially once you've reached 40—life does indeed get shorter. Time does indeed speed up. There are only so many years your children will be young and happily accompany you on family adventures. Only so many years during which you have the strength and stamina to do what you've always wanted.

At different points in our lives we need to ask ourselves; "Am I living the life that provides meaning and joy, and allows me to be healthy? If not, why not? Am I spending sufficient time with those I love, doing what I love? Am I feeling good about how I spend time at work, with my family and friends, and for myself? Is there something I truly want to do right now in my life—alone or with my partner or family? Am I creating the life I want to live?"

No one who has made a significant change in their life has ever told us that taking time off, traveling, or embarking on something different was a waste of time. What they did say was, "Why did I waste so much time living in fear? What took me so long?"

Many people postpone their dream because they think they can't afford it—they don't have enough savings, they are in debt, they are worried about funding their children's college years, or their retirement, or day-to-day living. We completely understand, because we felt the same way once until we realized that the answer is actually quite simple.

If you want it badly enough, you will find a way. You can make small incremental changes that add up or you can save for a few years, sell your new cars, rent out your house or sell your home and buy something lovely and affordable. You can ask for an early inheritance (some lucky people have!), find hourly work, teach English as a second language, exchange houses or make other trades or barters, or volunteer to help out somewhere on this planet. There are a million ways to make changes in your life, big and small. What it takes is a strong desire, the dream, and the recognition that the decision is worth it. Minimally, you can begin planning and focusing on the dream—that part is totally free.

Coming to terms with the fact that we preferred to spend money on a lengthy family sabbatical versus saving money was a difficult, and yet easy, decision. Yes, today we would be financially richer if we had plowed the money into retirement (though with the cyclical stock market plunges, even that isn't guaranteed) and kept on working. The trade-off, however, was not one we were willing to accept: a further energy depletion of body, mind, and soul. We would never have developed the intimate relationship we have with our daughter, traveled to the fantastic places we did, or enhanced our life so much if we had not made an unconventional decision.

Life changes, however, don't have to be huge to make a significant difference. They can be as small as making a commitment to family dinners once a week, finding time to pursue a long-lost interest, going back to school to study something that interests you, taking a vacation to a place you have never been, or reserving one day to be free of obligations and stresses. The question to ask yourself is what do you and your family need to live a healthy, joyful life? What changes—big or small—would enhance your life experiences and feed your heart and soul? As Abraham Lincoln said, "And in the end, it's not the years in your life that count. It's the life in your years."

Chapter 30

Three Kisses and Much Confusion

One's first step in wisdom is to question everything—
and one's last is to come to terms with everything.

Georges Lichtenberg,
German Scientist (1742-1799)

O UR TIME OFF IN France was moving on fast, and soon we
would have to start making decisions as to what was next:
what we were going to do with our careers, and where we were eventually going to live.

Sitting at a café in the late afternoon, Jean and I watched eight
teenagers talking and sipping their drinks. A few minutes went by,
and two more teenagers walked up to the group. Instead of saying
hello, they moved around the table, kissing each friend three times,
first on the right cheek, then the left cheek, and then the right cheek
again. The entire ritual took approximately five minutes. Finally,

having acknowledged each person fully, the latest arrivals plopped down in empty chairs and continued happily chatting, laughing, and cracking jokes.

Our hearts were warmed by the ease and genuineness among the group of young friends. We had been saying hello to our friends this way, but to watch adolescents take the time to greet each other so enthusiastically and lovingly made us feel as though all was well with the world. A minute later, two new friends walked up and started the process all over again.

There is something about the time it takes to give three cheek-to-cheek kisses that allows for a deeper, longer, and more feeling connection. A hug is great, too, and a handshake is okay, but the three kisses seem to signal a sheer, welcoming joy. It allows for that extra couple of seconds of contact that makes you feel cared for and recognized.

Living in California, I'd never realized how different my native culture was from Jean's. Part of this is because Jean is of the nature to try anything, go anywhere, and find a way to fit in with almost any group of people. He loves to learn how people think, and is always amazed, impressed, or saddened by the excitement and pain in which people live. His curiosity leads him to quickly connect with people of all kinds. Because of his adaptability and interest in other cultures, I'd never truly recognized how difficult it must have been for him when he first moved to California. Now, the tables had turned on me, as I adjusted to living in an entirely new culture with its unfamiliar—albeit lovely—customs.

"I know, I can see you struggle," Jean said. "Learning French as you have, without any formal language foundation, is difficult. You are progressing, but I don't know if you will ever be totally fluent, and therefore independent." It was true—being dependent on Jean was totally against my character. Plus, I missed my girlfriends. Unlike Jean, who had explored new places for his entire life, this was completely new territory for me.

But I also knew how much Jean loved it here. He seemed so contented and truly at home, as though he was sitting in front of a warm fireplace on a cold night.

"I do love it here," he agreed. "I don't know if it is a mixture of genetics and the fact that we grew up European in an African context. I just understand the logic here in France, how to do things, and how to get things done."

He went on to tell me how living in America was not always easy for him, partly because of the way people think. The American logic was illogical to him at times. Why, for example, would some managers believe it is okay to call or e-mail their employees on their vacations? Didn't they work hard enough during the rest of the year? Didn't they deserve time away from work? Why did so many companies talk about work-life balance, but not practice it? Why did our generation seem to evaluate themselves in terms of how much money they made, how productive they were, and how many goals they achieved, but not in terms of their quality of life?

Though it was less foreign to me, I still didn't miss the Puritan work ethic in which materialism, perfectionism, and work above all else are the measure of our worth. In France, it is more about living life well, having time for family and yourself, and doing good work. All three are integrated and balanced.

The next day, we attended a dinner party at our neighbors': Gabriel, a glass blower from the north of France, and his Swiss-German wife, Agnes, who made her living by being a companion to a few of the elderly in the village. Situated in the couple's courtyard were five small, round, iron tables with folding chairs, and a long table filled with pâté, *fromage*, salads, baguettes, and a French country stew made from freshly picked mushrooms, tomatoes, green beans, potatoes, and chicken stock.

"Don't worry," Agnes said. "We had the mushrooms checked out with the pharmacist today, and they are all good to eat." She explained that, every year at this time, they would go mushroom hunting in the Cevennes and find the most delectable varieties. "Gabriel knows which ones are safe, but just in case, we check them out at the pharmacist," she told us. "If you find mushrooms on your hike in the woods, pick them and just take them to the pharmacy, and they will verify that they are okay to eat or not."

"What a great service," I said.

Jean mumbled, "Can you imagine the local chain drug store in California offering to examine mushrooms?"

Sitting down to eat with a few other neighbors, Jean was in his element, conversing with Brigitte and her husband David, whom he had always wanted to meet but hadn't yet had the chance. She was the Cultural Director of our village. Next to Brigitte and David was Laure, the potter, and Serge, her boyfriend, and then Jules and Henriette, a retired French couple from the village. Perched on the edge of my seat, I said to myself, *Talk, talk. Say something in your good French now.* My heart was beating wildly.

"*Où irez-vous pendant les vacances?*" (Where are you going on vacation?) I asked Brigitte, feeling proud for remembering to use the future tense.

"*On va voir mes parents,*" Brigitte replied. (We are going to see my parents.) Third person, I thought. The one they never teach to foreigners, but that everyone uses all the time. However, there I was, having a French conversation, exactly as I wanted. So what could I say next?

"*Oui, oui!*" Oh, and remember to smile, as Jean had told me often before.

My brain was in knots trying to keep it all straight, and I felt as though I was moving in slow motion. However, for another few minutes, we conversed about easy subjects: the kids' school, where her parents lived, and how work was going for her. I craved more. I wanted to know her better. I wanted to be her friend so badly. But I could tell that her patience was wearing thin, my mistakes were fatiguing both her and me, and my accent was causing mass confusion.

The next morning, Jean told me over coffee how he had talked to a variety of people at the party about why they chose our village, and what they loved about living here. By and large it was because it was different from many French towns: this was a lively village with a reputation for being open to newcomers, hence the many artists who have come to live here. People were carving out livings as potters, property managers, teachers, translators, tour operators, computer repairmen, technical consultants and, in some cases, corporate professionals who commuted to England or Paris weekly for work. All had felt, like us, that there had to be more to life, and had gone in search of creating something different for themselves.

Though the village was so eclectic and unique, it was also very French insofar as English was very rarely spoken, and newcomers had their incorrect French corrected on the spot. We knew our year off had been exactly what we needed to do, but while staying in France was becoming very attractive to Jean, the idea of living here, well, *forever*, was beginning to make me anxious.

We began to think about moving toward Montpellier, where there were more ex-pats, more English-speaking people for me to meet, and more stimulation—something we were both starting to crave a bit more of these days. At the same time, we had become accustomed to slower days, in which reading was a central part of our lives, not something tagged on for a few minutes before you fell asleep. I was gobbling up all sorts of books, and it wasn't just because of the slower pace. I was looking for answers, wondering whether anyone had come up with the perfect place to live a quality life while working and raising a family.

Soon we realized that perhaps the question we were always asking ourselves, "Where do we want to live?" wasn't the right question. It had become more complicated than that, and now sounded more like, "Where can we both live that will give us the lifestyle we want with the fewest tradeoffs?" Whatever we chose to do, there were tons of tradeoffs, but we wanted to make each sacrifice mindfully, with a full understanding of why it was worth making.

My spirituality began to blossom with more yoga, meditation, and exploration of my sixth sense. Jean, who had always naturally been very intuitive, was happy to indulge me and play with the tarot deck and involve our higher selves, angels, guides, and prayers in helping to answer the questions we had for ourselves. And yet, our analytical minds always intervened, giving way to thoughts and making us doubt our instincts and our hearts. We were so focused on the outer circumstances that we were again forgetting what each other needed *inside* to feel whole and at peace.

ᴗ ᵛ ᴗ ᵛ ᴗ

One week, when Jean had to travel to Texas for his research project, I was left alone in France with Zoé-Pascale. We had a great time, but I was lonely, isolated, and teary. I went shopping in Nimes and bought too much because I thought it would make me feel better, which, in retrospect, it did—for about a day. Yes, I had neighbors to borrow a cup of sugar from. Yes, I could call a friend of Zoé-Pascale's and ask her parents whether she could come over for a play date. But what I didn't have were other moms and daughters with whom I felt comfortable enough to ask them over for a day's activity—partly because of language, partly because I wasn't sure how they would react, and partly because I felt intimidated that my French was not adequate for an afternoon or day of conversation. The social aspect of my personality was being starved.

It wasn't like we hadn't become more intimate with new people; in fact, we had, but the individuals I felt most comfortable interacting with intimately for any length of time were mainly English. The

English families who had kids were heartwarming and kind, and yet I felt a need to not overburden them. Besides, some of them were far more fluent in the language and integrated in French family life than I was. From time to time, they would say, "We don't want to mix just with English-speaking people." Jean and I understood and agreed, but it also made us a bit timid to deepen the relationship.

Besides the language and culture, there were other things to which I found it difficult to relate. For example, Zoé-Pascale's friends' parents were fifteen years younger than we were. I felt like a professional grandmother, staying home with my family while the other parents went out dancing after midnight every Friday. In California, it was far more common to be fifty years old with a young child. Many of the other parents hadn't had careers like we had—yet another disconnect. And yet Jean loved it so much, and so did I…

"I don't think we're ready yet to decide, are we?" I whispered to Jean, leaning on his shoulder, my head spinning with options and reasons and possibilities.

"One year isn't enough. We've just gotten started," he said, softly. We were on the journey to find the place where we could all belong, doing good work that financially supported us, and surrounded by people who fed our souls. It was just taking longer than we anticipated.

And then we looked at the two smiling teenagers at the table next to us. When their friends walked in to join them, their ritual started up again. Everyone had big grins and happy eyes. The newly arrived friends went first to one seated friend, then to the next, planting a light kiss, then another, and finally a third, so that each was fully acknowledged as part of each other's universe and each knew that they were eternally bound in deep friendship. For today, that was more than enough.

Chapter 31

Across the Oceans

*It's not so much that we're afraid of change or so in love with
the old ways, but it's that place in between that we fear... It's like
being between trapezes. It's Linus (from "Peanuts") when his
blanket is in the dryer. There's nothing to hold on to.*

MARILYN FERGUSON,
American New age author and speaker (1938-)

"As I GREW UP, I knew one day I had to come to France—that
one day I had to live here, in the home of my ancestors," Jean
said one afternoon over a glass of Perrier. We were discussing his
roots in France, and how his ancestry came to mean so much to him.

Jean's paternal French Huguenot grandfather, who was adventurous and proud and the youngest of seven strong brothers, worked
as a pioneering teacher in the dangerous frontier of South Africa at
the beginning of the twentieth century. Later in life, he met and
married a sixteen-year-old student of his, a pretty and talented
young girl of German-Jewish origin. Together, they made a rich life

in colonial South Africa, which had historically been a Dutch and British colony, thriving on their love for each other and their passion for the wild African bush. They balanced their differences amidst a hodgepodge of melting cultures and languages.

His story made me think of my paternal grandma Rose, who lived a full ninety-nine years, but began her young life in Lithuania during the violent attacks against Jews in Russia in the late nineteenth century. On both sides of our families, we are descendants of people who were persecuted for their beliefs, but who were fiercely devoted to religious freedom. At the age of eight, Grandma Rose and her mother and brother packed everything they could carry—including her mother's one and only green dress, worn with a lace collar on special occasions—in two little brown satchels, and set out by foot to meet her father, who had left for America five years earlier.

Hopping on a donkey cart, boarding a train, and then trekking on foot, the little family made its way across Europe. Miraculously, many months later, they found themselves huddled aboard a ship with hundreds of other tired but optimistic immigrants, waving kisses to the Statue of Liberty as they began a new life in America.

For most people in English-speaking countries, our generational identities extend across the oceans to other continents. Alex Haley talked about how "in every conceivable manner, the family is the link to our past, a bridge to our future." For us, our time in France was another opportunity to not only assess our current lives, but also visit our roots. It was like finding a doorway into our spiritual cores, realizing that we are traveling on the same magnificent and mystical journey as our ancestors.

Jean grew up in what can be referred to as a "third culture" in South West Africa. As the child of culturally mixed French, Dutch, and Afrikaans descendants, he was living in an old German colony, molded by African culture, in the center of South West Africa (what is now called Namibia).

Jean's father was the president of the country's premier teachers' college, and his mother was a teacher and college instructor. They lived a life typical of ex-pats in a little-known arid country: kudus grazed at the outskirts of the family's two farms, rhinoceroses chased their car on Sunday drives, leopards dined on the farmers' sheep, baboons stole their food, knitting was the primary skill taught in Jean's German kindergarten, golf courses were made out of sand and oil, and a snake killed a boyhood friend.

During Jean's childhood, the strange status of the country—formerly a German colony, it was a protectorate of the United Nations and administered remotely by South Africa—led his family to believe, quite rightly, that they were citizens of the world. What mattered most were their own cultural histories, the origins of their families, and the stories of their ancestors. "Where is your family from?" was always the question asked upon meeting someone new. The answer was always highly descriptive of the person and his or her links to the past. Sometimes Jean would actually introduce me as descended from Eastern Europe. "I'm just a plain Californian," I said once. "You want me to be more European. I know that's what you are really getting at," I teased him.

"Well, I said *originally* from, because your grandparents did come from Romania and Lithuania," he explained. It made me think more about my Eastern European roots, and how my own history and DNA must, on some level, affect who I am today.

In a small corner of the Cape Province, about an hour from Cape Town, a large French Huguenot settlement called *Franschoek* (Dutch for "French corner") survived as a tiny enclave far from the mother country. The valley, given to the French settlers by the Dutch in the mid-1600s, proudly sports its own French tricolor flag in red, white, and blue, with an elephant in the center to honor the huge herds that once lived there. The French immigration began when Louis XIV, the Sun King, declared his egotistical political slogan, *l'état c'est moi* (I am the state), and persecuted the fiercely independent Huguenots, who were unwilling to convert to Catholicism. The settlers in South Africa enriched their new land, bringing worldwide fame to the region by making some of the most highly-prized wines in the world.

During childhood, when asked where he was from, Jean's standard reply was, "We live in Windhoek, my father's family originates from Orange, France, and my mother's family is partially from Belgium." At school, his French name stood out in the midst of all the other Dutch, German, English, and African names.

Jean began his education at the local German school playing with African children who spoke Herero and Okavango. At home, his family spoke a smattering of European and African languages, reflecting the multicultural diverse environment, in a house filled with prized heirlooms from old Europe.

For long stretches at a time, they would visit Jean's grandparents, who then lived an hour north of Pretoria in a huge villa that had been converted from an Italian hospital during WWII. With his brother and sister, Jean would run through the fruit orchards, chase the farm animals, swim in the pool, play tennis, and learn golf. The inside of the house was a replica of a French country manor house, with flowery wallpaper, lace curtains, and French music playing loudly on the phonograph.

Sunday family lunches resembled those in France today, with long tables set out under the grand oak trees, and platters of peaches, melons, berries, grilled eggplant, peppers, grilled meats, fresh cheese from his grandfather's goats, and freshly baked bread.

Jean was expected to know French, even though his family rarely spoke it to him. It was simply considered part of his heritage, as if carried in his DNA. By the time he was nine, he had started to sing along to the French records that were playing daily in the family's home and was teaching himself to read French.

"At dinner, my dad would often quiz my brother, sister, and me about French geography and language," Jean said. "'What is the Côte d'Azur?' my dad would ask. 'Where is *Orange*? What is the name of the famous wine region where grandfather's family came from?'"

If Jean didn't know the answers, his father would take out the atlas and point to the location in France where the family had originated.

Years later, traveling to France for the first time, Jean was lying in a country *gîte* (a furnished, self-catering cottage or apartment hosted by an owner), feeling strangely and completely at home. The lace curtains and flowered wallpaper were just like his grandmother's, and the heavy dark wood furniture was exactly like their living room table. The food was similarly spiced, and the music was familiar. "I felt as if I had finally come home, to the real place that my family had forsaken to seek a better life in Africa—a land that had been buried deep within their hearts for so many years," he said. "I felt taken in, welcomed, cozy and complete."

Now, in France, he was no longer the little boy with a French name living in an old German colony on the huge African continent, or an ex-pat living in America, where most people couldn't pronounce his name correctly. Here, Jean was seen and accepted as one of the French who had gone to Africa and returned. Like birds, salmon and bees, who will migrate long distances and then find their way home, the love of my life had found his heart and soul in France once again.

ᵕᵛᵕᵛᵕ

"It's time I go to Orange to check out the cemetery," Jean said one spring morning. Walking among the grey tombstones and dead plants that had been left by visiting relatives, he searched for the name "Roux" etched in barely readable script. His mind wandered to his grandfather: a great teacher, farmer, and businessman, along with his great grandfather and the long line of ancestors before him who had left France's cultural imprint so deeply on him.

Climbing up the medieval tower in the cemetery, he spotted the caretaker and asked, "I'm looking for the grave of my ancestor, Jean Pierre Roux. Can you help me?"

"No problem," the caretaker said as, to Jean's surprise, he pulled out a laptop. He typed in the name, and waited for the search results. Laid out before him was a professional-locking spreadsheet, cross-referenced with the cemetery markings for the names of each person in each grave.

Studying the map on the computer, the caretaker gave Jean directions. "Go down three aisles, turn to the left, and then straight ahead to the third plot on the end."

Thrilled, Jean set out. However, after circling the cemetery twice and reading every tombstone to no avail, he gave up in frustration and returned to where the caretaker was weeding.

"I just can't find it; can you please help me?" he requested.

Retracing Jean's footsteps, the caretaker walked along, removing dead flowers from the old plants along the way, picking up empty containers, and casually swishing his head from right to left as he read the names on the gravestones. Abruptly stopping, he pointed and said, "This is where he is buried. As you can see, there was no gravestone placed here. I can tell you by the records that he was buried alone, and that your family did not pay the funeral and burial bill. Will you be paying it today?"

Quite shocked, Jean mumbled something about the family having left for Africa.

"Take your time," the caretaker answered. "I'll be in my office. Come see me and we can work something out."

Not quite trusting the French bureaucracy, Jean roamed further among the tombstones and then slipped out the back gate of the cemetery as fast as possible.

For days, Jean asked our French friends whether he should pay the bill. Was it customary? "Of course not," they answered. "Just make sure you bring flowers on *Toussaint*—the day of the dead."

ᴗˇᴗˇᴗ

Our year in France grounded Jean deeply to the ancient land, to his ancestors, and to something bigger than himself—a connection and quality that only the heart truly understands.

The truth is that our identities are complex, and we are all mixtures of different cultures, ancestors, races, and histories. In spite of (or maybe because of) that truth, often there is one place on Earth that calls out to us in a deep, heartfelt way. Writer James Baldwin, who explored issues of identity, race, and sexuality in the middle of the twentieth century before it was *à la mode*, said something that rings truer than ever as a necessity for this changing world: "Know from whence you came. If you know whence you came, there are absolutely no limitations to where you can go."

Chapter 32

Swimming with the Bulls

*We live in a moment of history where change is so speeded up,
that we begin to see the present only when it is already
disappearing.*

R.D. Laing,
Scottish Psychiatrist (1927-1989)

Serge, the chiseled-cheeked Italian potter who lives next door, peeked his head of black shoulder-length hair into our ground-floor office window and called out to Jean, *"Taureau piscine ce soir!"* (Bulls in the swimming pool tonight!) He continued, gesturing wildly, "You must be ready at 21:00 hours, 9 p.m. tonight."

It wasn't an invitation, really, but more of a command, that we join Serge and his family to see the bulls in the swimming pool. Jean mumbled okay, and we glanced at each other warily. Why in the world would there be bulls in a swimming pool?

At ten to nine, with Zoé-Pascale in tow, we gathered outside on the street between our houses with Serge, Lauré and their gang of children from two marriages. We walked swiftly down the hill to the Grand Rue, passed the *boucherie* and the crowded *Bar du Marché*. Situated just below the *Place du Marché*, in a vacant dirt lot in front of a stone farmhouse, stood the temporarily constructed *Taureau* stadium.

The makeshift oval-shaped arena was made of wood and metal, with rickety wooden bleachers rising up from either side. Two concentric circles were built in the center of the stadium, with a one-meter gap between them. The outer circle was fenced with a ten-foot-high metal barrier, upon which testosterone-rich boys perched daringly, ready for action. Practicing their running jumps over the lower red interior fence, the boys hitched their toes into the slats and bounced over like rabbits.

As she glanced out into the middle of the field, Zoé-Pascale exclaimed. "Look, there *is* a swimming pool!"

"She's right," Jean affirmed. "It looks like a very large baby's wading pool. *Voilà*, we have the *piscine*. Now, where are the bulls?"

As Jean prepared to pay our entrance fee, Serge whispered, "Why pay to see from inside the stadium when we can see just as well from the outside?" Making their livings as potters, with four kids to provide for, Serge and Lauré had to be creative. A few minutes later, Serge and his son were pushing trash bins against the outer wall of the stadium and boosting the kids up to see over the top.

Jean didn't want to offend them. "Okay, let's try it," he whispered. "If we get tired of standing on trashcans, we can always go inside."

"I have to admit, they do know how to make the best of their budget," I whispered back to him.

Ten minutes later, Lauré and Serge's sons had finagled their way over the wall and into the stadium, with the idea that they might participate in the games themselves. "Let's go," Lauré said. "The kids got in free, so now we only have to pay for us—plus, I don't quite trust the boys in there by themselves."

Leaving our standing-room-only trashcan seats, Jean and I gratefully followed them inside, eager to participate from the purchased seats.

Once inside, we deliberated on where to sit. Jean proposed on top, far from the potentially dangerous bulls, as Serge and Lauré's boys sat casually on top of the metal fence, waiting for the bulls to arrive. As we maneuvered our way through the crowds, we stopped to greet neighbors and friends who had turned out in full force to see the *Taureau Piscine*.

Toward one end of the oval field was a large truck, backed up flush against the interior red fence. Zoé-Pascale cried out, "Look, there are the bulls in that truck!"

"Mooo, brahh..." responded the *taureaux*, bucking wildly and kicking the sides of the truck.

"They are ready to go!" said Serge. Four Camargue cowboys, dressed in their Provençal shirts, denim jeans, and leather farm boots, stood on top of the high truck, looking down through a barred opening. They poked, jabbed, provoked, and pushed the first bull out into the ring with the metal points on their long wooden prods. "*Va, va!*" they yelled, as the crowd cheered them on and the bull bucked down the ramp and into the stadium.

As we perched on the edge of our seats, the first bull burst into the arena, jumping, kicking, snorting, and sneering. Looking around, the bull zoomed in on a young boy standing in the middle of the ring, dressed in blue jean shorts and a T-shirt printed with "*Club de Taureau.*"

"Who are these boys?" Jean asked Serge.

"Anyone from the village can join in the *piscine* games. Many of these teenagers are part of a club in which they train throughout the year. I think they use a calf for their training to learn how bulls behave," he told us. "I've also heard that sometimes a boy dresses up as a bull, and they practice on each other. Besides chasing the bulls and *abrivados* down the street each night during the *feria*, this is what they practice for all year. You win the grand prize, good money, if you get the bull to go into the pool because you know, bulls hate water."

Aha, that's why there's a pool involved.

The announcer in his Provençal accent shouted through the speakers, "It is ten euro, going for ten euro."

"The announcer will present the bet and challenge the boys to meet the bull," Lauré explained. "In some games, they have to touch a horn or lasso a ribbon around it, and other times, they have to get the bull into the *piscine*. The award increases as the bull gets bigger or the stunt becomes more dangerous."

The ten-euro game, we soon discovered, involved one of the players facing the bull, whose head was lowered in charge position with hooves shuffling the dirt, running past him, touching his tail, and jumping onto the red fence and over the divide, with the snorting bull in furious pursuit. Meanwhile, ten other boys tried to distract the bull by jumping and running in chaotic patterns, as though they were playing soccer, eventually causing the bull to stop and stare.

For the next twenty minutes, an assortment of big, small, strong, and not-so-strong teenagers and young men traversed the ring, encouraging the bull to chase them. Bouncing up the fence, they clambered up and swung to the outer rails for safety as another player took off, teasing the bull and hoping to distract him before he had the chance to inflict mortal injury.

One player, riled up by the excitement of the crowd, flew through the air over the interior divide, leaving his torn T-shirt hanging on the bull's horns.

"Bravo, bravo!" the crowd cheered. As the young man stared down at his naked chest, realizing his close call, he heard the crowd yelling, burst into a wide grin, and stood tall, thrusting his arms into the air over and over again. *"J'ai gagné!"* (I won!)

"Bravo, bravo," the announcer said, "This young man wins an extra twenty-five euro for his daring!"

The Camargue cowboys then brought a bigger, meaner bull to up the ante while the boys sat on the fence, yelling at each other, "You go, let's see you do it! I bet you can't do it!"

Suddenly, one sweaty, pimply-faced young man ran across the ring, the bull butting up right against his *derriere*. With a lurch forward, the bull gouged the boy's pants with his horns and tossed the young man over his head and up into the heavens.

In an instant, a bunch of boys who had been sitting on the rails across the arena leaped into the ring and surrounded the bull, yelling, *"Allez, allez."* Staring them down, the bull snorted and pawed the ground, then suddenly whipped around and ran after one of the kids standing behind him. Off went the boy, flying over the red fence like he was Superman.

"Ce n'est pas grave," the announcer yelled as the cowboys gathered around and lifted the first young man, who was still on the ground, out of the ring. When he walked away on his own two feet, the crowd shouted "Bravo, bravo!" and applauded wildly.

"Ce n'est pas grave," I said to Jean. "I guess it's not serious when you get tossed by a bull and land on your head, because at least you get to walk away a real man."

"These events are a throwback to the reenactment of the Romans in the arenas of southern France and Spain," Serge said. "The chance to be a gladiator, to chase and survive a fierce bull is a rite of passage many of these boys go through in their late teens. It's actually quite a good sport for the boys of the area. Much safer than motorcycle riding—and great for the admiration they receive from the girls."

"Some things never change," I whispered to Jean.

"It is now time for the young members of our community to try their luck at running with the bulls," the announcer said as we saw a calf run into the ring. "This is your chance to run with your children. Come on down!"

"Let's go, Papa," said Zoé-Pascale, "I want to run with the bulls, too."

Jean, having had a bit of experience being chased by his grandfather's bull when he was a boy in Africa, was less than excited about the idea. However, a few pulls on his shirt and his heartstrings, and the two of them were climbing over the metal barrier and the red fence, and facing down a calf the same size as Zoé-Pascale. "Let's make him chase us," she cried, and off they went, Zoé-Pascale chasing the calf, and Jean chasing Zoé-Pascale. I nervously waited for the fledgling to turn around and say, "Now it's my turn to chase *you*."

Meanwhile, a few other dads and kids had joined in the chase, and a game plan was being developed. Like an impromptu pick-up basketball game, positions were being appointed and a play was in action.

Bravely circling the calf, Jean edged up and reached out to tug his tail. From a distance, I could see Zoé-Pascale shouting to him. He turned around to see what she wanted. The calf, deciding it was his moment, sprinted towards Jean and thrust his diminutive dagger-like horns against him, propelling him forward, straight into another observing dad.

"Time to get out of here," Jean hollered to Zoé-Pascale as he pulled himself off his new compatriot, grabbed Zoé-Pascale around the waist, and scurried out of the arena to the applause of the crowd.

"Proved yourself, huh?" I said, smiling at them. Both smelled of sweat and dust, grateful to be safely back on the bleachers.

"We touched the baby bull, we touched the baby bull!" Zoé-Pascale sang.

Returning to the stadium after the playful intermission, it was clear that some of the audience had had a little too much to drink. "Come on, you can do it," we'd hear from groups of teenagers. "Go show us what you can do!"

Suddenly, a svelte young *jeune fille*, about eighteen years old, dressed in stiletto sandals, a breezy summer skirt, a stretchy tight tank top, and a long, flowy pink scarf wound around her neck, waved her arms wildly. The next game was for 80 euro, and it was time to show everyone how it was done. The audience started to yell *"Allez, allez!"* spurring her on to accept what she already seemed eager to embrace.

"Only in France would someone so stylish get in a ring with a bull," I said to Jean. "She's either going to break her leg in those heels or strangle herself with her scarf."

Climbing on top of the metal barrier and passing through the safety area, she climbed over the red fence and down into the ring, her fellow players shouting encouragement and advice. Weaving through the crowd of boys, she meandered in a semicircle around the wall, stopping every few feet as though to get her balance. She would stare at the bull and then smile up at the crowd as though she was a high-fashion model on the runway in Paris.

Suddenly, waving her scarf in the air, she danced across the ring, having great fun taunting the boys, the crowd, and the bull. We could see the bull rubbing his right hoof back and forth on the dirt, appearing ready to make a run for it.

Sensing the bull's hot breath, the girl twirled around and plunged forward, diving into the pool of water with a splash. Powering after his target, the bull jumped over the pool as though he was in a ballet, spun around, and pawed at the water, stomping toward the girl with his hoofs, and pushing her with his horns.

"What's going on?" I cried. "This is awful."

"The bull is afraid of the water," replied Lauré, "but he wants her."

From the right, her group of friends bounced off the fence and began distracting the bull. Looking up with stringy wet hair, the girl waved to the crowd, proudly rising out of the swirling water, yelling, *"J'ai gagné!"*

Just as the crowd went wild for her bravery, the raging *taureau* spun around and charged at her once again. "Ohhh!" the crowd yelled in unison. A great splash was heard as the girl dove back underwater. Angrier than ever, the bull came up with a different idea. Seemingly unaware of his supposedly inherent fear of water, he jumped into the pool, scooped the girl up in his horns, and threw her up and over the side. She flew through the air, kicking her legs, wind-milling her arms, and screaming "Ehhhh!" as the crowd stood stunned and silent.

"Oh mon Dieu, oh mon Dieu!" the crowd cried out.

Falling to the dust like a rag doll, she rolled over on her back, looked at the sky, and meekly raised her arms up, waving to the crowd. "Bravo, bravo!" yelled the crowd in delight as the disheveled young woman rose onto her knees, touching her bruised body gingerly to make sure she was all in one piece.

Off to the side, we could see the Camargue cowboys wrestling the bull back into the truck with their long wooden prods. Enough was enough, as far as they were concerned.

As we walked home from the adrenaline-pumping, vociferous evening, we excitedly recapped our experience.

"I loved it," Zoé-Pascale said. "I felt like I was a Roman living in Roman days."

"I have to say," I observed, "running with the bulls seems like a perfect metaphor for how our life was in California before we took this time off." It had been like we were being chased from all sides to own our time and attention, and we were cornered into a space from which we felt we couldn't escape. It's so easy to get caught up in the adrenaline of the experience of running with the bulls, but I was so grateful we had the courage to break away. While we didn't know what was next and were striving to be patient and enjoy our journey, one thing was for sure: we needed to create our life in such a way that the raging bull didn't overtake us. Life was just too short.

Chapter 33

What Is Life About?

Where am I? Who am I?
How did I come to be here?
What is this thing called the world?
How did I come into the world?
Why was I not consulted?
And If I am compelled to take part in it,
Where is the director?
I want to see him.

SOREN KIERKEGAARD,
writer in the Danish "golden age" of intellectual and artistic activity (1813-1855)

LIKE ANTS ALWAYS FEVERISHLY working, thumbs quickly moved over BlackBerries as our visitors were busy catching up on emails that came in from around the globe the night before. Alternatively the little black boxes were attached to their belt loops hanging off their vacation shorts. Even though they were on holiday they felt obliged to check into work a few times a day. The newer portable technologies, wonderful for all the benefits they provide, were in desperate need of being managed aggressively. It wasn't that PDAs and cell phones weren't widely used in France, it just seemed that the French had a sense of the turn on-turn off button which paralleled their work-life balance philosophy.

The morning after our friends left, a notice went up at school that said the CP class (first grade) would end at noon on Tuesday, as the teacher was attending a conference.

"What is this about?" I asked Lorraine.

"They don't bring in substitutes unless it is for a long-term absence. The kids can either go home, or they can sit in another class and basically draw pictures and color."

Back in Marin, if I was told unexpectedly that I had to find childcare for Zoé-Pascale, I would be in a panic trying to juggle her needs and our work obligations. As a friend pointed out to me, life in California works until a big bump in the road comes along and everything breaks apart at the seams. Upon receiving this news, however, I was calm, curious, and vaguely excited, wondering what we could do with the extra time.

At noon on Tuesday I picked up Zoé-Pascale and her new friends Perrine and Christophe, whose moms were working, and whom I had offered to take for the afternoon, their mothers' smiles confirming the relief that my offer afforded them.

"Let's see what games you have," said Perrine. "Chutes and Ladders? Great."

"My turn to pick a game." Zoé-Pascale said some time later. "Let's do this puzzle. It's very hard, though."

And later still, "I think we did as much as we can with the puzzle," chirped Christophe. "Can we play with all those marbles you have? I'll teach you how."

"*Je vais gagner! Je vais gagner!*" (I'm going to win!) I overheard from the kitchen, followed by laughter.

"Let's make cupcakes!" I said to the kids when the game ended, feeling like a kid myself. I was a novice baker but had never had the time to make a cake, let alone cupcakes.

As they lined up in new Provençal aprons, I assigned tasks

to the children in my broken French: break the eggs; measure the flour; stir in the milk, butter, and vanilla; and mix. Circled around the table, they poured the batter into the pale blue, green, and yellow cups and then licked the bowl with their fingers until it was sparkling clean. As they stared into the oven, watching the cupcakes rise up and over the edges of the paper cups, the three squealed with delight. They had placed a bet on which cupcakes would overflow, and cheered them on as though they were at the horse races.

"J'ai gagné," I heard again, thinking it must be a favorite saying among six-year-olds.

"Let's frost and decorate the cupcakes," I said to the kids.

"C'est bon," said Perrine, licking her lips.

"C'est bon," said Christophe.

"Mommy, these are wonderful! Can we make them every week?" Zoé-Pascale asked.

After working full-time for twenty-five years, the simple act of making cupcakes with three children gave me a sense of heartfelt fulfillment so uniquely different than any I had ever experienced from my rewarding career or the money that came with it.

⌣˅⌣˅⌣

"What makes a life worth living?" Jean asked me one day when the rain had fallen for most of the morning and then burst into sunshine by lunchtime. This was a question he had been asking himself ever since he left Africa so many years before. He told me that he would catch glimpses of what a life worth living felt like, only to have the idea elude him once again. He wondered whether it was God's way of getting us to pay closer attention and be more conscious of our decisions.

Ralph Waldo Emerson said, "Nothing is secure but life, transition, and the energizing spirit." Was that what our lifestyle experiment was about: moving the energizing spirit around? Or was it all the stories we were hearing of people who were forced to slow down and take a good look at the way they were living due to debilitating disease or loss?

We are extremely grateful that we weren't compelled to take stock of our lives due to illness, but that we made a conscious choice to take this time when we were healthy. Our willingness to exchange our house with a view, modern conveniences, comfortable income, luxury cars, shopping sprees, and prepared meals for something simpler was not easy by any measure, but it was ever so gratifying. We discovered that savoring a glass of local wine in an outdoor café provided as much pleasure as an expensive bottle in a five-star restaurant. Having time to build relationships with neighbors and eat meals together as a family every single day fed our souls and reinforced our connection to each other. We still loved and desired beautiful things, but our newfound focus on small, everyday pleasures shifted our perspective and moved us toward a willingness to make tradeoffs that we hadn't been prepared to make before. Our values and priorities were starting to become clearer with each passing day.

"Listen to this," I said to Jean one evening, reading a quote from Henry David Thoreau. "'Go confidently in the direction of your dreams! Live the life you've imagined. As you simplify your life, the laws of the universe will be simpler.' I think that is what is happening," I added. "The laws of the universe seem to be simpler than they were before. Or is it just my imagination?" We truly felt that our workaholic behaviors were being replaced by health, joy, and balance.

Every few weeks on one of our walks, Jean and I would check in with where our life was headed and explore how we'd reprioritize and create a more balanced lifestyle once we returned to the States. Our time off had been about rejuvenation and re-establishing what was important to us in living a good life, deciding upon the work we wanted to do and the lifestyle we wanted to have. We had begun to unlearn how we had been living, and learn instead how to live well. Not only were our priorities changing, but we were changing also. We were beginning to feel truly free to go anywhere and do anything we wanted.

"One thing I realize now," I said, "is that our time off is allowing me to truly take care of myself without guilt, and is teaching me what I must do to live a long, healthy, and balanced life. Here, we don't have excuses to eat unhealthily, not exercise, and not take time for ourselves." In our old life, we would have persevered, paid a therapist for weekly visits, and indulged in massages and other bodywork in an attempt to speed up the healing process. I was beginning to see that putting Band-Aids on top of psychic wounds just doesn't work. I remember the chills that swept through me when the therapist had said to Jean, "Suzanne's soul is dying." How right she was. It had been withering slowly and imperceptibly. Only with this dramatic lifestyle shift was it beginning to flourish again.

With time to truly cocoon through the winter months, we basked under the luminescent blue sky wrapped in warm coats and boots, and lounged by the fireplace each night. Partly because we didn't have family or many long-term close friends nearby, our intimacy as a family grew. We were able to listen to each other, to embrace our daughter with extreme patience and love, and to live tranquilly, quietly, and peacefully. Marcel Proust, the French novelist, wrote, "Let us be grateful to people who make us happy: they are the charming gardeners who make our souls bloom." We had the time to cultivate ourselves and each other, and as a result, we flowed with the seasons and were all blossoming brightly.

༺ ༻ ༺ ༻

One year turned into two, which rolled into three. Time seemed to slip by like a long unending warm summer day. We had more to taste, explore, and learn, and our appetite for living the simpler life of *joie de vivre* was unquenched.

Without a doubt, our time off changed us. We are no longer the same people we were. Even though we recognized that we once again needed to find a way to make a good living, we are no longer interested in climbing someone else's ladder or keeping up with the Joneses. Yes, life would probably throw a few wrenches in the works, but with renewed energy and focus on a balanced lifestyle, we want to make deliberate choices and be intentional in what we are trading off.

Taking this path had not been easy, nor would it be any easier going forward. But, we realized, the very notion of life, transition, and the energizing spirit that Emerson spoke of requires us to stay on the edge of our comfort zone and live consciously, with adventurous hearts.

Epilogue: It Has Made All the Difference

A journey of a thousand miles begins with a single step.

Lao Tzu,
Chinese Taoist Philosopher (c 600 BCE)

Sure enough, as our journey continues, we've encountered numerous roadblocks. When we eventually returned to the states thirty-six months after moving to France, the economy took a turn for the worse, and the dollar was falling. We sold our home in the small French village and couldn't find another one we wanted in our price range. No matter how hard we pushed, nothing seemed to move. Then, recalling how we'd made the move to France possible to begin with, we decided all we could do is focus on good-feeling thoughts and use everything that we have learned as we continue on this path. What we have learned is that we can't plan a perfect journey, but that we can live from the heart, from a place of what we feel as well as what we think is right for us.

Like a meandering river, the path to a dream is not linear, but often circuitous. Day-by-day we continue to create, refine, and realize the life we want to live; nurturing the process one step at a time...

The simple country life in France warms our hearts and through persistent focus on what our souls crave, we eventually bought a spacious house in the south of France where the sun shines three hundred days of the year. Incorporated in the house is Zoé-Pascale's love of Greek Ionic pillars with archways and ivy that grows onto the side of the house. The garden is idyllic for entertaining, with a long wooden table, wicker chairs and cushions covered with Provençal designs. A crystal clear azure infinity pool, a nearby pond with koi fish, and a little willow tree are a complement to the blue skies and lavender fields waving in the breeze off the Mediterranean. The land is planted with Jean's beloved silvery olive trees, which he harvests and trades for olive oil. Jean and Zoé-Pascale have their hands full collecting eggs from the hens and milking our five goats, while I read up on how to make chevre fromage (goat cheese). We are surrounded by rows and rows of Côte du Rhône vineyards and swim frequently in the nearby river. A short drive takes us to the sandy Mediterranean beaches of Languedoc, and we can easily drive to neighboring countries, giving us a rich playground to explore. We feel wea thy beyond our dreams in every way, and live in abundance and simplicity, close to nature and with friends and family around the world. We have also managed to create the work we love. Part of that is this book. Since not getting this message out into the world—the one that says that you, too, can create the life you want to live—was not an option, we forged ahead with revision after revision for four straight years. You are all part of the road we have chosen to take and, as Robert Frost said, "it has made all the difference in the world."

We found ways to integrate our professions with our love of travel and adventure through our global nonprofit foundation that focuses on global education and health to those in need. It is something we can do together as a family, and that we would never have conceived of if it weren't for the internal shifts brought on by our journey and the generosity of others to support our work.

In the book The Second Half of Life, Angeles Arrien describes the Four Rivers of Life: challenge, surprise, inspiration, and love. This image depicts our continued journey well. The river of challenge pulls and pushes us to grow and stretch and go beyond our comfort zone in ways we may or may not choose. The river of surprise opens us up to the possibilities of what may come our way, even if we can't imagine them now. The river of inspiration asks us where are we in relation to our creative fire and our life dream, and assures us that if we can touch these things, we can live fully. And the river of love invites us to stand in intention and in each present moment, focusing on the joy, laughter, and all that which touches our hearts.

Today, the smell of lavender permeates our senses as we drive through the French countryside, happy and grateful for our ability to reside in the south of France for most of the year. For the other part, we engage in the stimulating life of the Bay Area. Both worlds have become part of us, and we part of them. It was—and is—the right thing for us.

We are more attentive to our bodies now, and Jean and I show up at the yoga studio twice a week with a group of like-minded men and women. We get into our poses, stretch, relax, breathe, and stretch a little further. I no longer worry about what the teacher is saying in French. I feel like I breathe the language as I absorb the various poses. The practice of yoga translates well. Meanwhile, Jean's aches are dissipating as he flexes and stretches further.

Jean has taken up painting again after having let it go for many years in pursuit of his career. His large, bold, abstract paintings are coming to the attention of viewers as he plans his first exhibit in an eighteenth-century French chateau. He has named his series of thirty paintings "Personal Abundance"—something that is definitely depicted in the deep, rich colors, radiant light, and untold mythical symbolism of the work.

Zoé-Pascale's adventuresome spirit continues to blossom. She is more fun to be around than ever, and the three of us are very close. Our love of travel and learning has led us to plan several adventures in the coming months and years. We are training to climb the Himalayas, and are planning the Nile cruise that Zoé-Pascale insisted on, as well as a trek in Kenya with Jean's brother and his family, an exploration of the Greek antiquities, and a visit to the home of Zoé-Pascale's favorite goddess, Artemis. These trips aren't lavish sorties, but are done as simply as possible and always on a budget.

Our friends and families love to visit us in France and share in the local culture. It makes it even lovelier when they come to visit—they always
leave a little lighter, happier, and with bigger smiles.

We feel deeply connected to our global village and to our loved ones
through the wonders of technology and air travel. We are finding that the
world is smaller than ever, and that it is possible to live in multiple communities both physically and virtually, keeping all ties and relationships
intact. The issues of time and space have greatly diminished, allowing us
to embrace each other over continents with ease.

Will I ever be truly French? No, but in some way I have absorbed the
country's best qualities and have integrated the American culture with the
French joy of living. Jean and Zoé-Pascale are definitely much more integrated into French life, but together we have found our unique rhythm,
appreciating the qualities of both cultures and living simply—our own
unique life based on our family's own unique needs.

Today, Zoé-Pascale reads a book a day, stretching her mind with mystical characters, historical facts, and great stories. She has wonderful
friends and family in three continents to hang out with, laugh, and play.
Her love of theater, classical ballet, and dance feeds her creative spirit, and
she is becoming a star in her own right. In spite of challenges that she may
encounter, we know that what we have created with her will inspire her to
create her own dreams as her life evolves.

Many mornings and most evenings we snuggle and read in bed together; like bookends holding the books on a shelf tightly together, our
snuggles unite us together as we go our separate ways during the day. As
the world becomes more technological, we recognize that the basic routines that bring us comfort and joy are what make our relationships with
each other worthwhile.

Is it all perfect? No, there are the occasional problems. The car breaks
down or someone gets sick. We experience everyday challenges: managing our budget, weight, and bills; being caught in traffic jams; keeping up
on emails; and making time to do everything we want to and need to do.

The difference now, however, is that we have achieved a sense of balance and reprioritized family as the center of our lives. We balance time and money, and no longer feel crazed trying to stay on the treadmill.

For the most part, life flows easily and simply, and at the same time is stimulating and full of adventure. We recognize that we will always be transitioning and searching—after all, life is ever-changing, and we are endlessly curious about it. But for now, life is good. Our hope is that we have planted a seed of inspiration that might allow you to go after your dreams and live the life you want for yourself and your family—whatever that looks like to you.

Did we have doubts? Sure. Do we still have doubts? Of course. Did we expect it to work out? Yes. Did we think it would take such a circuitous route? Not really. Was it easy? No. Would we do it again? Yes. Are we continuing to do it? Yes. Is there another choice? Not really—not if you want to live your dreams.

The only real limitations we ever truly have are our own fears and limiting beliefs. All we can do is say yes to our dreams and follow the path that appears before us, using the guidance of our hearts. Then surrender, trusting that all will work out as it is meant to.

With this in mind, we wish you bon courage along the path to your unique dream, and hope it finds you munching on hot croissants (or some other delectable) along the way. Be strong, bold, and courageous, and be open to wonderful surprises.

The only real stumbling block is fear of failure. In cooking you've got to have a what-the-hell attitude.

JULIA CHILD

Part V

Life Guidebook Tips

It takes a lot of courage to release the familiar and seemingly secure, to embrace the new. But there is no real security in what is no longer meaningful. There is more security in the adventurous and exciting, for in movement there is life, and in change there is power.

ALAN COHEN,
Inspirational Author and Speaker (1954-)

Recognize What Is Not Working

If you change the way you look at things,
the things you look at change.

Wayne Dyer,
Self-help advocate, teacher, and author (1940-)

Western culture tells us to keep on pushing on: run faster, do more, never give up, keep going, push, and push some more. The paradox is that the harder we push, the more resistance we encounter. In fact, according to Albert Einstein, the definition of insanity is "to keep on doing the same thing, expecting a different result."

If you are paying attention, it is easy to recognize whether part of your life is not working. The hard part is taking the time to stop and assess whether it is time to do something different. Is it time to stop pretending, stop pushing, and stop trying to fit a square peg into a round hole?

Once you stop and analyze the situation, you may realize there are many alternatives to the way you've been living, and at least one of them may be worth a try.

A few ideas for assessing what is and is not working in your life

Exercise

1. **Identify what is no longer working for you (and your family or partner).**

    Either alone or with a partner, family member, friend or professional, discuss what is no longer working. Following are some questions to guide your discussion.

    - What aspects of your life are no longer working? Is it a part of your life or the whole package?
    - What do you feel fed up or done with?
    - What in your life is working well?
    - What is it you want to stop doing, or do more of/ less of/ differently?

    » *We came to the realization that being older parents of a newborn with two full-time, all-consuming careers—not to mention the high expenses we had accumulated to make our life work—was leading to depression, unhappiness, and exhaustion.*

    What was working was our commitment and love for each other and sense of adventure. We felt passion for doing something new and felt we had the courage to take a risk.

2. **Get clear on what you dream of doing differently**

    Have a discussion based on the following questions:

    - What is missing in your life that you want to create?
    - What does your dream look like? How would you know that

you have achieved the dream you want?

- Will the change you wish to make move you towards what you want in life? Will you always regret it if you don't give it a try?
- Will the change bring you long-term gratification or just short-term satisfaction? Which are you seeking?
- Is the dream something that empowers you?
- What is calling you?

» *After a great deal of soul searching, it became clear that we wanted to take time off and live in a different culture, travel the world, and experience a simpler life together as a family. Beyond that, we weren't sure what we wanted to do.*

3. **Identify fears, limiting beliefs, and "shoulds".**
Have a discussion based on the following questions:

- What fears are you going to have to face to create what you want? Are you willing to face them?
- What limiting beliefs do you need to address to make a shift happen?
- What seeming obligations, or "shoulds," will you have to eliminate in your thinking? Are you willing to replace them with your dreams and desires?

» *Many fears came up for us as we made our plans: not having money, not having work, and leaving what we knew. Every time those limiting beliefs surfaced, we acknowledged and talked about them until they lost their power. They were simply fears that needed to be dealt with in order for us to move forward.*

4. **Learn about what it takes to make changes in your life, and gather the support you need.**
Read books, listen to recordings, and watch programs that will inspire and motivate you on your journey. Surround yourself with supporters and eliminate naysayers.

A few of our favorite books and CDs are:

- *Your Heart's Desire, Using the Laws of Manifestation to Create the Life you Really Want* by **Sonia Choquette**. A sixth-sensory look at how to create what you want in life.
- *Transitions* by **William Bridges**. A small classic on what happens as you go through a transition.
- *Personal Power and Awakening the Giant* by **Tony Robbins**. We have listened to the Personal Power CDs over and over again.
- *The Success Principle* by **Jack Canfield and Janet Switzer**. An all-encompassing book that is easy to pick up and put down as needed.

Determine Your Options— Then Decide and Act

It all depends on how we look at things,
and not how they are in themselves.

CARL JUNG,
Swiss Psychiatrist and founder of Jungian Psychology (1865-1961)

Making a decision requires doing research, gathering information, and using both mind and heart to guide you. The more complex the decision, the more tools you might want to use to help
you weigh the different choices. In addition, each individual does
make decisions differently depending upon their own way of
thinking. Keep this in mind as you weigh your options.

A few tips for making decisions

Here we have provided a few key decision-making tools, along with examples of how we used them.

1. *Identify the problem you are trying to solve.*
What exactly is the problem? How would you benefit from solving it? Will the result of this choice add to your happiness, or will wrestling with the problem rob you of your energy?

>   » *We wanted to figure out where and how to live a more balanced, higher-quality life. We felt we needed to change not only the speed at which we were living but also the physical surroundings. Why? Because our current pace and environment were no longer working for us. Our hearts—as well as our heads—made this very clear.*

2. *Gather information.*
What considerations do you need to make to address the problem? What information would be useful in identifying your options?

>   » *We spent a few years reading about and traveling to different towns and cities to which we thought we might potentially move. We listed a set of criteria: weather (top of our list), education, environment, culture, community feeling, business environment, recreation, housing, proximity to other things we needed, cost of living index, medical care, natural disasters and manmade hazards, traffic, friends, and family.*

3. *Determine the criteria by which you will evaluate your choices.*
Are you going to make a decision based on a set of fact-based criteria, subjective criteria, your intuition, or a mixture?

» Once we began comparing all of the potential new cities by giving them quantitative ratings, we were shocked at how similar the numbers were. Nothing jumped out at us as particularly different or special about any of them. For us, this led to a huge revelation, and served as a jumping-off point to focus on the heart of what we wanted and needed—to take a risk.

At this point we needed to shift our attention to our hearts, instincts, and intuition, as the data alone provided too little information toward a clear-cut solution. In the end, the questions that drove us were things like: What feels right? What excites us? What makes us willing to make the sacrifices needed? What do we dream about day and night? What were our intuition and guts telling us? For what end would we willing to take a leap of faith?

4. Brainstorm and generate different possible choices.

Once the list of criteria is solid and resonates strongly with heart and mind, start listing out possible solutions that match the criteria.

» We had actually done most of our brainstorming as we were gathering information. What were the cities and towns we might want to move to? What did we want to do with our careers? What choices were available to us: time off, traveling the world, bringing in a business partner, managing the business from afar, selling the business, a combination, or something else entirely?

5. Evaluate each choice in terms of the pros and cons.

Using both analytical tools and intuitive feelings is critical in the evaluation process. One fun way to do this is to use the "Thinking Hats:"*

- **The Data Hat.** What does the quantitative data say? What information is missing? What can you predict from the data?
- **The Intuitive or Gut-Check Hat.** What does your gut tell you?

What do you feel is right or not right intuitively?

- **The Pessimistic Hat.** What can go wrong? Where are the holes in your plan? This hat allows you to plan for contingencies and be prepared for obstacles that might come your way.

- **The Positive Hat.** What are the benefits and the real value of the choice? This hat helps you keep going regardless of the obstacles you may encounter.

- **The Creativity Hat.** What creative solutions might help you overcome hurdles? What creative ideas do you have for making your dream come true?

- **The Facilitator Hat.** This hat helps you to keep moving things forward even when they get difficult. This hat asks the questions, "What would be most helpful now?" and "Which hat would help us to move along?"

*Adapted from Edward De Bono's "Six Hats" method.

» *During the hours we spent evaluating our options, one or both of us would ask questions wearing different hats. Asking the questions of each other was enlightening and thought-provoking. It soon became very clear that our decision needed to be made more from the Intuitive/Gut-Check hat. We made sure, however, that the data we were seeing would support our choice, and that we were also aware of worst-case scenarios. With this in mind, we made contingency plans so that we would not be derailed completely.*

6. *Determine the best alternative by defining what success looks like.*

Now that you have used the above tools to arrive at what you'd like to do, what does success look like to you? How would you know if you have achieved your goals? How will you measure success?

» *It soon became clear that what we wanted to do was to take time off and live in our village house in the south of France for at least year.*

We had done enough analysis and planning that we knew it was the right choice for us. We also became very clear about what it would take to create the dream. There was no doubt that it required our full attention in every realm: mental, financial, physical, and spiritual. We were both not only up for the challenge, but determined to remain focused on and support each other in pursuit of our goal.

Our first measure of success would be to get on that airplane and fly away. After that, we set more specific milestones in order to ensure we were creating what we envisioned. We checked in periodically about whether we felt healthier and happier. Were we being creative? Were we feeling more balanced now that we had made the shift to a new way of life? Were our priorities shifting like we thought they would?

During our journey, whenever doubts surfaced or something new came up, we went back to the list of ways we had originally defined success. This became even more important as time moved on and new goals emerged, by assuring us that the decisions we had made and were making were in line with what we had wanted from the beginning.

7. **Develop and execute an action plan, and keep believing that you will create what you want.**

Transform your decision into specific action steps and then go for it.

» Once we were focused, clear, in total agreement, and determined, our action plan came together quickly and easily. Continuing to believe while taking action was a key element in manifesting all the components of our plan.

Our first order of business was to focus on getting our business in great shape to sell, as well as developing the sales proposal and networking. This one action item took us eighteen months from beginning to end. As this was happening, we listed out what actions

*were required to address the following: living year-round in a vaca-
tion house, schooling for Zoé-Pascale, how we could work, how Jean
could continue his Ph.D. program, travel, renting out our house, obtaining the required residency permits, and budgeting and financial
planning.*

*We worked together to execute the required actions, believing
that the dream was well worth the work. We divided up tasks and
asked for support when needed. We checked in often, re-evaluated
whether we were on track, and developed new contingency plans as
more information was revealed.*

8. **Evaluate the outcome of your decision and action steps. What
    lessons can be learned? This is an important step for further
    development of your decision-making skills and judgment.**

We never doubted that our decision to sell the business and
take time off as a family was the right one. Sometimes we wished
we had done a few things differently (such as selling our house in
Tiburon before the real estate market crashed), but we did the
best we could with what we knew at the time. What we learned
was that you can take on only so much at one time, and that each
"wrong" decision is merely a step towards the next dream.

Determine How to Fund Your Dreams

*Middle Age is that perplexing time of life when we hear two
voices calling us, one saying, «Why not?» and the other, «Why
bother?»*

SYDNEY J. HARRIS,

American Journalist (1917-1986)

Focusing on the Dream

If you are clear on what you want but have trouble obtaining
it (as many of us do), you may wish to explore the principles of
the Law of Attraction. In their work, *Money and the Law of Attraction*, Esther and Jerry Hicks emphasize the importance of
thoughts—namely, how thoughts help to raise our vibrations
and attract what we want into our lives. If you want to attract
things—money, experiences, people—into your life, you have
to offer substantially different vibrations, which means that you
have to think thoughts that actually feel different to think. Make
an effort to find good-feeling thoughts all the time. For example,
even in times of financial difficulty, focus on feeling prosperous
and, according to the Law of Attraction, more prosperity will
come your way.

You have to find a way to feel the essence of what you desire
before the details and reality of that desire will appear. If you can't

bring yourself to focus on feelings of abundance, focus instead directly on your dream—what does it FEEL like to live the life you desire? Holding this picture in your mind is of paramount importance, far more significant than coming up with the money itself.

So much of the work is done on this level. However, as far as time-space "reality" goes, we offer you ...

A few thoughts on financing your dreams

First, figure out how much money you really need to fund the dream. This is often where the rubber meets the road. What are you willing to do to create the necessary budget? Depending on your timeframe and how much money you need, different choices will have to be made. Following are a few things to consider.

1. **Can you reduce expenses or cut back? What might you be willing to give up to create the life you want?**

   This is where the "latté factor" comes in. What small expenditures can you give up in order to fund the dream: a latté a day, babysitting, cable television, a gardener, dinners out? It all adds up, so you may wish to consider what you can eliminate or reduce.

   > » *A major expense we gave up was our live-in nanny. Zoé-Pascale was going to a full day of preschool at the French School and the au pair was becoming a luxury and convenience versus a necessity. In addition, we socked more money away in the bank and reduced our dining out and entertainment budget. We also knew we'd be willing (and wanting) to live a simpler life once we made the move.*

2. **Do you need to save money from current income? Do you have a plan for doing so, and are you on target?**

If you can put away 10% of your paycheck, you will be surprised how fast it adds up. Comparison shop, buy at consignment stores, use coupons, and figure out ways to save on food, clothes, entertainment, healthcare deductibles, insurance, and more to reserve that 10% as fast as you can.

3. **Do you have another source of income on which to rely if you weren't working?**

Perhaps you are in a position to have some other sources of income, such as a future inheritance or stock options? Can you make some additional income through a second source (i.e., second job, internet-related work, part-time work, selling services) now to help fund and sustain the change? Get creative, brainstorm ideas, and think outside of the box.

4. **Can you make money while you are living the dream? (e.g. teach ESL while living in a foreign country, work via the internet, etc.)**

The Internet has made it much easier to work from anywhere in the world.

> » *For six months as we transitioned our business to the new owner we logged in and did business via the phone and webcam, and traveled for work when needed.*

5. **Are you planning on coming into an inheritance soon? Might you ask for the inheritance early?**

For some fortunate people this is a possibility. It may be worth the conversation with your parents if you think it is an option.

6. **Can you sell some investments? Do you want to? Is it better to invest in yourself for a period of time?**

Do a cost/benefit analysis to see whether this makes sense

for you and your family. Sometimes it is cheaper to spend money now versus later on when a crisis is brought on as a result of how you've been living.

7. **Might you sell a business, a house, land, etc. to fund the change? Is there a plan in place?**

Selling a business or house is a longer-term strategy to consider, but a viable one for some people. If you are feeling burdened with what you have rather than enjoying it, you might consider this option. Not only does it free up funds, it simplifies life overall.

8. **Will you need to lengthen your timeline in order to save? What is the cost of time versus money?**

Patience is key here. The journey of creating the dream can be as important and satisfying as the dream itself. Enjoy the ride, which is not a straight line, but more of an undulating curve as it slowly and with its own speed moves you forward to your dreams.

9. **Do you want to—or can you—borrow the money?**

We would suggest this only if you believe you will be making enough income (via your dream) to pay down the debt within a time period that you are comfortable with and makes sense. If, for example, you are borrowing to increase your education and marketability, it might be worth the cost in the long run. Otherwise, having debt hanging over your head could actually decrease your enjoyment of your long-held goal, not to mention reduce your freedom.

10. **Affirm that the answers are coming to you. Keep your mind open to the possibilities.**

Ask every day for signs, ideas, people, and information that will help you to figure out how to fund the dream. Meditate, affirm, pray, and share your dream with others. Be open to signs and answers when they appear.

Remember, funding your dream is a combination of taking practical steps and having constant good-feeling thoughts of abundance, prosperity, and the life you want. Let your positive thoughts propel you to take those practical steps and you will be amazed at what you attract into your life to support you along the way.

In all realms of life it takes courage to stretch your limits, express your power, and fulfill your potential—it's no different in the financial realm.

Suze Orman,
American Financial author and motivational speaker (1951-)

Get Outside Your Comfort Zone

Challenges make you discover things about yourself that you never really knew. They're what make the instrument stretch— what make you go beyond the norm.

CICELY TYSON,
American actress (1933-)

Confirming the old expression "use it or lose it," research now shows that we have to keep our brains and bodies active and learn new things in order to combat the diseases associated with aging. Stepping out of your comfort zone enables you to live a longer, healthier, and fuller life overall.

Not surprisingly, most of us will do whatever it takes to stay within our comfort zone. Many people never venture further than fifty miles from the place they were born, and fewer than 25% of Americans own a passport. However, traveling is only one of many ways to expand your comfort zone. The important thing is taking steps to expand your own horizon.

The reward of pushing your own boundaries is an incomparable feeling of vitality and new energy. And, the more you step out, the more comfortable and competent you become at doing so.

Your comfort zone comprises 4 distinct areas: Place, People, Pursuits, and Power (of the brain)

1. Place:

Being in a new place for the first time is an experience for many in living outside of their comfort zone. Traveling, putting yourself in new situations, and enjoying different physical environments are wonderful ways to grow and learn. Marcel Proust said, "The real voyage of discovery consists not in seeking new landscapes but in having new eyes."

> » *Living in France and traveling around Europe and Africa gave us the opportunity to see and experience things that were new, different, and exhilarating. We felt as fascinated as children as we walked down a cobblestone street, scaled a sand dune in the Namib Desert, or stared up at an ancient church built in the 10th century.*

2. People:

Venture out to meet and interact with people you don't know. Go to a lecture or networking meeting, volunteer, or attend a class or a party with the intention of meeting new people.

> » *Being understood and understanding others in the French language was—and continues to be—the ultimate push out of my comfort zone. The reason I stick with it, however, is that when I am able to have a conversation I am thrilled and walk on air for the rest of the day with added excitement and confidence.*
>
> *Jean pushed himself out of his comfort zone while conducting his Ph.D. research. He reached out to a professor at the Université de Montpellier and asked for her assistance. He was able to involve her in the project as a research supervisor and, as a result, was able to conduct his study with both US and French subjects.*

3. Pursuits:

If you continue to engage in activities with which you are familiar and competent, you are in your comfort zone. When you endeavor to learn a new sport, skill, or activity, you start to push the boundaries of your comfort zone.

» In France, we would constantly venture out as a family to new towns and villages and explore the countryside. These adventures pushed us out of the known and into areas that challenged us. Our senses were on high alert, from reading the roadmap to deciding the best place to eat lunch or go for a hike. We often found that driving sixty kilometers to a new village or region was as exhilarating as touring the whole continent.

4. Power of the Brain:

Completing tasks with which you are already familiar keeps you in your comfort zone. Stretching yourself to try a new skill or task takes you outside of it.

» Currently, our brains are being constantly stretched as we endeavor to learn new social marketing tools. We decided a while ago that we can't learn all of them at once but will take on one per month, allowing us to build competence and confidence.

Why don't we step outside our comfort zones more often?

In many ways, humans are still functioning on the biological instincts that tell us to play it safe, stay with the herd, and protect ourselves from possible danger. This was important at one time but no longer serves us today. As children, it is our nature to grow and develop, but as autonomous adults, we are faced with the choice to either stagnate or continue to learn.

A few tips for stepping outside your comfort zone

1. **Take small steps. Pick one or two domains in which you are willing to experiment.**

   Say, for example, you want to learn how to knit and decide to take a class with all strangers. What is the worst that could happen? You stab yourself with the knitting needle and someone laughs at you. But wait, if it is a beginner's class, they won't know how to knit either, and the teacher is sure to show you how to properly handle the needles. Breaking it down this way often helps allay our fears of entering into something new.

2. **Stick with it until it becomes comfortable.**

   Keep going to the knitting class until the basic principles become second nature. Suddenly, you might find yourself signing up for the more advanced class or trying a more difficult pattern.

3. **Repeat the process over and over and over again.**

   As you practice stepping out of your comfort zone, you will find that you become bolder, more courageous, and want to try out new things. Take your first experiment into another domain. After knitting, you might travel to an unfamiliar state, learn to sail, or develop a new relationship with someone who stretches your interests.

   Find the joy in stepping out of your comfort zone.

   Acting on your dreams, desires, goals, and wishes will require that you move out of your comfort zone. If you want to create the life you hope for, keep practicing moving out of your comfort zone. You may suddenly find yourself captivated by the feelings of joy, liberation, and accomplishment.

Enjoy the Simple Things in Life

It is the sweet, simple things of life which are
the real ones after all.

LAURA INGALLS WILDER,
American author (1867-1957)

Living in one place and going through the same motions day after day often leaves us numb to our surroundings. A big change—be it a geographical move or a change in our career, health, or relationships—provides an opportunity to see our lives from a different perspective. Mostly, however, living in balance and joy requires us to pay attention to and enjoy the things in life that give us most pleasure.

Moving to another culture, we became amazed at the joy we experienced from simple things in life, such as:

- *Walking our daughter to school (versus being in the car all of the time)*

- *The success of being understood when conversing in French*

- *Cooking a scrumptious meal made from fresh, seasonal foods*

- Sticking our heads out the window to smell the scented air
- Picking lavender on our walks or fresh figs from the nearby orchards
- Reading together on the couch in front of the fireplace every night
- Carrying colorful baskets everywhere
- Driving through the roundabouts versus stopping at red traffic lights
- Drinking great local wines
- Talking to old friends and family back in California or Africa
- Working with clients for the sake of the work itself
- Writing our book together
- Painting en plein air
- Meeting new friends and fellow travelers

A few tips for enjoying the simple things life offers

1. Get rid of clutter in your life, in your house, and in your mind

Wherever there is clutter, there is no room to see what is in front of you or derive much pleasure or meaning from life. Start by taking the time to clean out the physical clutter around you; anything you haven't used in the past year is obscuring your vision from enjoying what you do have.

> » All of the tchotchkes we bought in our travels and throughout life seemed important until we realized how crowded they were making us feel, how many more bookshelves we needed to store them... not to mention the storage units we had to pay for when we left for France! Cleaning out and saving only the items most precious to us made us appreciate what we had, and caused us to be more mindful of what we bought for our home in the future. After all, how many wood-carved hippopotamuses, tapestries, or ponchos does one household need?

2. **Surround yourself with supportive people (and avoid negative people and energy).**

It is difficult to appreciate the simple things around you when your space is clouded with negative energy. Get rid of negative energy—yours and other people's—so it isn't pervasive in your life.

> » From time to time we would encounter angry people who felt the world was against them. Most often they were chance meetings with strangers in a store or with colleagues at work. We both learned to recognize what that energy felt like and would take ourselves away from it as quickly as possible.
>
> Sometimes, when the negative energy of another rubs off on us, we literally rub it off our shoulders until our energetic space feels clean once again. We call it an energy dusting, and it helps us to clean off negative energy that can sometimes stick.

3. **Focus on what you are doing and whom you are with.**

Distractions deter you from seeing, hearing, feeling, and smelling the simple joys that occur in each moment. The more you are able to be present, the more you are able to enjoy the treasures life has to offer.

> » Though it is easier said than done, we try to give our full focus to things like dinnertime conversation, a yoga class, or a walk in nature.

We also strive to be present while doing things by ourselves, such as reading books, cooking dinner, or taking a walk.

4. **Make a list of all the simple things you enjoy and make sure to do at least one of them daily.**

By listing things you enjoy, you begin to focus on making them a priority in your life. Whether it is cooking a special meal, planting a garden, walking hand-in-hand with your child, or reading a good book, declare in writing what you most desire in life. It is much easier to make time for and create things on which we put our focus and intention.

> » *Our list includes a walk, a good book, just being with our daughter, art and creativity, making love, connection to friends, and a great film.*

5. **Practice going outside your comfort zone to experience new simple pleasures.**

Though travel is one of the easiest ways to do this, there are plenty of ways to experience new delights closer to home. Meander over to a new hiking trail, tune into a new radio station, or invite neighbors you don't know well over for a glass of wine or a cup of tea. You'll be surprised at how these little adjustments can lift your spirits.

> » *This year we are going to try something new: a ballroom dance class. A bit of exercise, a new endeavor to try together, and certainly a source of many laughs.*

Include Creativity in your Life

I have learned, as a rule of thumb, never to ask whether you can do something. Say, instead, that you are doing it. Then fasten your seat belt. The most remarkable things follow.

JULIA CAMERON,
American teacher, artist, and author of *The Artist's Way* (1948-)

One simple way to change your view of the world is to tap into your creativity. Whether it is through a traditional art form, playing an instrument, or cooking up a new dish for your family, exploring creative endeavors helps us reduce stress and live healthier lives, as well as giving us the joy of providing something from the heart for others.

A few reasons to include creativity in your life

1. **Creative activities slow down time and relieve stress.**
   When you are immersed in a creative project, time slows down and expands at the same time. Numerous creative people

report that when they are engaged in a creative project, time seems to go on forever.

> *If I ever want to relax and slow down time, I take out my paints or my knitting. My focus shifts, my mind expands, and time slows down.*

2. Creativity increases self-esteem, self-confidence, and competence.

When we are creating, there is no right or wrong—there is only what we create. As a result, our minds open to the vastness of what we can do.

> *Cooking is a great example of a creative process in which there is no right or wrong, just experimentation. Sure, we can follow a recipe, but we can alter it just as easily. When Jean or I give ourselves the time to creatively cook, we are often thrilled with the results, as are our family and friends.*

3. Creative activities stimulate the mind and help us recognize that anything is possible.

There are many forms of creative expression so if you don't like to paint try something physical like dancing. If you feel intimidated or embarrassed, take classes. If you don't know where to start get ideas from magazines or check out the local community college for classes. Just do something that taps into your creative side and frees up your mind and body to express itself with the pure goal of having fun.

> *In our sculpture class, we were amazed at how every student's sculpture was completely unique, and yet we were all using the same tools, at the same time, with the same instructor. That realization opened our minds greatly, and the notion of anomalous possibility— that there is never just one way to see, be, or do things—remains with us today.*

Live in Gratitude

*If the only prayer you said in your whole life was, "thank you,"
that would suffice.*

MEISTER ECKHART,
German philosopher (1260-1328)

According to the Law of Attraction, one of the easiest ways to attract positive things into your life is to be grateful for the things, people, ideas, and events that already exist. It makes sense—when you focus on good things in your life, you aren't focusing on the negative. But how often do we stop to adjust our focus?

A few tips for practicing gratitude on a daily basis

1. **Keep a Gratitude List**

    A gratitude list is an easy tool that can be used to make a good day even better and, used each day, brings a great deal of positive healing energy into life.

Each morning when you wake up, or in the evening before you go to bed, list in your journal all of the things in your life for which you are grateful. Every once in a while, go back and read it. You will be astounded at all the small things that make you feel good!

Another idea is to create a Gratitude Board. Use colored pens and draw or write on a large poster board what you are grateful for. Keep the board in a place where you can glance at it daily and add new things as they come up.

> » While living in our French village, it was easy to write down everything we were grateful for as we were living our dream each day. It's when life isn't so easy or when it is super busy that it becomes even more important to keep writing down what you are grateful for—that's when we realize how many good things in life are there to support us through the more trying times.

2. Give thanks as a family

Share what you are grateful for with your family at dinnertime. Talk about why you are grateful and how it makes you feel. Each night when you tuck your children into bed, ask them to list as many things as they can think of that they are grateful for (aim for 10-15 items). Then, ask them whether there is anything that didn't go well in their day—usually the list is pretty short. Pointing this out to them goes a long way in teaching kids to see the good things in life, and helps them to build resilience when things don't always go their way.

> » We have been doing the above rituals with our daughter for the last four years. Some days it is harder to do this than others, for all of us. Sometimes she asks us to go first; sometimes she wants to go first. What is startling is that, when she sees that there are ten or fifteen great things that happened and only one negative thing, she immediately feels excited. We then talk about how she might address the negative event the next day, which empowers her to turn her situation around, whatever she may face.

Do Now What You've Always Wanted To Do—Now Is The Time!

You always do what you want to do. This is true with every act.
You may say that you had to do something, or that you were
forced to, but actually, whatever you do, you do by choice. Only
you have the power to choose for yourself.

W. CLEMENT STONE,
businessman, philanthropist, self-help author (1902-2002)

What is stopping you from doing what you really want to do? What is inhibiting you from creating the life you desire, and fulfilling your heart and soul? Is it fear or a lack of belief, self-confidence, or self-esteem? Is money the issue, or do you just not know what you want?

The present moment is all we have. The past is behind us and the future is waiting to be created. Why not create what you want versus letting it happen to you? You are the master of your destiny.

A few tips on creating the life you want

1. Visioning

Ask yourself the following questions, and answer them as honestly as possible.

- Do you have a vision of what you want to create?
- What is your heart's desire? What are the passions you want to fulfill before you die?
- Review your entire lifestyle: health, career, relationships, environment, creativity, life-long learning, spiritual, financial, leisure, and travel. Where are you out of balance? Are you using your strengths? What do you want to be doing more of, less of, or differently?
- What's aggravating you, bugging you, frustrating you enough that you want to do something different?
- What is calling to you? What is important to you in your life? What is no longer working for you?
- What do your instincts whisper to you?

» *Our vision when we left for France was clear: to live in another culture and experience the simple joys of life, travel to other countries, and rejuvenate ourselves for the next phase of life.*

Now, as we enter that next phase of our journey, we are creating a new vision that guides us toward the life we want to actualize. We want to design a fulfilling, balanced life in which we have time for the things we love: creativity, travel, exercise, healthy living, reading, and being with family and friends. We want to be doing work we enjoy while living in a place that feeds our souls and earning an abundant income to support our needs and desires. We have defined in detail each element of what the dream means and looks like. One day at a time, we continue to move towards our ideal vision in an ever-evolving journey.

2. Gathering the support you need

Ask friends, family, and colleagues to be part of your "dream team." Let them know what you need in terms of support and ideas. The more specific you are, the better they can support and challenge you to reach your goals.

At certain times in your life a coach, consultant, therapist, or objective good friend is needed to motivate, provide input and feedback, or help you to get over life's hurdles. Reach out and find people who can support you in achieving your dreams. This is not work that is easy to do alone; we all need a support network to call on as catalysts of change.

> » In this virtual world, we've come to find out that our support network comprises not only close friends, family, and colleagues, but an entire world of like-minded people connected via the Internet.

3. Eliminating obstacles

Recognize that the number one obstacle is your own system of limiting beliefs—those which you hold in your mind and body.

- **Practice believing it can happen.**
  Eliminate beliefs that are holding you back (e.g. "Who am I to think I can do this?" or "I can't be rich and have friends"). Replace them with positive ones that support your dream. For example, "I can do work I enjoy with great people, make a good income, and have balance and flexibility in my life."

- **Find time and be patient.**
  Unless we find time to focus on creating what we want, it will not happen. Put it in your calendar, make it a priority, and

eliminate distractions. At the same time, be patient as the steps are executed—it takes time (sometimes a lot of time) to create something new.

- **Make room for the new.**
  Is there physical, mental, or emotional clutter that you need to eliminate to make room for the new dream? Clear out all energy suckers that deter you from moving forward.

- **Let Go.**
  Let go not only of limiting beliefs and clutter, but also of the old behaviors that no longer serve you. Your beliefs and actions may have protected you from harm, cruelty, or embarrassment in the past, but are they still serving you today?

  » *Having grown up with asthma, I had the belief that I needed to be cautious of overexertion. Over the years, I let go of the belief that my asthma dictated what I could do, and I ended up trekking through Europe alone, hiking arduous trails, running in the San Francisco Bay to Breakers race (albeit slowly), and skiing downhill and cross-country.*

4. **Using the Law of Attraction**
   The Law of Attraction is an amazing principle that has to be carefully observed daily to be effective. It says that we create whatever we focus on, and invites us to speak in terms of what we want, *not* what we don't want. For example, instead of saying, "I don't want any bills" (in which your focus is on the bills), say, "Money is flowing to me easily and abundantly, allowing me to pursue my dream." This takes the focus and energy off the bills and puts it onto the dream.

   » *We learned about the Law of Attraction by watching the DVD The Secret, reading Esther and Jerry Hicks' books, and listening to Sonia Choquette speak about developing your sixth sense. Now that we* know how it works, we are convinced that the Law of Attraction has been at work in making our dreams come true. We love watching for signs that we are attracting more of what we want. Every phone call, conversation, and e-mail we receive regarding our vision is a sign that we are moving forward on the right path.

5. **Creating your plan and sticking to it**

The best plans can be developed, but if you don't execute and follow through, they become worthless.

- Develop three to five courageous goals and an action plan that identifies tasks and timelines to guide you in moving forward
- Define your success criteria, and identify support and resources you will need
- Identify the perceived challenges and brainstorm ways to overcome them
- Get a coach or friend to support you in executing your plan by keeping you motivated and holding you accountable
- Periodically re-evaluate whether your plan needs to change, brainstorm alternative actions and contingency plans, and keep on moving forward, even in the face of setbacks
- Keep readjusting as you receive new information and, most importantly, never give up

6. **Believing and creating**

There are two major reasons people don't create their dreams and do what they want:

- **They don't truly believe**

  Not only the person with the dream, but his or her significant other, children, or family may have doubts. Or, you and your partner may have mismatched beliefs that contradict each other and slow momentum.

  » *Small and large dreams need support. Even a simple dream of los-*

ing weight and getting in shape can be derailed if a partner or family is unable to support you. The easiest times we have found getting fit is when we endeavored to do it together, aligning our goals, and believing in and supporting each other along the way.

- **Impatience**

  It takes time for miracles to happen, or to become an expert in something. It may seem that others create dreams quickly, but most successful endeavors are born through hours of practice, focus, and attention.

  In his book *Outliers*, Malcolm Gladwell consistently shows how an expert is seen as a true expert only after they have practiced their craft for 10,000 hours. Patience and persistence are key to creating your dreams.

7. **Managing setbacks**

   As life throws us its inevitable curve balls, we have to be sure to maintain focus on our vision and the belief that we can create it. Patience, focus, belief, support, and using the Law of Attraction are key factors for ultimate success. Adjust as needed, work with and around the problem, seek new solutions, and focus on the longer view.

   » *When my business partner Virginia died and Zoé-Pascale was born a month later, Jean and I set our attention on gathering support both in business and at home. In a short time, we hired a fantastic nanny who even did night duty and we enlarged the team at work to execute our business plan. Asking for help from friends, family, colleagues, and even strangers was critical in helping us maintain focus during that turbulent time in our life.*

Step off the Merry-Go-Round

When I am traveling in a carriage, or walking after a good meal, or during the night when I cannot sleep; it is on such occasions that ideas flow best and most abundantly.

WOLFGANG AMADEUS MOZART,
classical composer (1756-1791)

Like the roundabouts we so often encountered in France, it often feels like we are going around and around in circles. We invite you to pick a direction, jump off the roundabout, and take a break from the busyness and routines of life.

When you do something new, you actually transform your emotional and physical states. Your adrenalin starts pumping, your eyes see things that once were a blur, and your body responds with more alertness. This allows you to view the world from a different perspective, giving you a jolt of healthy joyful living.

A few tips for taking a break from your routine

Here are a few ideas for what we call "spinning off"—taking a break from your routine and doing something completely different. Often these activities are free, easy, fun and, most importantly, make you smile.

- Take a new route to work or school and enjoy the different scenery.
- Have a picnic dinner on the living room floor, red wine and all.
- Change your exercise routine. Instead of yoga, go out for a walk. Instead of your usual run, take a swim.
- Instead of having coffee with an old friend, invite a new one.
- Listen to different music or watch a program or movie you wouldn't normally see.
- Call someone you haven't spoken to in a while—or better yet, write a letter on paper and mail it.
- Take a day off from technology and turn off the cell phone, computer, iPod, and PDA. Notice how being unplugged makes you feel.
- Pretend you are on an exotic island and make yourself a Piña Colada.
- Do something spontaneous and different: go to a museum, a comedy show, or an art gallery.
- Hold a popcorn feast in bed for the entire family. Add a few books and hang out awhile.
- Turn a dinner party into an evening in which everyone cooks a new dish together and stays until past midnight.

Prioritize Family and Partner Time

To put the world right in order, we must first put the nation in order; to put the nation in order, we must first put the family in order; to put the family in order, we must first cultivate our personal life; we must first set our hearts right.

CONFUCIUS,

Chinese thinker and social philosopher (551 B.C.E.–479 B.C.E)

In most religious traditions, there is a designated day of rest. The word "Sabbath" derives from the Hebrew, Shabbat, "to cease." This sacred pause has been provided to hardworking people since the beginning of time. Today, though it is harder to protect and honor, taking at least one day or block of time a week to slow down, rest, and rejuvenate is critical for a healthy, joyful life.

A few tips for prioritizing family and partner time

1. Create a special weekly (or more frequent) time together as a family

Though nightly family dinners are ideal as kids grow up, the reality is that the more schedules you are coordinating, the greater the chance that someone will be missing or late. Strive to have dinner together as much as possible, and make a minimum of one mealtime a week sacred and protected.

Whether it's Friday night dinner or Sunday brunch, designate a time when everyone in the family knows that they are to be available and present. Cook a great meal together or order pizza, play games, go for a hike or to the beach, tell stories, laugh, light candles. Make the time an anchor for your kids, so that as they grow up and leave home, they know they can always return for this sacred time together.

> » *Everything is closed in France on Sundays and, as a result, Sunday is the day when friends and family get together for a leisurely meal and a walk. The entire country slows down and everyone embraces the time out. Taking a cue from our time there, most nights we sit down to a family dinner (albeit a rushed one at times), light the candles, and catch up. One day of the weekend is always reserved as our sacred family day, when we have spontaneity, no plans, no schedules, no stress. It usually includes a walk in nature, a meal, and time to read and relax together.*

2. Step out in nature

There is no better way to quickly move from a state of work to a state of relaxation than by being in nature. Find a time each week when you (and family and friends) can hike, walk, bike, swim, ski, picnic, and play outdoors. Feel the earth, smell the seasonal scents, and disconnect from the everyday world. The natural beauty around us is ours to enjoy—make use of it, and take care of it for future generations.

> » Every weekend, we go for a hike as a family with the dog. Walking out in nature allows us to connect at a deeper level, and often our conversations take on new meaning. Unlike our dinner table conversations, we talk more openly, naturally, and easily for hours on end. We are amazed at how our daughter processes countless ideas and concerns in one hour during our hikes that we would not hear about otherwise.

3. Protect your family and partner time

Sacred time is the first thing to go when life starts to get out of control or new demands are put upon you and your family. However, it is the easiest way to manage stress when life gets busy in the first place. Everyone has different needs for alone time and together time, for time to be with extended family or friends. Strive to figure out what you and your family's needs are, and make a plan to help each other protect this essential time for yourselves. Go to bed early, get up late, or reserve one day to replenish yourself and loved ones.

You may have to begin to set limits and say no to dinner every Sunday night with your extended family and negotiate that you get together every other week or once a month for a longer afternoon and evening. When a social invitation or event begins to feel like a burden or an obligation it is time to rethink how you are spending your time.

Guidebook Tip #11

Consider the Importance of Time versus Money

It's pretty hard to tell what does bring happiness.
Poverty an' wealth have both failed.

Kin Hubbard,
American humorist, cartoonist, and journalist (1868-1930)

The age-old question of which is more important—time or money—is a personal one.

At different times in your life, your answer will likely be different. One thing we have discovered, however, is that life is not just about money. Phenomena like the simplicity movement (in which you live an examined life focusing on what is important), the demise of the American Dream, our need to save the environment from ourselves, Sarkozy's *Gross National Happiness* revolution, and the downfall of our financial institutions are all pointing us toward the realization that money and things are not the only measure of success as many of the baby-boomer generation were raised to believe.

In her book, *Your Money or Your Life*, Vicki Robin writes, "Money is something we choose to trade our life energy for. Our life energy is our allotment of time here on earth, the hours of precious life available to us. When we go to our jobs we are trading our life energy for money ..."

Those who have experienced death, ill health, and tragedy know all too well that life is precious and can be taken away at any moment. We each have to decide how we want to spend our life energy, our time, and our money, now and going forward.

For instance, it may make sense to pay a gardener to keep the yard neat while you work at a job you enjoy making a great deal more money. However, this can be taken to an extreme when a family begins adding expense upon expense into their budget, only to eventually find themselves working just to keep up with the expenses that were originally intended to make their lives easier.

On the flip side, it is important to be fiscally responsible and plan for our future, our children's education, and our retirements. The key is to find the balance that provides a healthy, joyful life.

A few tips for thinking about Time versus Money

Consider the following when you think about how you are spending your time, and how you are spending and saving money. The answers may point toward imbalances between time and money—either in reality or in your thoughts—and how you might bring about more equilibrium.

- *Are you fulfilling your life's purpose? Are you making money in a way that feeds that purpose?*

- *Are you satisfied with the money you are making in comparison with the time you spend? If not, what needs to change to make it more balanced?*

- *Are you able to disconnect from work and does your employer encourage it?*

- *Are there ways to make passive income that would give you more free time?*

- *Is it time to downsize, right size, or lower expenses in some other way?*

- *If you had "enough" money, what would you be doing differently?*

- *Are you saving and paying down debt?*

- *Do you have enough free time for creative endeavors, relationships, leisure, and ongoing learning?*

- *Are you working yourself to death with no end in sight?*

- *Are you living beyond your means?*

- *Are you and your partner in agreement on the issues of money and time?*

- *How can you create more time for yourself? What would you have to trade off or give up? Is it worth it?*

- *Do you have a way each day to replenish your life energy?*

- *Are you fulfilled with how you spend your free time?*

- *Do you believe that a sufficient and abundant amount of money and time are coming your way to live the life you want? How does that change how you live today?*

Review these questions and take action where needed. Read books, talk to friends and professionals. Take a look at all areas of your life that are out of balance and develop a plan to get as much positive life energy in your life as possible.

A quick check on how satisfied you are with your life

On a scale of 1-10, rate how satisfied you are with the following areas of your life. For those areas that are below 5, think about actions you might take to improve your level of satisfaction. For areas that are 8 and above, congratulate yourself and learn from those things that add abundance and delight to your life.

	Not at all								Extremely
Financial sufficiency and abundance	1	2	3	4	5	6	7	8	9	10
Learning/education	1	2	3	4	5	6	7	8	9	10
Leisure time	1	2	3	4	5	6	7	8	9	10
Recreation/sports	1	2	3	4	5	6	7	8	9	10
Creative pursuits	1	2	3	4	5	6	7	8	9	10
Hobbies	1	2	3	4	5	6	7	8	9	10
Good health	1	2	3	4	5	6	7	8	9	10
Career/business/livelihood	1	2	3	4	5	6	7	8	9	10
Retirement plans	1	2	3	4	5	6	7	8	9	10
Spirituality	1	2	3	4	5	6	7	8	9	10
Family relationships	1	2	3	4	5	6	7	8	9	10
Friend relationships	1	2	3	4	5	6	7	8	9	10
Positive contributions to the world	1	2	3	4	5	6	7	8	9	10

Choose **three** areas that you want to **address**, and make a plan. If not now, when?

Continue to Learn

Anyone who stops learning is old, whether at twenty or eighty. Anyone who keeps learning stays young. The greatest thing in life is to keep your mind young.

HENRY FORD,
American industrialist (1863-1947)

We all have the potential to be lifelong learners. Teachers can be found in traditional institutions of learning or prayer; in books or films; on the web or in conversations with colleagues, friends, support groups, professionals, and family. Other times, we learn very unexpected lessons from people and places we never would have assumed had anything to teach us.

A few tips on continuing to learn

1. **Make a list of all the things you want to learn or do before you die.**
   Some of the items may cost more money or take more time, but many can probably be done right in your home or community.

To get started, consider these ideas:

- Travel anywhere, either to a local site you haven't visited, or to the unfamiliar environment of a foreign country. If you don't like to travel or can't afford it, read travel stories, watch travel films, take day trips, or go to travel lectures.
- Learn to cook, knit, paint, or sculpt—any new skill that involves your hands and energizes your mind.
- Take classes in your profession and develop your career. Or go back to school and learn something you have always been interested in.
- Find out how your kids, friends, and colleagues are using new technology to help them in their lives and work. Investigate new ways of working and communicating.
- Take up a musical instrument, take a singing class, or learn how to ballroom dance. Or challenge yourself to learn a new sport, or sign up for a marathon or a two-day walk to benefit a worthy cause. Pushing the limits of your body automatically serves to stretch your mind.
- Challenge your mind and learn how to play chess, bridge, or canasta.
- Use your mind to reflect back on your life—start writing short stories about your life or better yet, your memoir.
- Look up words you don't know—perhaps ones that you run across while you're reading—and try to use them in a sentence that day.

» *As lovers of learning, we focus on learning one new thing every day. When we were in France, it was often as simple as a new French word or a phrase we kept hearing, a way to prepare a vegetable, or a new route found on a map.*

Take Pleasure in Good Food and Healthy Living

Tout est question d'équilibre. (It is a question of balance.)

MIREILLE GUILIANO,

French-American author (1946-)

One of the reasons the French are so well known for their slim figures is that they walk everywhere. They also take their coffee black and never eat in between meals. These are just a couple of the many valuable lessons we learned from the French when it comes to food, mealtime, and good health—lessons we've brought into our own lives.

A few tips on taking pleasure in good food and healthy living

---

- **Never eat while walking, driving, or sitting at the computer.**
  Sit down and enjoy your food. It's good for your health. You

become aware that you are eating and actually taste your food. In France, even *emporter* (take-out) dictates that you find a park, a bench, or a table to eat—no eating while walking, driving, or on the go.

- **Sit down at the table to eat with your family or friends as often as possible.**
Light the candles and enjoy the conversation and the food. Turn off the TV, the computers, the cell phones, and even the home phone. Slow down, have a glass of wine and take time to connect to the people and the food no matter how simple or elaborate it may be.

- **Drink an Espresso or a noisette (an espresso with a dabble of milk).**
In France, nonfat milk is hard to come by and ruins the taste of a good cup of coffee. A café crème is delightful but deadly for the waistline. A great espresso or noisette served in a tiny espresso cup provides the jolt and the sense of well-being we love. We do admit that in California, we also enjoy a tall, nonfat Starbucks latté (after all, a little nonfat milk is good for the bones).

- **Breakfast is small, and lunch and dinner are either medium or large (whichever is medium dictates that the other is large).**
All meals are eaten off china plates atop a decorative tablecloth. Treat yourself by eating off pretty pottery dishes that make you feel good. The plate is just as much a part of the meal as the food. If you don't like your dishes, the food just doesn't taste as good.

- **Eat healthy and well at home, and go out once a week and live it up with dessert and wine.**
It is much easier to eat healthy at home, allowing us to manage our weight and our budget. Conversely, when we do go out

for a Saturday lunch or dinner, we make sure we have time to enjoy the meal and the company. Avoid restaurants that are noisy or rush you out the door. Instead, choose restaurants that encourage you to linger and enjoy the company and conversation as well as the meal.

- **Buy fresh produce from farmers' markets and cook seasonally.**

Seasonal vegetables and fruits get cheaper as the season comes to a close. Stock up and use ingredients readily, freezing the leftovers. Take your kids along as you shop and have them pick out the olives, strawberries, and ripe fruits. Once home, ask them to help prepare the dishes, even if it is only to decorate the plate with some pretty leaves and fresh fruit.

- **Experiment with new recipes using seasonal food.**

It is hard to go wrong with fresh ingredients. Check out the thousands of online sites for great recipes.

- **Walk after dinner.**

Walk on Sunday. Walk whenever you can.

- **Don't take things so seriously.**

Ce n'est pas grave. If there is anything we have learned, it is to just not take anything too seriously.

- **Go slow and, once in awhile, take time to sit in a café and watch the world go by.**

- **Enjoy a glass of red wine.**

It's cheaper in France than a diet Coke and healthy for you too!

- **Drink lots of water.**

You can never drink enough water.

- **Watch the frites.**
I usually ask for the French fries to be replaced with salad as one sniff and I lose all willpower. When I do indulge I borrow a few frites from my daughter's plate.

- **Reserve one day for enjoying a family meal or picnic, getting out in nature, and relaxing.**

- **Have people over for Sunday lunch.**
Outdoors, when the weather permits. Take a walk afterwards no matter what the weather.

- **Share desserts, and use the three-bite rule: the first bite is delectable, the second bite is a must, and the third bite satisfies the palate.**

- **Enjoy sharing funny stories and laughing at the table.**
It is a wonderful way to keep us healthy and joyful.

Surrender Your Fears

Courage is not the absence of fear, but rather the judgment that something else is more important than fear.

AMBROSE REDMOON,
author and rock band manager (est. 1950-1996)

If there is one thing that stops us from doing what we want, it is usually fear. Sometimes these fears are conscious, but more often they are hidden deep in our psyche. Many of our fears may be left over from childhood, instilled in us by our parents, or from other past experiences that no longer apply to our lives. Limiting beliefs are actually fears dressed up a bit differently.

Of course, fears never seem to dissipate completely; it is a constant challenge to keep them at bay. With this in mind, we have provided a few creative tools that we have found to be of great use in conquering our fears.

A few tips for surrendering your fears

Releasing Exercise

1. On a large poster board using different color pens or markers, write or draw all of your fears. Keep writing for at least five minutes. No fear is too mundane, too irrational, or too big to write down. Allow both your conscious and unconscious mind to empty all of the fears you hold onto the board.

2. Once your board is full, read all the fears to yourself or a person you trust, and then let them go. To do this you can:
    *   meditate on letting them go
    *   visualize them leaving and vanishing into the universe
    *   name each one and then say goodbye to it
    *   use gestures to physically move the fears away into the universe and out of your mind and body

3. Once you have released them, spend five minutes experiencing what it feels like to be clear of fears.

4. Each day, when the fears start to pop up, repeat the exercise of letting them go.

5. If you encounter a new fear that wasn't part of the initial exercise, write it on the board, and then let it go.

6. Keep the board somewhere you will encounter it often, but not in your constant, direct view. Alternatively, you might want to burn the poster board as an exercise in releasing the fears. However, I find that glancing at it from time to time helps me to continue to release the fears on deeper and deeper levels. I often find myself laughing at how silly many of them are.

> »   Jean and I did this exercise recently and had a good laugh at how obscure, insane, and truly silly many of our fears were. Yes, they did have some basis in our experience and reality, but to worry about them did not serve us in any way. Rather, it inhibited us from moving forward and attracting what we wanted in life. Some examples of these types of fears were: fear of earthquakes, fear of terrorists, or fear of getting dementia in our old age.

Bridging Exercise

1.   **Write down or state the fear or limiting belief.**

For example, from childhood, I used to have a limiting belief that if I was rich no one would like me. Rich people were show-offs and often looked down upon others.

2.   **Write down what achieving this state or engaging in this activity may support what you believe in, and what you want to do in life.**

I began to realize that if I had an abundant amount of money and a house in France, I could share it with others. I could invite people over to experience a different way of life and the joie de vivre of France. Purchasing our first home in France became linked with sharing the experience with others.

> »   In this way, I was bridging my fears of having money with something that I felt good about, which naturally removed the fear and allowed me to move forward.

3.   **Write, talk, and discuss how achieving what you want will make your life—and the lives of others—better as a result. Feel that result in your body, and repeat it in your mind until it feels true.**

Cleansing Exercise

1. ***Whenever a fear arises, take a minute and wipe the fear off your body.***

   Literally brush it off with your hands—you might even ask someone to help you. Brush the fear off your shoulders as though it is lint. Move down to the arms and legs, continuing to brush until you feel lighter. As you brush, say to yourself, "I am brushing the fear away. It is no longer attaching itself to me," or, "Off, off, off."

2. ***Stand tall, shake the remaining fear from your body, and feel the lightness, knowing that the fear is no longer grabbing or holding on to you.***

   You have let it move away and dissipate.

   » *Jean, Zoé-Pascale, and I do this whenever we feel something is holding us back. It also works if negative energy from some other person has attached itself to us. This may sound odd, silly, or just plain weird, but we promise it works in the same way a warm bubble bath relaxes your body and cleans away any grime, leaving you feeling clean.*

Lean into Creating the Life You Want to Live

Take the first step in faith.
You don't have to see the whole staircase.
Just take the first step.

MARTIN LUTHER KING JR.,
American civil rights leader (1929-1968)

Having a clear vision is one of the best motivators for creating the life you want to live. However, sometimes we just aren't that clear. We have a fuzzy idea, a sense of what we want, and a hope that clarity comes to us sooner than later. This is similar to painting a fantastic landscape: we don't know exactly where it is going to take us, but we are willing to continue to put layer after layer of paint on the canvas.

Even without a vivid vision, you can start to live the life you want by going with the idea. Just start and let the momentum take you with it. Experiment, let it guide you, learn along the way, and use the feedback to become clearer on the direction you want to go.

A few tips for leaning into the life you want to create

Create Momentum

1. **Be willing to start without seeing what the end result might look like.**

    Simply start doing what makes sense and let the next logical action present itself to you.

    Suppose you have always wanted to run a marathon. Start by walking, run a few steps, and before you know it you might be running a mile, joining a running club, or training with a group. A variety of options will present themselves to you if you just start.

2. **A fuzzy idea or dream is a great place to start.**

    Bill Gates, Steve Jobs, and thousands of other successful entrepreneurs didn't know exactly what they were going to build when they started their companies. What they did have was a fuzzy idea, a purpose, and a passion to start where they were at—in a garage, a dorm room, or their bedroom.

3. **Keep leaning into your hopes and dreams and the answers will come.**

    As you take action on your hopes and dreams, you are attracting more of what you want: opportunities present themselves, people come into your life to support you. One thing builds upon another. You might be surprised by the path you follow, so be open, be curious, and keep leaning into the dream and let the breeze take you with it.

Keep your fuzzy dream in the forefront of your thoughts and see where it leads you. Be open to new ideas, a different direction, and support from others. Pay attention to the signs that are coming your way as you lean into your dreams.

4. Take responsibility for living the life you want

We will all have excuses why we can't do something, why it just isn't the right time, or how someone else's demands take precedent. The question is, however, are you taking responsibility to make things happen or are you waiting and waiting and waiting? Be your own magic genie and make your wishes come true.

The American Dream: The Facts

THE FACTS THAT lead up to this story and life guidebook all started in 1931 when James Turslow Adams in his book, *The Epic of America*, first coined the term The American Dream.

Growing up as baby-boomers, we were all told to follow the American Dream. These two words were discussed at dinner tables, in the workplace, in schools, churches, in government, and at the bars—all as code words for creating the perfect life. It was based upon the belief that with hard work and determination, anyone can prosper and achieve anything and everything they wanted. With this hard work ethic, there was a secondary belief that parents would be able to easily provide more for their children than they themselves ever had: a bigger house, education, opportunity, and better jobs.

The idea is still alive, but many things have changed since 1931. Today there is a growing belief that the American Dream of devoting your life to your work in order to reap the rewards is no longer valid. The cost to one's family, one's health, and one's own well-being can be sustained only for a period of time, not for forty years. This focus on the importance of well-being is not new, but is reflected in the Declaration of Independence, written over 200 years ago. *"We hold these Truths to be self-evident, that all Men are created equal, that they are endowed by their Creator with certain unalienable Rights, that among these are Life, Liberty and the pursuit of Happiness."*

In the late 1970s, as an unprecedented number of women entered the workforce, the notion of work began to change. It was no longer a job but a career. Slowly but surely, the notion of work starting at 9:00 and ending at 5:00 became a thing of the past. For working couples, this meant more income and the ability to buy bigger homes, better cars, private education, and abundant luxury items, but it also meant they were building a lifestyle based on the requirement of two incomes. Working moms became super moms and taking time off to raise a child was unheard of for most women (and often not financially possible). Soon, this was followed by a move away from working in one company for your lifetime to becoming your own brand and being told "you have to take care of yourself." The Catalyst organization reported, "...by 2005, the family structure changed dramatically in which only 17% of households had a husband in the workforce and wife who was not bringing in a paycheck, down 63% since 1950. That means over 83% of households have two working adults and approximately half of those have children under 18." This shift in lifestyle alone has drastically changed how Americans and people in other countries as well, spend their time. The net result is that a lot less time is available for anything but developing your career and taking care of the children and household chores.

Simultaneously, many of us were led to believe that if we were loyal, hard working, productive, and continuously added value, jobs would be plentiful, our retirements would be secure, careers would keep on developing, and the American lifestyle would be a given. Even as we lived through recession after recession, layoff after layoff, companies taking away retirements, benefits, and our overall security, we still believed in the elusive dream. We trusted in the growth of the GNP, the finance markets, the stock markets, and our leaders. The irony is that we kept on believing, working harder than ever, and ignoring all the indications around us.

The American Dream as we knew it was shifting like sand from under our feet. By 2001, the signs were crystal clear that our view of the future was changing at lightning speed. By 2008, everything was up for grabs. We had to begin to rethink work, life, family, careers, jobs, retirement, and the pursuit of happiness.

Today calls for a harsh reassessment focused on our pursuit of life (as we want it to be), liberty (the freedom to do what we choose) and the pursuit of happiness (living a happy and healthy life). Sarkozy, the President of France, recently proposed that the G-20 world leaders join together in a "revolution" to shift the measurement of economic progress from gross domestic product to account for factors such as health-care availability and leisure time. "The global financial crisis," reports Sarkozy, "doesn't only make us free to imagine other models, another future, and another world. It obliges us to do so." As early as 1972, the small Himalayan country of Bhutan announced that it was focusing on Gross National Happiness as its measure of development. It is based on the premise that the development of society takes place when both material and spiritual developments occur side by side and reinforce each other. It is not just one-sided, focused on stressing economic growth—both ideas of the equation matter equally. The four pillars measured in Bhutan are sustainable development, preservation and promotion of cultural values, conserving the natural environment, and establishing good governance. Not a bad way to measure development. Imagine if we integrated these concepts into our GNP.

The American Dream is being replaced with the New American Lifestyle. This lifestyle is based upon quality of living indicators. It is no longer just about work, but about the total quality of the life we live. In 2005, the Economist developed an index based upon nine quality of life indicators: material well-being, life expectancy, political stability and security, family life, community life, climate and geography, job security, political freedom, gender equality. The key in the study was to understand the interplay of modernity and tradition in determining life satisfaction. It doesn't matter how much money you have in the bank or how new your car is, but how secure you feel and satisfied you are with your overall life—physically, mentally, spiritually. The time is coming in which the public will demand that these qualities are included as key measures for developed nations.

In the past twenty-five years, the interplay between the quality of life indicators has been severely affected by the advent of women in the workplace, two career couples, long commutes, business travel, periodic stock market crashes, declining home values, layoffs and resizing, devaluation of retirement accounts, and a decline in company benefits. Added to these ongoing grating trends are increasing healthcare costs, an erosion of a quality public education for all, the need to stay connected 24/7, and the demands placed on workers and families to balance it all. As a result there has been enormous erosion in healthy, stable family and community life and our overall sense of well-being.

Taking it further, Marcus Buckingham, in his book *Find your Strongest Life* (2009), reports that women are generally less happy than they were forty years ago. He reports, "In the past four decades, women have secured better job prospects, greater acknowledgement for achievement, wider influence, more free time, and higher salaries. And yet, recent studies reveal that women have gradually become less happy than they were 40 years ago, and less happy than men—and unlike men, they grow sadder as they get older." Additional research shows a trend toward overall anxiety and stress becoming paramount in society. As early as 2000, the Gallup poll reported that 80% of workers report feeling stress on the job, and the CDC states that 70-80% of all visits to the doctor are for stress-related and stress-induced illnesses.

Coinciding with the rise of stress-related illnesses has been the increasing recognition that the workplace does need to examine old assumptions, policies, and human resource practices—quality of life for employees does matter. Companies such as Deloitte Touche have implemented what they call career lattices. Different from the career ladder, which is upward only, the lattice allows employees to take their careers in many directions without being looked upon negatively. Instead of one career path, the realization of retaining and hiring good talent is dependent on their ability to customize career paths for each person in four domains: pace, workload, location/schedule, and role. Mirroring real life, Deloitte Touche and other "Best companies to work with" are beginning to recognize that at different times in your life, you will have different needs that require changing how you work and live. Companies that are serious about retaining top talent are embracing flexible work arrangements ranging from part-time to telecommuting, to compressed schedules. In a survey of Fortune 500 male executives (Miller and Miller 2005), 84% of male executives said they would like to work flexibly to allow them to pursue their professional aspirations while having more time for activities outside of work. Thankfully, some of these forward-thinking companies are betting on attracting and retaining great employees by building programs for career flexibility and encouraging living a more balanced life.

Complementing this movement is the push for each and every employee to brand themselves, focus on their strengths, determine their identity, their value, and their expertise, and continue to keep on growing and learning in their chosen field. The idea is that expertise and talents are what people will pay for and each person is individually responsible for managing their career and their financial retirement needs. The stated and unstated contracts of a company taking care of you are long gone. As long as you perform well and the company needs your services, you will have a position. If and when either is no longer true, you are on your own. This shift is both welcoming and unsettling as the new American Lifestyle continues to redefine itself.

Today, we watch the courageous surge of experienced professionals, voluntarily and involuntarily, moving towards entrepreneurship. Today's internet technology has enabled anyone to work, market, and compete globally with low overhead and a high level of flexibility. The attraction to be one's own boss has a similar ring to the American Dream, but is somewhat different. It's not just about work, but it is about creating a lifestyle of flexibility and fullness, being your own boss and doing work you love. The sense of false security working for a corporation is replaced by the belief in oneself above anything else.

As the new American Lifestyle continues to evolve, corporate America will as well. The shift from an obsession with work to living a full life will continue to be challenged by every type of worker from entrepreneurs, to skilled talent, to college graduates, to dual career couples and families, women, men, and experienced retirees. The new American Lifestyle we speak of is gaining momentum in every walk of life.

More recently, the global ethical and financial crisis has pushed us to look more closely at how we are living our lives. The spiraling greed and illegal business practices of Enron and the risky behavior of Wall Street were only the tip of the iceberg. We truly don't know what other surprises will come our way, but we are now aware that nothing will ever be like it was before. The American Dream was all mom and apple pie—it never spoke of greed, corruption, and the possibility that trusted professionals would be either unethical or *laissez-faire* about the long-term and global implications of their decisions. The American Dream blindly screamed out, if you work hard, it too will come.

Millions of Americans now realize that our lives, our global economy, the world of work, and our institutions have to change. The old rules, the old expectations, and old behaviors are no longer serving our country, ourselves, or our planet. Whether voluntarily or involuntarily, we are becoming environmentally conscious and need to change our ways. Our habits of being consumers, focusing on instant gratification, and living with a "we deserve it" mentality have shifted. Our habits of being the "throw-away" society are being closely re-examined. The simplicity movement has become main-streamed. It is no longer about living off the land, but about taking care of our planet and enjoying the simple things in life, first and foremost. It's about using our natural resources wisely and choosing not to always want more at the expense of what is most important. It's about living a full, healthy, joyful life and fulfilling our dreams. Our challenge is riding the wave as the pieces realign towards the new American Lifestyle. The need to be creators of our own destiny, communities, and planet is more important than ever.

A strong economy, political stability, and safety are still critically important, but of equal value is our right to pursue good health, well-being, and happiness. More specifically, this new American Lifestyle can be defined as having meaningful work that provides a sense of well-being, living in a safe and healthy environment, being with people you care about, and living a pace of life that allows you to pursue other interests. The pendulum is moving from material-ism to a full, quality life. This sounds like the pursuit of life, liberty, and happiness redefined once again as our forefathers intended.

Thank you and Best Wishes
Suzanne and Jean

Questions for You and for Book Club Discussions

1. Is your pace of life working for you? If not, how would you like to change it?

2. What is working or not working in your life today?

3. What have you put off doing that you truly want to do before you die?

4. What practical steps can you take to simplify your life today?

5. What risks can you take to push yourself out of your comfort zone?

6. Where is the one location on the planet that aligns with your heart and values and that supports your soul?

7. Where are your deepest roots? Who are your ancestors and what do you want to know about them? What values of your ancestors are you embodying in your daily life?

8. Are you taking time to eat fresh food and enjoy your meals with good company and conversation? Have you stopped eating at your desk or in your car? Are you taking a two-hour lunch at least once a week with a good friend or romantic partner?

9. How can you simplify and exclude any unnecessary consumerism for your life? Are you still trying to keep up with the Joneses? Are you staying within your budget each day, week, and month?

10. How can you enhance the beauty of your environment? What can you do to make your living and work space more tranquil, peaceful, and soothing to your soul?

11. Are you out walking in nature often? When's the last time you walked where the sounds were not of cars, but rather birds singing or twigs crackling beneath your feet?

12. What do you need to do to nourish your body, mind, and spirit?

13. Have you traveled or are you planning to travel to a foreign country or a new environment? When will you do it and where will you go?

14. Have you carried a beautiful basket to the farmer's market recently or are you still schlepping plastic bags? How does it make you feel if you carry a beautiful basket?

15. Is creativity missing in your life? Are you itching to learn to paint, write poetry, sing in a choir (or just learn to sing)? In what ways can you and your family find joy in creative pursuits?

16. What life lessons and experiences do you want to give your children, nieces, or nephews while they are young enough to share them with you?

17. When's the last time you took a big risk? When did you last do something on the spur of the moment, something completely spontaneous? When was the last time you went topless (publicly or privately) or engaged in an activity that took you out of your comfort zone?

18. What have you done to support your community, business, and political leaders who have influence over improving the

quality of our lives? How might you get involved in your community or take political action to inform politicians that quality of life is essential to a healthy, vibrant society?

19. When's the last time you splurged on something impractical just to feel sensual, sexy or beautiful? When was the last time you went to the boutique lingerie store and indulged yourself fully?

20. When was the last time you talked to your partner about your deepest dreams and started to jointly move forward in creating the life you want to live?

Acknowledgements

We express our heartfelt thanks to those who have played a role in the creation and editing of this book: Karen Leland, who got us started on writing the book proposal years ago, and Linda Watanabe McFerrin, our writing teacher at Book Passages in Corte Madera. A heartfelt huge thank you goes to Joy Mazzola, our editor, who helped shape and edit the final version and Morgan Chase, our proofreader. We would also like to thank Linda Jay Gelden, our copy editor, who cleaned up the manuscript, and Tara Weaver, our initial editor, who helped to set us on the right path with the book. Thank you to Jean Baillargeon, who provided proofreading of the French translations. To the various reviewers who provided numerous ideas along the way, we appreciate and thank you. A special acknowledgement goes to Cynthia Keefe, who was our cheerleader throughout the whole process.

We hold deep gratitude for the people of our village community in the south of France. Thank you all for welcoming and accepting us into your midst with such warmth. Especially, we want to thank Maryse Tonnelier for her guidance and friendship. To all of our wonderful neighbors and friends from our quartier and in the south of France, we say you are terrific and thank you for continuously enriching our lives. Special mention and huge thanks to: Lucy and Peter Till and their kids, Lilou Milcent and Philippe Gallot, Alain Monteuil, Tom and Mary Gibbs, who shared many great times with us, Marjorie Genest, Anne, Thibaut and Emily Peyroche d'Arnaud, Mireille Laurens, and Beatrice Marcoux, the cultural director, and her husband, Denis. Thank you Astrid and Brian French, Mary and Mike Faigle, Mimi and Anton Liss, Sasha and Paul Liss, Luc Venet, Robert and Pat Bradley, Amy and Matt

Lillard, Françoise Janosse, Lilyane De Brauwer from Presence Choréographie d'Uzes, and Nathalie Tzorig Nichanian our yoga teacher. To Zoé-Pascale's teachers at the Ecole Primaire and all the friends she made especially, Perrine Cadaze and Priscillia Nallet, we say merci beaucoup.

We especially honor the memory of Madame Claudine Laurens, Zoé-Pascale's adopted French grandma who always took great care of us and cooked Zoé-Pascale five course lunches every Friday. We think of her often and fondly as she passed away right at the end of our adventure.

To our California friends, who hugely supported us in our journey and in the writing of this book. Thank you Roxanne Howe-Murphy and Jim Murphy, Kirsten and Farnum Alston, Shelley Katz and Ken Polowitz, Kathy Collard and Don Bauer, Paul and Susie Segal, Anne and Peter Albano, Darcey Sears and Ted Wilson, Debbie and Mark Spohr, Craig Garshelis and Mike Andrews, Christine and Claris Gallais, Jan Bein and Ken Hickey, Mike and Mindy O'Toole, Nico and Connie Yiangou, Carrie Messina, Beverly Pinto and Elliot Levine, Lynda McGlone, Mia Benedict, Dina Hatchuel and Tim Tabernak and to Greg Baker, thank you for taking such good care of Advance Consulting, Inc. A special thank you to the Wild Women's Group for welcoming me back after my sojourn and travels and to Virginia LaGrossa's angel who is always sitting on our shoulders. And for all our friends and colleagues who are too numerous to name specifically, please know we appreciate and thank you.

One major expression of gratitude: while most names throughout this book have been changed to respect your anonymity, you may recognize yourself and we thank you for sharing in this great experience of joy and living.

We also thank all of our wonderful friends and the terrific faculty at Lycée Francais La Perouse in Marin and San Francisco as well as the

French community for their fabulous support and friendship over many years. To all of Zoé-Pascale's classmates many of whom started together in maternelle at age 3, thank you for being her extended family

Deep appreciation, love and thanks to Suzanne's parents, Gerald and Marilyn Saxe as well as Margaretha Roux, Jean's mom; you three are always understanding and supportive of everything we do. We also acknowledge and thank Cynthia and Michael Keefe, Bari and Latimer Lorenz and their families in Southern California, Janus, Daniel, and Retha Roux and their families in South Africa, the Stals families in Australia and Daniel and Alain Roux and their families in France.

We also appreciate all of those people whom we met randomly, often in airports, while we were traveling and writing this book who said to us, "You are living our dream." Their stories and encouraging words always solidified that we were not alone and that by taking the critical time out to rejuvenate, it was not only the right thing to do, but also a courageous and essential heart step, even when it flew in the face of reason.

Most especially we want to thank and acknowledge each other; we are ever so grateful for having a partner, best friend, lover, and soulmate to share our life with and for supporting each other in our own growth, development, and passions through thick and thin. The writing of this book, as husband and wife, is a feat in itself.

Finally, our biggest appreciation goes to our daughter, Zoé-Pascale, who was patient when we were busy on the computer, kind in her encouragement to keep on writing, flexible in every way, and always made us laugh and enjoy. But mostly, we thank her for being part of the fantastic journey and for the great times we have shared.

The Authors

THE HUSBAND AND WIFE team, Suzanne Saxe-Roux, Ed.D., and Jean P. Roux, Ph.D., LMFT, have over the last twenty-five years developed, consulted, coached, and trained thousands of people to become the best they can be both personally and professionally. As successful professionals and entrepreneurs in their own right, Suzanne and Jean-Pierre, offer a fresh slant on adventuring through change, life transitions and recommitting to live a balanced and quality life. Suzanne is author of *The Consultative Approach, Partnering for Results!* and numerous workshops and articles. She is a columnist for the SF Examiner online, an avid blogger for www.healthyjoyfullivingblog.com and a national speaker inspiring busy professionals to take responsibility to create a life that embraces joie de vivre. Jean is the author of a variety of health and wellness related workshops and articles and is a health psychologist and clinical psychotherapist working with individuals and organizations.

Suzanne and Jean, married for many years, divide their time between Marin County, California and the south of France with their daughter, Zoé-Pascale and their dog, Pantoufle, constantly paying attention to attracting what they desire into their lives.

To learn more about Suzanne or Jean, their coaching, consulting or workshops, or to donate to the Roux Foundation dedicated to cross-cultural education and health initiatives, please visit www.healthyjoyfulliving.com or send an email to info@HealthyJoyfulLiving.com.

You can join the authors on Facebook, Twitter, and LinkedIn and at www.Healthyjoyfulliving.com

www.twitter.com/suzannesaxeroux

www.twitter.com/couragecroissan

www.facebook.com/pages/Courage-and-Croissants-Inspiring-Joyful-Living

www.facebook.com/healthyjoyfulliving

www.linkedin.com/in/suzannesaxeroux

www.linkedin.com/in/jeanprouxphd

For more information

Please visit our website at:

www.healthyjoyfulliving.com

or contact us at:

Info@HealthyJoyfulLiving.com

Info@Saxe-Roux.com

Coaching and Consulting

Lifestyle Planning, Life and Career Coaching
Business and Entrepreneurial Consulting
Leadership Coaching and Facilitation

Workshops and Speaking

See our website for upcoming events. Contact us about speaking for your group or organization or designing a speech or workshop customized to fit your needs.

Newsletter, Blog, Articles

Keep inspired and gain new ideas on creating a healthy joyful life day-by-day.

Books and Great Stuff

Visit our website for books and e-books on lifestyle and business planning as well as other Great stuff for living a healthy joyful life.

Roux Foundation

Dedicated to promoting Cross Cultural Learning and Health in the Global Community.

Bon Courage—Go with Courage!

Suzanne Saxe-Roux and Jean P. Roux
Tiburon, CA and the south of France